THE FEDERAL
DEFICIT

edited by ANDREW C. KIMMENS

THE REFERENCE SHELF

Volume 57 Number 4

THE H. W. WILSON COMPANY

New York   1985

THE REFERENCE SHELF

The books in this series contain reprints of articles, excerpts from books, and addresses on current issues and social trends in the United States and other countries. There are six separately bound numbers in each volume, all of which are generally published in the same calendar year. One number is a collection of recent speeches; each of the others is devoted to a single subject and gives background information and discussion from various points of view, concluding with a comprehensive bibliography. Books in the series may be purchased individually or on subscription.

Library of Congress Cataloging in Publication Data

Main entry under title:

The Federal deficit.

    (The Reference shelf ; v. 57, no. 4)
    Bibliography: p.
    1. Budget deficits—United States—Addresses, essays, lectures. I. Kimmens, Andrew C. II. Title. III. Series.
HJ2052.F43   1985   339.5'23'0973   85–22651
ISBN 0–8242–0712–2

Printed in the United States of America

CONTENTS

PREFACE

For much of its modern history, the U.S. government has spent more money than it has taken in. This situation, called *deficit financing* or *deficit spending,* is a term economically neutral but politically opprobrious. Conservatives have long held that liberals, whom they see as advocates of increasing government's size and cost, recklessly add to the national debt by policies of "tax and tax, spend and spend." Liberals, while believing in the value of creative, often expensive government programs, have striven to appear fiscally prudent, and have often welcomed or initiated national budget-balancing schemes.

The fairly rigid political alignment over the question of deficit financing broke apart during the early 1980s, in the face of the huge deficits included in the successive budgets of President Ronald Reagan. Reagan is generally regarded as the most conservative president in five decades, and his early political career was founded on balanced budgets as the cornerstone of fiscal responsibility. Since 1981, questions of budget balancing and debt maintenance have occupied business people, economists, and politicians as never before.

The scope of the deficit problem may be succinctly illustrated by the table on the following page.

Two disturbing trends are evident. (1) The deficit has grown at an unprecedentedly rapid rate since the 1970s. (2) Although the fluctuation between surplus and deficit was fairly steady between 1915 and 1970, the amount of interest payable on the public debt has never ceased growing, because the aggregate debt itself has never ceased growing. Each fiscal year's deficit is added to the national debt, which in 1983 amounted to $1.377 trillion. In the month of December 1984 alone, for example, the federal government had to spend $22 billion on interest to service the debt. These interest payments will probably continue to rise, because only a budget surplus—an eventuality not even contemplated in mid-1985—can reduce the national debt, and then only if Washington decides to apply such a surplus to debt reduction instead of some other purpose.

THE FEDERAL DEFICIT, selected years
(in millions of dollars)

Year	Interest on public debt	surplus (+) or deficit (-)
1915	23	-63
1918	190	-9,032
1929	678	+734
1933	689	-2,602
1943	1,808	-57,420
1945	3,617	-53,941
1950	5,750	-3,122
1956	6,787	+4,087
1960	9,180	+269
1965	11,346	-1,596
1970	19,304	-2,845
1975	32,665	-45,108
1980	74,860	-58,961
1981	95,589	-57,932
1982	117,404	-110,658
1983	128,813	195,354
1985[1]		-178,000
1986[1]		-195,000
1987[1]		-216,000
1988[1]		-238,000
1989[1]		-263,000

[1]Congressional Budget Office deficit estimates, August 1984
Source: U.S. Treasury Department data

The origins and salient features of the federal deficit and the political storms swirling around it are the subject of this volume. Section I inquires into the origins of deficit financing. Section II examines the growing controversies over the very large deficits of the 1980s. Section III considers the arguments for and against the proposition that large deficits are primarily stimulative in their economic effects, that they have no deleterious impact on the national economy. Section IV outlines the difficult policy choices facing political leaders today in their efforts to reduce deficits that are widely considered far too high, if not actually out of control.

ANDREW C. KIMMENS

August 1985

I. ORIGINS OF DEFICIT FINANCING

EDITOR'S INTRODUCTION

Deficit spending has its origins in theoretical economics, a rarefied specialty within a specialized field. The articles comprising the first part of this book are all exercises in theory, and were all written and published before the 1980s, when the question of national budget deficits became a prominent political football. The arguments for and against deficit spending, however, are usually clear.

The first article, by James M. Buchanan, is a terse summary and definition of the terms employed throughout the debate: the various kinds of public debt, how that debt is connected to fiscal policy, how it may be managed and financed, and the essential controversy over its size and function.

Abba P. Lerner, in the second article, presents what is even today the best defense, in U.S. terms, of the Keynesian model of deficit financing. Lerner singles out for demolition various "imaginary" aspects of the national debt—several of these are still being repeated as truth nearly four decades later by apparently respectable commentators.

In an equally classic contribution to the debate from the supply-side, anti-Keynesian position, James M. Buchanan and Richard E. Wagner examine the history and practice of the paradoxical Keynesian doctrine that deficits and mushrooming national debts are economic assets to be encouraged, because they stimulate wealth, growth, and employment.

PUBLIC DEBT[1]

Public debt is an obligation on the part of a governmental unit to pay specific monetary sums to holders of legally designated claims at particular points in time. The sums owed to creditors may be defined in standard monetary units of the debtor government or in units of an external currency. The United States national debt represents, predominantly, an obligation of the federal government to pay specific sums of United States dollars to creditors. On the other hand, national debts may, and local debts must, be defined in units of external currency. The monetary obligation may be that of paying either interest or a return of principal, or both. Specific issues of debt may or may not be characterized by definite maturity schedules. Consols, which represent obligations to pay interest in perpetuity, involve no obligation for a return of principal.

Public debt must be distinguished from currency outstanding. The obligation on the part of a money-issuing governmental authority to the holder of currency is not public debt, since the claim can also be met in currency units.

Public debt is created by the act of public borrowing, or, in other words, the act of floating public loans, the act of selling government securities. This is a process through which governmental units, in exchange for money (currency or demand deposits) give promises to pay, this exchange being normally voluntary on the part of the lender. For governments the purpose of the exchange is that of securing current purchasing power with which they may purchase resource services, or final products. The issue of public debt is one means of financing government expenditures, alternative to taxation and to direct currency creation.

Public debt is amortized, or retired, by a reverse transfer in which government gives up money for debt instruments, either through purchase on the open market or through scheduled maturity payments.

[1]Reprint of an article by James M. Buchanan, professor of economics, from International Encyclopedia of the Social Sciences, David L. Sills, editor. Vol. 4, pp. 28–34. Copyright © 1968, Crowell Collier and Macmillan, Inc. Reprinted by permission.

Measurement. Public debt is normally measured in nominal maturity values. This does not represent the "size" of the public debt in such a manner as to make comparisons over time and among separate governmental units fully accurate. Varying composition of debt can affect its degree of liquidity for holders, as well as other characteristics. To the extent that debt instruments are valued for these nondebt features, the effective size of public debt, as such, is reduced. A more accurate measure of debt is produced by capitalizing the annual interest charges at some appropriate rate of discount, normally that rate which approximates the return on risk-free investment in the economy. An example will clarify this point. In terms of nominal maturity value, national debt may be of equal size, say $300,000 million, at two points in time. In the one case, however, if the debt is composed primarily of short-term issues possessing a high degree of "moneyness," the annual interest charges may amount to, say, only $6,000 million. In the other case, if the debt is largely funded, the interest charges may be as high as, say, $12,000 million. Clearly, the "size" of the public debt is not identical in the two cases; other dimensions than nominal maturity values must be included in any appropriate measure. For purposes of making intertemporal and international comparisons, the most appropriate measure is perhaps the ratio of annual interest charges to gross national or gross domestic product.

Public debt may characterize both national and local fiscal systems. Data are much more readily available for national debts, and that of some selected countries may be introduced for illustrative purposes. Table 1 shows the national debts of several selected countries in 1960, defined in nominal maturity values, local currency units being converted into United States dollar equivalents at official exchange rates. The right-hand column of Table 1 indicates the ratio of national debt to gross national product of the issuing country.

The most significant fact that emerges from any comparative survey of national debts in the various countries, and one that is indicated from the data summarized in Table 1, is that no single country was, in 1960, dangerously "overburdened" with national debt. Among the major countries of the world, only for the United

Kingdom was the size of the national debt larger than GNP. And for relatively few countries, developed or underdeveloped, is the ratio of national debt to GNP more than 50 per cent. There are several reasons for these results, some of which make their significance less than it might initially seem to be.

Table 1.   National debt in selected countries, 1960

	National Debt, 1960[a]	Ratio of Debt to GNP[b]
	(In millions of dollars)	(Per cent)
Brazil	4,911	19
Canada	17,679	49
France	24, 925	40
Germany	611	1
India	13,159	35
Japan	2,551	7
Norway	1,293	29
United Kingdom	77,652	124
United States	286,471	57

[a]Includes intragovernmental debt. Converted to U.S. dollars at official rates.
[b]Rounded to nearest percentage point
Source: International Financial Statistics.

Countries that are characterized by large national debts, measured proportionately to GNP, tend to be those that have enjoyed reasonably stable government, that have been victorious in wars, and that have experienced reasonable monetary stability over a relatively long period. Great Britain and the United States, both victorious in two world wars and both characterized by political stability and relatively moderate inflation, carry relatively heavier national debts than most other countries. Causality seems to work in only one direction here, however. Political and monetary stability do not result from large national debts; instead, large national debts emerge only in conditions of reasonable political and monetary stability. In the absence of these conditions, public borrowing will rarely be important as a means of financing public spending, and, even when it is successfully carried out, the creditors of the state may be subject to confiscation through inflation or through default.

Historically, the large increases in national debts have been associated with the financing of war emergencies. This is illustrated by the growth of the United States national debt, shown for selected years in Table 2.

Table 2.   Growth of United States national debt,
                          selected years

Year	Nominal Maturity Value (In millions of dollars)
1917	1,023
1919	26,349
1930	15,774
1940	42,376
1946	277,912
1949	249,509
1960	286,471
1965	317,270

Source: U.S. Treasury Department data.

Composition. Public debt assumes many forms, ranging from consols at the one extreme to treasury bills of very short maturity at the other, with other characteristics not relating to maturity schedules. The form in which debt is marketed affects the interest rate that must be paid, since various features, desired in themselves, may be offered complementary to what may be called "pure debt." Consols, which have no maturity and which obligate the issuing government only to pay a specific interest charge periodically and in perpetuity, provide a useful bench mark for comparative purposes. These come close to representing "pure debt," and as other features are added the cost of carrying debt tends to decrease. The fixing of a definite maturity, which obligates the government to return the principal to the holder of claims, increases the liquidity of the claim, especially as maturity is approached. Hence, as maturities are shortened, liquidity is increased to the point at which short-term treasury bills take on a high degree of "moneyness." For this reason bills can normally be sold at considerably lower rates of interest than long-term bonds.

Certain countries have been successful in floating issues of debt that obligate the government to return monetary sums of fixed purchasing power to holders of claims. These constant-value bonds, which provide holders with apparent protection against inflationary erosion in value, have been marketed at very low rates of interest. Great Britain, in the years since World War II, has successfully introduced "premium bonds," which incorporate certain features of a lottery.

The terms "funded debt" and "floating debt" have been used, historically, to refer to long-term and to short-term debt, respectively. Any definitions are, to an extent, arbitrary, but all issues of more than five-years maturity are generally called "long-term," and all issues with shorter maturities are called "short-term." The rubric "floating debt" is most explicitly used with reference to issues of less than one year maturity.

The names given to specific debt instruments reflect the maturity category. Bonds are securities issued for long term. Notes and certificates are intermediate-term, and treasury bills are short-term. The term "government securities" is used to refer to the whole range of public debt instruments.

Ownership. The pattern of ownership of public debt is an important factor in determining its impact on the national economy. In almost all countries national debt is held in significant amounts by various governmental or quasi-governmental agencies. For some purposes it is desirable to include only debt held outside the governmental sector in measuring total debt. For other purposes intragovernmental debt should be included. Insofar as the agencies holding debt are, in fact, treated as being independently accountable units, both in their investing and in their paying functions, the public debt that these agencies hold is not different in effect from that held by the nongovernmental public. However, insofar as these agencies holding debt are not independent of direct treasury control, their holding does not constitute debt at all and could as well have been canceled at the outset. For the most part, intra-governmental debt represents some combination of these two institutional situations.

It is also important to distinguish between the debt held by the nonbanking public and that held by the banking system and by certain categories within the banking system. To the extent that government securities are held by the central banks, they provide reserves for the commercial banking system, and changes in central bank holdings are indicative of important monetary movements in the economy. To the extent that commercial banks hold securities, potential reserves are available to them.

Traditionally debt held internally and debt held externally have been sharply distinguished. In a national accounting sense, the servicing of internally held debt does not require the transfer of income resources out of the national economy, whereas, of course, such a transfer is required for the servicing of an externally held debt. This point is relevant, even though it must be kept in mind that, other things being equal, the income base from which the transfers are to be made must be larger in the case of externally held debt, precisely by the amount of the necessary interest transfer.

Management. Public debt management may be defined as that set of operations required to maintain an existing nominal debt. Again, consols provide a useful reference point; if all public debt should consist of consols, management reduces to the payment of interest charges. Significant problems of management arise because issues must be refinanced, must be "rolled over," at periodic intervals. These problems become more difficult as the proportion of floating debt in the total becomes larger and also as economic conditions over time become less stable.

Recognition of management difficulties explains the traditional policy objective of funding the national debt to the maximum extent that is possible. This objective may conflict with other objectives that have been introduced into public policy. As national debts grow in importance, the annual interest payments assume relatively large shares of the governmental expenditure budget. This fact prompts recognition of the minimization of interest cost as an objective of debt management, one that is sharply in conflict with funding. Modern developments in the theory of macroeconomic policy have also forced the recognition that debt management exerts significant over-all effects on the economy. This produces a third possible management objective, that of supplementing macroeconomic policy in promoting stabilization-growth aims.

In a period of threatened inflation both the funding and the macroeconomic objectives would dictate a shift out of short-term into long-term issues, but this would increase interest costs. By contrast, during a period of recession both the interest-cost and the macroeconomic objectives dictate a shift into short-term issues from long-term, but this runs afoul of traditional notions about funding. The experience of the United States since World War II suggests that the best explanatory hypothesis is that management has been directed toward maintaining substantially the same maturity structure over time.

Monetization. Interest costs on national debt could, of course, be reduced to zero through direct monetization of public debt. This is a process through which interest-bearing issues are refinanced through the issue of money, currency, or bank deposits. Because of the interest saving alone, monetization is always to be recommended insofar as it can be accomplished without inflation. Only the threat of inflation provides a barrier to monetization.

As the national economy grows, an increasing stock of money is required in order to maintain a constant level of product and service prices. One means of injecting increments to the money stock into the system is through debt monetization. Given the improbability that modern governments will retire public debts through the deliberate creation of budgetary surpluses, monetization provides the primary means through which national debts will be reduced. Monetization of debt is possible only for governmental units that possess independent money-creating powers.

National debt and fiscal policy. There is no simple connection between fiscal policy and the issue or retirement of national debt. Budgetary deficits need not be financed by the issue of debt, defined in a meaningful way. And, if such deficits are generated purposefully for the supplementing of aggregate demand, national debt should not be used as the means of financing. Instead, money should be directly created, which is always an alternative means of financing. In such a setting, the issue of debt exerts a deflationary, and undesirable, impact on total demand.

The elementary confusion about all this arises because, institutionally, national governments tend to disguise money creation through so-called "borrowing" from the central banks, and "public debt" is, nominally, created in this money-creating process. It is essential, however, that these two methods of financing deficits, which are conceptually quite different, be distinguished in the analysis.

The same analysis applies, in reverse, when budgetary surpluses are created. If the purpose of generating the surplus is that of reducing total demand, debt held outside the central banks should not be retired. Instead, the surplus should be disposed of by drawing down treasury balances or retiring debt held by central banks, which is the institutional equivalent of destroying money.

Principles of public debt. The preceding sections of this article summarize the institutional elements of "public debt," on which there exists broad agreement among professional experts. It is the "theory," or "principles," of public debt that has traditionally generated controversy, and the debate shows little sign of being resolved, although essentially the same arguments have been advanced for two centuries. For those who remain skeptical about the progress of economic science, the debt-theory controversy provides ample corroboration.

Nominally, the central question has been: *Who* bears the burden of public debt, and *when*? Analysis is clarified if this question is more carefully stated as follows: Who bears the real cost, or burden, of the public-expenditure projects that are financed by the issue of public loans, and when is this real cost incurred? What is sought is the incidence of debt, and the problem is comparable to that of locating the incidence of taxation, should this alternative financing device be employed.

This question is important because only if it is answered properly can a rational choice be made between debt issue and alternative financing devices. When should government borrow? This

ultimate policy question cannot be answered until and unless the
consequences of public borrowing can be predicted. Public spending may be financed in any of three ways: (1) taxation, (2) public
borrowing, and (3) money creation. The appropriate situations
for the use of the second alternative cannot be identified until the
differences between this and the remaining alternatives are ana-
lyzed.

For whom is the central question relevant? Failure to clarify
this point has also led to ambiguity. In any broadly democratic political structure, "government" is the institutional process through
which people make "public" decisions. Therefore, "When should
government borrow?" becomes merely a shorthand manner of asking, "When should individual citizens, as participants in the governmental decision process, as prospective taxpayers, borrowers,
or beneficiaries, borrow?" The question of the appropriateness of
public debt issue becomes analogous to the question concerning
private debt issue for the individual in his private capacity.

The answer to the central question posed above seems obvious.
Public borrowing should take place when it is desirable to put off
or to postpone the incurring of real cost until some later period,
in return for which, as in any act of borrowing, an interest charge
must normally be paid. The desire to postpone the incurring of
real cost or incidence of the public expenditure project may or may
not be related to the characteristics of the project itself. Public or
collective consumption may, in some cases, be legitimately financed from public loans, just as private consumption may be legitimately financed from private loans. A more normal or
standard reason for public borrowing is found, however, in the
temporal pattern of benefits that are expected to be produced by
the public spending project. If the project involves a large and concentrated outlay that is anticipated to yield benefits over a whole
sequence of time periods in the future, considerations of both efficiency and equity suggest resort to public loans, provided only that
direct money creation is predicted to cause inflation. Traditionally, public debt has been discussed with reference to the financing
of extraordinary expenditure needs, and specifically with reference to public capital formation. Historically, national debts have
been created largely during periods of war emergency, when

spending needs have indeed been extraordinary, even if the result
has not been public capital formation of the orthodox variety.

The controversy. Little more would need to be said with respect to the "principles" of public debt were it not for the fact that
the straightforward analysis has been recurrently challenged, and
by economists of great eminence. Ricardo's logic led him to enun-
ciate the proposition that the public loan and an extraordinary tax
of equivalent amount exert identical effects on the rational individual. Under conditions of perfect certainty, perfect capital markets, and under the assumption that individuals act "as if" they
will live forever, the future tax liabilities that are inherent in a
public debt obligation will be fully capitalized at the time of debt
issue, and the effects on individual behavior patterns will be identical to those that would be produced by a tax of the same capital
sum (Ricardo 1817). Within his own restricted model Ricardo's
basic proposition cannot be challenged, but its validity does not
contradict the elementary notions on public debt outlined above.
The individual, as prospective taxpayer-borrower-beneficiary,
confronts two financing alternatives—current taxation and public
debt issue. And to the extent that he interprets these two alternatives correctly, he knows that each of the two will impose upon
him a real cost, a burden that in a present-value sense is substantially the same. This Ricardian equivalence does not suggest, however, that the objective pattern of cost payments remains the same
over the two alternatives. Taxation and debt issue remain different, not similar, financing institutions, between which the individual may choose, for the simple reason that taxes require a transfer
of resource services from the individual to the fisc during the initial period, whereas debt issue postpones such transfer until later
periods. Whether or not the individual, under debt financing, correctly or incorrectly anticipates or "capitalizes" future tax liabilities as he "should" in the normative Ricardian model, is not
relevant to the determination of the objective pattern of real cost
payments over time.

A common fallacy. The most pervasive and recurring fallacy
in the discussion of public debt has been that which summarizes
the theory of internally held debt by the statement "We owe it to
ourselves." The fallacy here is not a new one; it was widely held

by both scholars and publicists in the eighteenth century. It almost faded out of the literature during the nineteenth and early twentieth centuries, only to reappear and to gain predominance after the so-called Keynesian revolution of the 1930s. In the immediate post-Keynesian decades the fallacy came to be almost universally accepted by economists. Therefore, if for no other reason, the importance that this fallacy has held in the literature warrants some consideration of it here. For purposes of discussion it may be labeled the "national accounting fallacy."

If the government borrows funds internally, so the theory goes, the public expenditure project is financed from internal resources. These cannot be brought from future time periods into the present; hence, the opportunity costs of the public project, regardless of the method of finance, must be borne during the period in which the resources are actually used. Public debt involves no postponement of cost or burden in time, and the view that it does so is based on a crudely drawn analogy with private debt. In periods after public debt issue, the required interest payments represent nothing more than transfers from taxpayers to bondholders, and, so long as both groups are members of the community, no real cost is incurred. External public debt, by contrast, because of the necessity to transfer interest payments to outsiders, is seen as wholly different from internal debt and analogous to private debt.

This conception of national debt contains a fundamental flaw in its failure to translate opportunity cost or burden from aggregative components into something that is meaningful to individual members of the community. What is the behavioral relevance of the fact that the resources actually used up in the public project are taken from current consumption or investment within the community until and unless those members of the community who must undergo the sacrifice of alternatives can be identified? Once this question is raised, however, and such identification is attempted, the fallacy is clearly revealed.

The members of the group who actually surrender purchasing power, command over current resource services, which is used by the government to carry out the public purpose, are those who purchase the public debt instruments, the government securities. No other members of the group sacrifice or "give up" anything di-

rectly during the initial period. But do the bond purchasers bear
the real costs or burden of the project? That they do not becomes
clear when it is recognized that their surrender of current funds
is a wholly voluntary and private transaction in which they exchange current purchasing power for promises, on the part of the
fisc, of income in future periods. These bond purchasers, or persons acting in this capacity, do not in any way consider themselves
to be exchanging purchasing power for the benefits of the public
spending, which would be the case if they should be really bearing
the real cost. If, however, it is acknowledged that bond purchasers
do not bear the real cost of the public spending, and if no other
members of the group bear such cost during the initial period, who
does pay for the project that is debt-financed? If, as the national
accounting fallacy suggests, none of this cost is shifted to future
periods, public debt might seem to provide for "fiscal perpetual
motion," since a means would have been located for financing beneficial public projects without cost.

The core of the fallacy lies in the equating of the community
as a unit, in some aggregated national accounting sense, with the
individuals-in-the-community, in some political sense as participants, direct or indirect, in collective decision making. In their capacities   as   prospective   taxpayers-borrowers-beneficiaries,
individual members of a political community can postpone the objective real costs of public spending through resort to debt finance,
even though they may sell the debt instruments, bonds, to
"themselves," acting in a wholly different capacity as bond purchasers. There are two exchanges, not one, involved, and it is the
neglect of this basic duality that has clouded much of the discussion   and   analysis.   Individuals,   as   taxpayers-borrowers-
beneficiaries, through the political decision process, "exchange"
the future tax liabilities that debt issue embodies for the promise
of expected benefits of the public spending, current or in future.
They are enabled to do this because individuals, in their capacities
as prospective bond purchasers, are willing to exchange current
purchasing power for the promise of future payments. The second
group makes an intertemporal exchange that is the opposite of
that made by the first group. And it is grossly misleading to think
of these two exchanges as canceling in effect merely because the
two groups may be partially coincident in membership.

The alleged differences between internal and external debt disappear in a model that corrects for this national accounting fallacy. In either situation individuals in their roles as participants in collective fiscal choice secure command over resource services initially without the necessity of giving up purchasing power. Whether other parties to the exchange be foreigners or some subset of individuals acting in their private capacity as bond purchasers makes no essential difference, secondary transfer considerations aside.

For individuals as they participate in fiscal choice, public debt is the institutional analogue to private debt as these same individuals act privately. Basically, the same principles apply in each case, despite all the disclaimers made by economists. This is not, of course, to equate public finance with private finance in all respects. The important difference lies, however, not in the effects of borrowing but in the fact that national governments possess powers of money creation whereas private persons, and local governments, do not. The power to create money allows national governments to generate budgetary deficits without at the same time issuing debt. The principles of public borrowing, which are at base simple, have been obscured by the failure of economists to make this elemental point clear. In part, as suggested before, this has been the result of institutional complexities present in modern fiscal-financial structures. Modern governments create money through issuing what they commonly call "public debt"; they do so by "borrowing" from central banks. This disguised money creation does not, of course, have the same effects as genuine debt issue.

The analysis of public debt which was dominant in the 1940s and 1950s, as a result of the Keynesian and post-Keynesian emphasis on deficit financing combined with the confusion between debt issue and money creation, was subjected to critical attack in the late 1950s and early 1960s. Predictions as to the development of analysis or the acceptance of ideas are risky at best, but it seems reasonable to suggest that the principles of public debt are on the verge of synthesis. Undue optimism is, however, surely to be avoided, especially if the history of debt theory is to be used as a guide.

THE BURDEN OF THE NATIONAL DEBT[2]

Millions of people are now taking time off from worrying about the prospects of atomic warfare to do some worrying on account of the burden of a growing national debt. But there are many quite different concepts of the nature of this burden. The purpose of this article is to examine the most important of these worries and to see to what extent they are justified and to what extent they are about imaginary burdens which only confuse the real issues.

I. Imaginary Effects of National Debt

1. By far the most common concern about the national debt comes from considering it as exactly the same kind of thing as a private debt which one individual owes to others. Every dollar of an individual's indebtedness must be subtracted from his assets in arriving at a measure of his net wealth. Indebtedness is impoverishment. It places the debtor in the hands of the creditor and threatens him with hardship and ruin. To avoid indebtedness as far as possible is undoubtedly an eminently well-established rule of private prudence.

The simple transferability of this rule to national debt is denied by nearly all economists. But nearly everybody who has ever suffered the oppressions of private indebtedness is tempted to apply the analogy directly, and the primary orthodoxy of the editorial writers, the dogma that sound government finance means balancing the budget, has no other basis.

One of the most effective ways of clearing up this most serious of all semantic confusions is to point out that private debt differs from national debt in being *external*. It is owed by one person to *others*. That is what makes it burdensome. Because it is

[2]Reprint of a *festschrift* article by Abba P. Lerner (1903–82), theoretical economist. From *Income, Employment and Public Policy: Essays in Honor of Alvin H. Hansen*, by Lloyd A. Metzler, et al., by permission of W. W. Norton & Company, Inc. Norton, '48. pp. 255–75. Copyright © 1948 by W. W. Norton & Company, Inc. Copyright renewed 1976 by Richard Musgrave.

interpersonal the proper analogy is not to national debt but to *international* debt. A nation owing money to other nations (or to the citizens of other nations) *is* impoverished or burdened in the same kind of way as a man who owes money to other men. But this does not hold for national debt which is owed by the nation to citizens of the *same* nation. There is then no external creditor. "We owe it to ourselves."

This refutation of the validity of the analogy from *external* to *internal* debt must not be interpreted as a denial that any significant problems can be raised by internal national debt. When economists are sufficiently irritated by the illegitimate analogy they are liable to say that the national debt does not matter at all. But this must be understood in the same sense as when a man who finds that rumor has converted a twisted ankle into a broken neck tells his friends that he is perfectly all right.

2. A variant of the false analogy is the declaration that national debt puts an unfair burden on our children, who are thereby made to pay for our extravagances. Very few economists need to be reminded that if our children or grandchildren repay some of the national debt these payments will be made *to* our children or grandchildren and to nobody else. Taking them altogether they will no more be impoverished by making the repayments than they will be enriched by receiving them.

Unfortunately the first few times people see this argument destroyed they feel tricked rather than convinced. But the resistance to conceding the painlessness of repaying national debt can be diminished by pointing out that it only corresponds to the relative uselessness of incurring it. An *external* loan enables an individual or a nation to get things from others without having to give anything in return, for the time being. The borrower is enabled to consume more than he is producing. And when he repays the external debt he has to consume less than he is producing. But this is not true for *internal* borrowing. However useful an internal loan may be for the health of the economy, it does *not* enable the nation to consume more than it produces. It should therefore not be so surprising that the repayment of internal debt does not necessitate a tightening of the belt. The internal borrowing did not permit the belt to be loosened in the first place.

3. Many who recognize that national debt is no subtraction from national wealth are nevertheless deeply concerned about the interest payments on the national debt. They call this the *interest burden* almost as if the interest payments constituted subtractions from the national income.

This involves exactly the same error. The interest payments are no more a subtraction from the national income than the national debt itself is a subtraction from the national wealth. This can be shown most clearly by pointing out how easy it is, by simply borrowing the money needed to make the interest payments, to convert the "interest burden" into some additional national debt. The interest need therefore never be more onerous than the additional principal of the debt into which it can painlessly be transformed.

Borrowing money to make the interest payments sounds much worse than simply getting into debt in the first place. Popular feeling on this score seems so strong that economists who are themselves quite free from the erroneous analogy have felt themselves constrained by the power of the prejudice to assume that the interest payments on national debt are never borrowed but raised by taxes.

The strict application of such a secondary orthodoxy would mean much more than these economists intend to concede to the popular prejudice. It would mean nothing less than the prohibition of all borrowing, and a meticulous adherence to the primary orthodoxy of balancing the budget at all times. For as soon as there is any national debt at all on which any interest has to be paid, *any* further government borrowing is indistinguishable from borrowing to pay the interest—unless we are taken in by bookkeeping fictions of financial earmarking which say that the money borrowed goes for other purposes so that the particular dollars used to pay the interest come from taxation.

4. Once the analogy with external debt is removed from the scene it is possible to consider various alleged effects of national debt on the economy to see whether they are real or important.

One of these is an alleged deflationary effect of the interest on the national debt. If the money to pay the interest is raised by additional taxes, these would probably reduce spending by more than the interest payments would increase spending. The net effect would be to aggravate any existing deficiency of spending or to alleviate any existing excess of spending. It would tend to deepen a depression or to mitigate an inflation.

But this deflationary effect is not really the effect of the interest payments. It only appears to be such because of a silent acceptance of the secondary orthodoxy of not borrowing to pay interest, but raising the money by additional taxation. The deflationary effect of such additional taxation is then misleadingly attributed to the national debt or to the interest payments.

With the unmasking of the implicit secondary orthodoxy it becomes clear that the interest payments are *inflationary*. They constitute additional income to the recipients and *increase* the rate of spending. If any additional taxes are imposed, their normally deflationary effects must of course be taken into consideration; but there is no reason for attributing these effects to the interest payments, since we need not impose such taxes if their effects are not desired.

5. The rational alternative principle to the orthodox one of balancing the budget, which means keeping tax revenues equal to government spending, is the Functional Finance principle of keeping total spending in the economy at a level which is high enough to prevent depression yet low enough to prevent inflation.

This is to aim policy *directly* at the real problems in terms of which any policy—including the orthodox policy of balancing the budget—must ultimately be justified: the prevention of both inflation and depression.

Whether the budget will be balanced or underbalanced or overbalanced will then be a *result,* more or less foreseen, of the application of the Functional Finance principle, depending on which of these is necessary for the prevention of inflation and depression.

Our main problem can then be reformulated in this way: Could we get into serious trouble from real effects of a growing national debt if we follow the principle of Functional Finance?

II. Real Effects of National Debt

6. Since the interest payments on the national debt increase private spending, a fiscal program which would have led to the right level of total spending in the absence of the national debt and the interest payments on it would now result in too much spending. Any increase in national debt (which increases money income and therefore also the spending out of income) must therefore be accompanied by a decrease in government spending or by an increase in taxation (or both). If this involves the abandonment of useful government undertakings or the enactment of harmful taxes, we really have a bad effect or "burden" of national debt.

This looks somewhat like the secondary orthodoxy which says that the money to make interest payments on the national debt must be raised from taxes, but the resemblance is only superficial. Since Functional Finance is interested only in total spending, it does not care whether the additional revenues from the taxes are equal to the interest payments. If more than an additional dollar is collected from the taxes needed to offset the extra spending due to an additional dollar of interest payments, tax revenue will have to be increased by more than the additional interest payments. On the other hand, if the efficiency of a dollar of tax revenue in reducing spending is greater than the efficiency of a dollar of interest payment in increasing spending, no increase in total spending will occur even though additional tax revenues are less than the additional interest payments.

But it is not really satisfactory to speak of tax revenues at all. Spending is affected by the tax *rates,* not by the tax *revenues.* The revenues are themselves effects of the taxes, and the efficiency of a tax in reducing spending is only indirectly connected with its efficiency in raising revenue. An increase in sales taxes which sharply diminished spending, for instance, might actually reduce the tax revenue. Functional Finance would then be served by additional taxes which offset the spending induced by the interest payments, even though tax revenues would actually be diminished just when the interest disbursements are increased.

7. In attempts to discredit the argument that we owe the national debt to ourselves it is often pointed out that the "we" does

not consist of the same people as the "ourselves." The benefits from interest payments on the national debt do not accrue to every individual in exactly the same degree as the damage done to him by the additional taxes made necessary. That is why it is not possible to repudiate the whole national debt without hurting anybody.

While this is undoubtedly true, all it means is that some people will be better off and some people will be worse off. Such a redistribution of wealth is involved in every significant happening in our closely interrelated economy, in every invention or discovery or act of enterprise. If there is some good general reason for incurring debt, the redistribution can be ignored because we have no more reason for supposing that the new distribution is worse than the old one than for assuming the opposite. That the distribution will be *different* is no more an argument against national debt than it is an argument in favor of it.

8. The growth of national debt may not only make some people richer and some people poorer, but may increase the inequality of distribution. This is because richer people can buy more government bonds and so get more of the interest payments without incurring a proportionately heavier burden of taxes. Most people would agree that this is bad. But it is no necessary effect of an increasing national debt. If the additional taxes are more progressive—more concentrated on the rich—than the additional holding of government bonds, the effect will be to *diminish* the inequality of income and wealth.

9. There are also effects on investment. Additional taxes reduce the net yield from investment, after taxes, and make socially useful investments unprofitable to the investor.

This effect is cancelled whenever there is the possibility of balancing losses against profits for tax purposes. If such offsetting were universally possible the taxation would not discourage investment at all. But the opportunity of loss offset is not universal, so that the interest payments on the national debt, by making more taxation necessary for the prevention of inflation, interferes with the efficiency of the economy by discouraging useful investments.

A failure to consider the cancelling effects of loss offsets is partially responsible for a common exaggeration of the bad effect of national debt on investment. This sometimes takes the form of a vivid nightmare of a vicious circle. Government investment to maintain prosperity by filling the gap left by discouraged private investment is financed by loans which increase the national debt still further. This calls for still more taxes, still greater discouragement of private investment, and the need for still more government investment to prevent depression with still more government borrowing—the cycle going on until by this insidious mechanism the economy is unwittingly led to complete collectivism.

Here it must be pointed out that as long as it is necessary for the government to prevent depression by filling a gap in investment, the economy is suffering from *too little spending*. There is therefore no need for more taxation and its possible bad effect on investment. Such extra taxation is necessary only if the economy is suffering from the opposite trouble—from *too much spending*. The vicious circle, apart from some other weaknesses, depends on supposing the economy to suffer at the same time from too much spending and from too little spending.

10. An increase in national debt, with its accompanying accumulation of government bonds by the individuals to whom the debt is owed, can make the owners of the government bonds less willing to work. One of the reasons for working, the earning of money to put away for a rainy day, is weakened (from the point of view of these bondholders) because there is more put away already for rainy days.

This has been pointed out as a bad effect of national debt. But work is only a *means* for producing the things that people want and is not desirable as an end in itself. (Any work that is so enjoyed would not be reduced for the reasons here discussed.) The decrease takes place because people *prefer* the leisure to the products of labor, and the change represents an *increase* in the welfare of the people.

The increase in leisure would be accompanied by an increase in consumption, both this and the increased leisure coming out of a reduction in *saving*. This saving which is prevented by the increase in national debt would have taken place not for the sake of permitting an increase in future consumption but for the sake of the security yielded by the savings. It would have made necessary an increase in investment to prevent depression. This shift of resources from consumption (including leisure) to investment is unnecessary, because the desired security is provided without it by the ownership of the additional national debt. Anybody who still wants to save for the sake of the interest yield (reflecting the marginal efficiency of investment) is free to do so. But the increased consumption and reduced efforts by people who are enjoying the ownership of government bonds is merely the result of the elimination, by the national debt, of an uneconomic, because undesired, shifting of resources from present to future uses.

Of real importance is the consideration that the taxes necessary to offset the inflationary effects of the interest payments may reduce the net reward for work below the value of the marginal net product. This would reduce the amount of work done below the optimum, and constitute a real impairment of the efficiency of the economy.

11. The effects of the national debt in discouraging its owners from working and in necessitating anti-inflationary taxes which may reduce the reward for work and for investment can be dramatized by imagining a fantastically large national debt.

If the national debt is so large that the interest on it comes to many times the national income from work (and if the interest payments are fairly widely distributed among the population), very little work will be done over and above that which is done for the pleasure of doing it.

This in itself is not anything bad. If such a state of affairs could be maintained without heavy taxation (which will be discussed below), nearly all goods will be free, and we will have approached the ideal of plenty where Marxism and Anarchism converge and economy is no longer necessary. This is perhaps not quite as far of attainment as one tends to suppose. In a rich country like the United States, if everybody had such an accumulation of government bonds that conspicuous consumption and display lost their significance, needs of material goods could be so simplified and reduced as to make their complete satisfaction feasible by the few hours' work that are necessary for health or may become necessary for social approbation.

The age of plenty is, however, not imminent. An income from interest on the national debt many times as large as the income

from other sources would result in expenditure on goods and services many times as large as the available supply of goods and services. There would therefore have to be very heavy taxes to keep
the demand from exceeding the supply and thus bringing about
inflation. If these taxes approached 100 percent of the income,
they would so reduce the net reward for effort that all work producing income subject to the tax (either when earning it or when
spending it) would come to a stop, and the whole economy would
break down. The continuation of life would depend entirely on the
degree to which black markets could avoid the taxation, for only
such activities would be worth while. Such heavy taxation would
be much more destructive than the inflation from which it was
supposed to protect the economy.

III. The Equilibrium Level of National Debt

12. Although this shows that too large a national debt can be
a most serious matter, it does not mean that Functional Finance
has to be supplemented by additional precautions to prevent the
national debt from growing too large. Functional Finance does
this *automatically*.

A tendency to depression exists only when people do not spend
enough—they are too eager to save. The amount they would save
if fully employed is greater than the amount privately being invested, so that unless the government augments investment or consumption expenditure we have a depression which prevents
people from saving more than is being invested.

The people want to save so much because they do not have
enough already saved up. The growth of national debt is an increase in the holdings of wealth, the past savings of the people, and
so it relieves the pressure to save. If we assume that the government borrows the money for its augmentation of spending, there
is an automatic growth of the national debt as long as people want
to save more than is being invested. This goes on until an
equilibrium level of national debt is reached when people are so
rich in claims to wealth that they no longer want to save more than
is compatible with the maintenance of full employment with a balanced budget. At that point the application of Functional Finance

calls for a balanced budget, and the national debt will not grow any more.

If the national debt is above the equilibrium level, Functional Finance calls for an overbalanced budget to prevent the excess demand for goods that this would bring about. The budgetary surplus could then go to repaying some of the debt, and so again there will be a tendency for the equilibrium level of national debt to be approached—this time from the other side.

This balancing of the budget is a *result* or symptom of long run equilibrium. The error of those who cling to the fiscal principle of balancing the budget lies in their prescribing as a *rule* for the short period what is properly only a *result* of the achievement of long period equilibrium.

If we assume a national debt many times greater than the equilibrium level, the taxes needed to prevent inflation may have to be so heavy, and their effects on the efficiency of the economy so pernicious, that this Functional Finance cure for inflation would be worse than the disease. Other and more drastic measures may then be proper, such as a capital levy to reduce the national debt once for all to something near the equilibrium (where Functional Finance could manage it) or perhaps to achieve the same thing by permitting inflation to wipe out the excessive national debt. In such an extreme situation the normal operation of Functional Finance may not be adequate.

It is, however, important to remember that such an extreme situation could never be the result of Functional Finance because Functional Finance would not permit so great a movement beyond the equilibrium level in the first place. Functional Finance, if it is not given too great a job, works steadily to move the economy toward the equilibrium where the budget would be balanced. From that point there would be adjustments only to the extent that the equilibrium position is affected by movements in the level of income, the age distribution of the population, the distribution of wealth in the population, and other such slow moving secular determinants.

13. It should be noted that the equilibrium level of national debt is quite different from the "manageable" or "reasonable" levels of national debt which Professor Hansen and others insist on

as limits to guide us in fiscal policy. The latter limits are *prescribed* limits which we are told not to pass because of dangers that lie on the other side. Sometimes they are accompanied by prognoses and estimates which indicate that there will be no tendency for these limits to be passed by a policy of maintaining full employment by borrowing to maintain adequate demand. But essentially they are signposts to guard against the dangers of permitting the national debt to go beyond the "manageable" or "reasonable" limit. Our equilibrium level is not a prescribed limit to policy. It describes an automatic tendency for the national debt to reach an equilibrium if we do nothing about it except merely follow the basic Functional Finance principle of keeping total demand at the proper level to prevent inflation or depression.

14. The equilibrium level of the national debt, with its balanced budget, is reached when the Functional Finance policy of preventing inflation and depression results in a yield from taxes just sufficient to pay all the expenses of government including the interest payments on the national debt.

These taxes may have serious effects on the economy even before the equilibrium level of national debt is reached. If there is not a proper arrangement for loss offset, the taxes may interfere seriously with useful investment. If the taxes fall heavily on the reward for marginal effort, they will prevent useful work from being done, diminishing the real level of national income. If the government has to restrict its own expenditures, many socially useful undertakings will be killed in the efforts to prevent inflation. And the diminishing desire to work, accompanied by an increasing desire to spend (which accompanies the growth of individual wealth in the form of ownership of national debt), will decrease the supply of goods on the market even while it increases the demand for them. Even though this last item must not be counted as a social loss, it does contribute to the inflationary pressures, and necessitates more taxation and greater government economies, both of which can mean real diminutions in the national income.

It is true that all these bad effects come only from the imposition of "bad taxes." If the additional taxes did not fall on the income from additional effort, the bad effects would be avoided. But it is probably impossible to avoid all "bad taxes," especially if the good ones are already being exploited to the utmost—so that the problem cannot be dismissed by simply recommending good taxes instead of bad taxes.

It is conceivable that even before the equilibrium level of national debt is reached a vicious circle would be encountered in which additional taxation failed to check the increasing inflationary pressure because, by its interference with the reward for extra effort, it reduced supply more than it reduced demand.

In such an extreme and very unlikely situation, there is a very easy and extremely satisfactory way out. The solution is to *reduce* taxes. This would increase supply more than it increases demand, and so would work to check the inflationary pressure even while it raised the national income.

More serious is the less extreme case where taxation reduces supply seriously but not more than it reduces demand. The tax increases needed to check the inflation might so reduce the efficiency of the economy and the real income that it would be better to suffer the evils of inflation. It may even happen that the increased tax rates resulted in a diminished yield because of the reduction in output so that the budget, instead of getting nearer and nearer to balancing, got more and more unbalanced. As the difference is added (we assume) annually to the national debt, the interest payments would increase year by year, while the tax collections lag further and further behind the government expenditures (including these interest payments) so that there is no tendency to equilibrium. The national debt would grow indefinitely— ultimately leading to all the evils of national debt much greater than the equilibrium level.

15. All these troubles not only assume extremely bad taxes, but depend on a basic misunderstanding of the function of government borrowing. The government is supposed to fight chronic depression by expenditure of money which it borrows at interest, so continually increasing the national debt until it becomes "unmanageable." Borrowing is thus seen as an inflationary activity, necessary to combat the tendency to chronic depression, and later necessary to raise the money to keep up interest payments on national debt even when the danger is one of inflation rather than of depression.

But borrowing is not inflationary. It is deflationary. It looks inflationary only if one fails to distinguish it from the expenditure of the borrowed money. This expenditure is more inflationary as a rule than the borrowing is deflationary, so that the net effect of the borrowing-plus-spending is inflationary.

Borrowing is deflationary because it takes money out of the hands of the lenders and puts government bonds there instead. People are somewhat less likely to want to buy other things when they have spent their money on government bonds. The sale of government bonds diminishes liquidity, tends to raise interest rates, and discourages investment. The government should therefore not borrow unless it wishes to bring about these deflationary effects. It can keep on making all the expenditures and investments it finds desirable without borrowing, merely by paying for these out of its stocks of money or creating new money if it should run short.

16. The government should therefore not borrow any money until the economy has passed out of the range of threatening depression into the range of threatening inflation. This will occur even without any incurrence of national debt simply as a result of the increase in the amount of money which gets into the hands of the public as the government spends it. As the amount of money in the hands of the public increases, the public feels itself wealthier—just as if they had more government bonds or other property. This is part of the "wealth effect." It diminishes the tendency to save, and to work for the sake of saving, and increases demand while it diminishes supply. The owners of the money do not get interest on their holdings as they would if there had been an increase in national debt instead of an increase in the amount of money. But in place of this there will be the increased liquidity of the economy, tending to lower the rate of interest, and thus to increase investment—and perhaps also some spending out of income by such as are discouraged from saving by the fall in the rate of interest. Instead of the "income effect" that would accompany the interest payments on the national debt there will be the "liquidity effect" of the increase in the amount of money, also tending to increase total demand. This is the other equilibrating mechanism. When the amount of money has increased sufficiently

the deficiency of demand which called for the government deficit will have to come to an end, and the volume of money will cease to grow. Full employment is maintained by an equilibrium level in the amount of money. There is no danger of inflation from the increase in the amount of money because the first signs of inflation are at the same time signs that the increase in the amount of money has gone too far. It will be a sign that the government must spend less money than it collects in taxes (or otherwise), and so bring back the amount of money to the equilibrium level.

17. The effect of government borrowing (in the sense of simply borrowing, not borrowing-and-spending) is to diminish the liquidity of the economy, to raise the rate of interest, and to discourage investment. The government should therefore borrow only when it wishes to diminish liquidity. This will happen whenever the government thinks it better to check low-yield investment than to check consumption by imposing more taxes, or to check useful government expenditures. Borrowing is a deflationary instrument like taxation and government economy, competitive with these in the battle against inflation.

But while the *act* of government borrowing is deflationary, the resulting *fact* of the existence of government debt is inflationary, because of both the "wealth effect" and the "income effect" on spending. The "wealth effect" is also produced by the *fact* of existence of money. If both the national debt and the amount of money increase together, the long period equilibrium will be the result of *both* influences on the rate of spending, and will be reached at the point where the "wealth effects" of both the national debt and the amount of money, together with the "income effect" of the national debt and the "liquidity effect" of the new money, bring about the required total rate of spending for full employment. The budget is balanced, and neither the national debt nor the amount of money need change any more (except in adjusting to secular changes in the determinants of the equilibrium).

18. The difference between government borrowing and the other deflationary instruments, government economy and taxation, is that while the other instruments have a once-for-all deflationary effect, borrowing only temporarily offsets inflationary effects until the time when the debt is to be repaid, and then the

inflationary pressure returns with interest—literally. And even before the debt is repaid, and even if the debt is destined to remain on the books indefinitely, the inflationary pressures come back in the form of inflationary interest payments in the "income effect" of the national debt and the constant "wealth effect" from the mere existence of the national debt. The deflationary effect of government borrowing is weaker than that of the other instruments, partly because it is offset by inflationary effects of the extra national debt which follows every dollar of government borrowing.

What this means is that government borrowing is not a real alternative to taxation or economy, but only a way of postponing these really deflationary instruments to a more convenient time in the future. Exactly the same relationships hold in reverse for the repayment of debt with its immediate inflationary effect through the increase in liquidity and its long run deflationary effect from the absence of the liquidated national debt.

19. The importance of this peculiarity of government borrowing as a deflationary instrument (and of repaying debt as an inflationary instrument) comes to light when we consider some attempts to derive rules for policy about national debt. It is pointed out for example that it is better for an economy to have a smaller rather than a larger national debt because the "wealth effect" and the "income effect" of the larger national debt cause more spending so that more taxes are necessary to prevent inflation. Since the taxes are not ideal taxes, they will to some extent fall on the marginal pay for effort, and they will also discourage useful investment and useful government spending. The national debt thus has a bad effect.

But is this remark of any use as a guide for policy? Hardly at all. For it is surely not intended to suggest that the debt or a part of it should be repudiated. The effects of this particularly arbitrary form of taxation would certainly be worse even than the imperfect taxes needed to prevent inflation, the bad effects of which it is hoped to avoid. Nor can it be intended to suggest that the borrowing should not have taken place in the past, if this borrowing was considered less harmful than the alternative deflationary instruments of taxation or government economies at the time. At the most it can tell us that the borrowing, which meant a postponement of the taxation or economy, was not wise if the taxation and economies would be more harm in the future than at the time from which they were postponed. The postponement was then a mistake. But that surely is no *general* reason for not incurring debt, since the postponement can very well be a very good policy. Certainly it is not intended to argue that it is better to permit unemployment if its prevention entails borrowing (the issue of new money being too shocking). Yet this is the lesson most likely to be derived by practical politicians from careless declarations that it is better to have a smaller than a larger debt. The statement is of the same category which says that it is better to have a larger than a smaller national income. Until it is shown what measures are proposed to increase the national income or to decrease the national debt, the statement is academic in the worst sense of the term.

The national debt cannot be made smaller by just wishing it so. It can be reduced only by repudiation, or by increased taxation, or by increased government economies on what are presumably useful activities. All of these steps immediately bring about in a more severe degree the very evils which the existence of the national debt threatens in the future.

IV. National Debt and National Wealth

20. It might be supposed that national debt could be avoided if appropriate and wise fiscal policy would result in *private* borrowing and investment taking place instead of government borrowing and investment or other expenditure. (This is independent of whether the activity is conceived as helping to prevent depression by providing investment, or helping to prevent inflation by borrowing.) There will then be no government debt. Is this a way in which the evils of national debt could be avoided without giving up the fight to prevent inflation and depression?

To suppose this to be the case is to make a most serious mistake. For the whole of the analysis of this article, *all* the effects of government borrowing and of national debt apply just as much to private borrowing and to private debt. We have seen that what is important about national debt is that individuals feel rich and have more income—the "wealth effect" and the "income effect."

These effects are just as much in evidence if the public, instead of owning government stock, owns stock in the private corporations which have done the investing instead of the government. The ownership of shares in private corporations has just as great a "wealth effect," and insofar as the yield in private investment is on the average greater than the interest on government bonds, it has a greater "income effect" even after allowing for bankruptcies. There will therefore be at least as great an inflationary pressure as if there had been the same amount of national debt; at least as much taxation will be necessary to prevent inflation, and at least as much harm will be done to the efficiency of the economy as in the other case. The evils cannot be avoided by having private instead of public debt.

All the other arguments developed above in relation to national debt will also be applicable in the same way to private debt. There will be an equilibrium level of *wealth* in the long run which will permit a balancing of the budget, though the wealth will consist of public and private debts, as well as money and real, physical goods.

Against this it has been argued that private investment results in an increase in the output of goods in the future to match the increase of demand out of the income of the recipients of dividends. But public investment may be just as useful in increasing future output, and it often may be more useful. Of course it is better to have useful private investment than useless public investment. It is similarly better to have useful public investment than useless private investment. In fact it is simply better to have relatively useful investments than relatively useless investments, irrespective of whether they are public or private. But this residual proposition is not really very helpful.

21. A final argument takes the form of pointing out that private investment is always built on the expectation of being able to charge sufficient for the product to be able to pay dividends to the shareholders, while public investment is often directed to enterprises which, however useful they may be socially, do not collect sufficient from the consumers to pay the whole cost of the investment and the interest on the money invested. Indeed it is just such enterprises which do not permit the consumer to be charged the

whole cost of the undertaking that are by definition the Public Utilities which tend to be run by public enterprise. It is therefore true that private enterprise is more likely to be less inflationary in the long run than public enterprise, and to need less taxation to prevent inflation.

But it does not in the least follow from this that it would be better to encourage private enterprise to undertake fully self-liquidating enterprise than for the government to undertake activities which are equally useful but would make more taxation necessary. For if these useful "Public Utilities," instead of being undertaken by the government and run on the socially most desirable scale (which results in losses and the need for more taxes), are undertaken by private enterprise (which will do so only if they can apply at least enough monopolistic restriction to get a normal return on their investment), the price will be raised above the marginal social cost to the average private cost. This inflicts exactly the same kind of social loss on the economy, interfering with its efficiency in serving the needs of the consumers, as is done by a very bad tax. Since the taxes imposed to prevent inflation are at least designed to some extent to avoid the evils of bad taxes, it would be most unreasonable to prefer the clearly bad "taxes" imposed by monopolists to make "Public Utilities" self-liquidating.

22. We see then that the kinds of evil most popularly ascribed to national debt are wholly imaginary; that some less serious evils are more real, but are not to be avoided by the obvious policies of avoiding national debt; and that the direct application of the basic principles of Functional Finance are an adequate general guide to fiscal policy. If the short run equilibrium is taken care of so that there is neither too much spending nor too little spending, and so neither inflation or depression, and a normal amount of reasonableness is applied in choosing between the different ways of achieving this short run equilibrium, the long run equilibrium of the size of the national debt will look after itself.

FIRST, THE ACADEMIC SCRIBBLERS[3]

John Maynard Keynes was a speculator, in ideas as well as
in foreign currencies, and his speculation was scarcely idle. He
held an arrogant confidence in the ideas that he adopted, at least
while he held them, along with a disdain for the virtues of temporal consistency. His objective, with *The General Theory of Employment, Interest and Money* (1936), was to secure a permanent
shift in the policies of governments, and he recognized that the
conversion of the academic scribblers, in this case the economists,
was a necessary first step. "It is my fellow economists, not the general public, whom I must convince." In the economic disorder of
the Great Depression, there were many persons—politicians,
scholars, publicists—in America and elsewhere, who advanced
policy proposals akin to those that were to be called "Keynesian."
But it was Keynes, and Keynes alone, who captured the minds of
the economists (or most of them) by changing their vision of the
economic process.

Without Keynes, government budgets would have become unbalanced, as they did before Keynes, during periods of depression
and war. Without Keynes, governments would have varied the
rate of money creation over time and place, with bad and good
consequences. Without Keynes, World War II would have happened, and the economies of western democracies would have been
pulled out of the lingering stagnation of the 1930s. Without
Keynes, substantially full employment and an accompanying inflationary threat would have described the postwar years. But
these events of history would have been conceived and described
differently, then and now, without the towering Keynesian presence. Without Keynes, the proclivities of ordinary politicians
would have been held in check more adequately in the 1960s and
1970s. Without Keynes, modern budgets would not be quite so
bloated, with the threat of more to come, and inflation would not

[3]Reprint of an article by James M. Buchanan and Richard E. Wagner, professors of economics.
Democracy in Deficit: The Political Legacy of Lord Keynes. pp. 23–35. Copyright © 1977 by Academic Press.
Reprinted by permission.

be the clear and present danger to the free society that it has surely now become. The legacy or heritage of Lord Keynes is the putative intellectual legitimacy provided to the natural and predictable political biases toward deficit spending, inflation, and the growth of government.

Our objective in this chapter is to examine the Keynesian impact on the ideas of economists, on the "Keynesian revolution" in economic theory and policy, as discussed within the ivied walls of academia. By necessity as well as intent, our treatment will be general and without detail, since our purpose is not that of offering a contribution to intellectual or scientific history, but, rather, that of providing an essential element in any understanding of the ultimate political consequences of Keynesian ideas.

"Classical Economics," A Construction in Straw?

Keynes set out to change the way that economists looked at the national economy. A first step was the construction of a convenient and vulnerable target, which emerged as the "classical economists," who were only partially identified but who were, in fact, somewhat provincially located in England. With scarcely a sidewise glance at the institutional prerequisites, Keynes aimed directly at the jugular of the targeted model, the self-equilibrating mechanism of the market economy. In the Keynesian description, the classical economist remained steadfast in his vision of a stable economy that contained within it self-adjusting reactions to exogenous shocks, reactions that would ensure that the economy as a whole, as well as in its particular sectors, would return toward a determinate set of equilibrium values. Furthermore, these values were determinate at plausibly desired levels. Following Ricardo and rejecting Malthus, the classical economists denied the prospects of a general glut on markets.

It is not within our purpose here to discuss the methodological or the analytical validity of the Keynesian argument against its allegedly classical opposition. We shall not attempt to discuss our own interpretation of just what pre-Keynesian economics actually was. The attack was launched, not upon that which might have existed, but upon an explicitly defined variant, which may or may not have been caricature. And the facts of intellectual history attest to the success of the venture. Economists of the twentieth century's middle decades conceived "classical economics" in the image conjured for them by Keynes, and they interpret the "revolution" as the shift away from that image. This is all that need concern us here.

In this image, "classical economics" embodied the presumption that there existed built-in equilibrating forces which ensured that a capitalistic economy would generate continuing prosperity and high-level employment. Exogenous shocks might, of course, occur, but these would trigger reactions that would quickly, and surely, tend to restore overall equilibrium at high-employment levels. Such an image seemed counter to the observed facts of the 1920s in Britain and of the 1930s almost everywhere. National economies seemed to be floundering, not prospering, and unemployment seemed to be both pervasive and permanent.

Keynes boldly challenged the basic classical paradigm of his construction. He denied the very existence of the self-equilibrating forces of the capitalist economy. He rejected the extension of the Marshallian conception of particular market equilibrium to the economy as a whole, and to the aggregates that might be introduced to describe it. A national economy might attain "equilibrium," but there need be no assurance that the automatic forces of the market would produce acceptably high and growing real output and high-level employment.

Again we need not and shall not trace out the essential Keynesian argument, in any of its many variants, and there would be little that we might add to the still-burgeoning literature of critical reinterpretation and analysis. What is important for us is the observed intellectual success of the central Keynesian challenge. From the early 1940s, most professionally trained economists looked at "the economy" differently from the way they might have looked at the selfsame phenomenon in the early 1920s or early 1930s. In a general sense of the phrase, a paradigm shift took place.

Before Keynes, economists of almost all persuasions implicitly measured the social productivity of their own efforts by the potential gains in allocative efficiency which might be forthcoming upon the rational incorporation of economists' continuing institutional criticisms of political reality. How much increase in social value might be generated by a shift of resources from *this* to *that* use? Keynes sought to change, and succeeded in changing, this role for economists. Allocative efficiency, as a meaningful and desirable social objective, was not rejected. Instead, it was simply relegated to a second level of importance by comparison with the "pure efficiency" that was promised by an increase in the sheer volume of employment itself. It is little wonder that economists became excited about their greatly enhanced role and that they came to see themselves as new persons of standing.

Once converted, economists could have readily been predicted to allow Keynes the role of pied piper. But how were they to be converted? They had to be convinced that the economic disaster of the Great Depression was something more than the consequence of specific mistakes in monetary policy, and that correction required more than temporary measures. Keynes accomplished this aspect of the conversion by presenting a *general* theory of the aggregative economic process, one that appeared to explain the events of the 1930s as one possible natural outcome of market interaction rather than as an aberrant result produced by policy lapses. In this general theory, there is no direct linkage between the overall or aggregate level of output and employment that would be determined by the attainment of equilibrium in labor and money markets and that level of output and employment that might be objectively considered desirable. In the actual equilibrium attained through the workings of the market process, persons might find themselves involuntarily unemployed, and they could not increase the overall level of employment by offers to work for lowered money wages. Nor could central bankers ensure a return to prosperity by the simple easing of money and credit markets. Under certain conditions, these actions could not reduce interest rates and, through this, increase the rate of capital investment. To shock the system out of its possible locked-in position, exogenous forces would have to be introduced, in the form of deficit spending by government.

The Birth of Macroeconomics

As if in one fell swoop, a new and exciting half-discipline was appended to the classical tradition. Macroeconomics was born almost full-blown from the Keynesian impact. To the conventional theory of resource allocation, now to be labeled "microeconomics," the new theory of employment was added, and labeled "macroeconomics." The professional economist, henceforward, would have to be trained in the understanding not only of the theory of the market process, but also the theory of aggregative economics, that theory from which predictions might be made about levels of employment and output. Even those who remained skeptical of the whole Keynesian edifice felt compelled to become expert in the manipulation of the conceptual models. And perhaps most importantly for our history, textbook writers responded by introducing simplistic Keynesian constructions into the elementary textbooks. Paul Samuelson's *Economics* (1948) swept the field, almost from its initial appearance early after the end of World War II. Other textbooks soon followed, and almost all were similar in their dichotomous presentation of subject matter. Courses were organized into two parts, microeconomics and macroeconomics, with relatively little concern about possible bridges between these sometimes disparate halves of the discipline.

Each part of the modified discipline carried with it implicit norms for social policy. Microeconomics, the rechristened traditional price theory, implicitly elevates allocative efficiency to a position as the dominant norm, and applications of theory here have usually involved demonstrations of the efficiency-producing or efficiency-retarding properties of particular institutional arrangements. Macroeconomics, the Keynesian consequence, elevates high-level output and employment to its position of normative dominance, with little or no indicated regard to the efficiency with which resources are utilized. There are, however, significant differences in the implications of these policy norms as between micro- and macroeconomics. In the former, the underlying ideal or optimum structure, toward which policy steps should legitimately be aimed, is a well-functioning regime of markets. At an analytical level, demonstrations that "markets fail" under certain conditions are taken to suggest that correctives will "make markets work" or, if this is impossible, will substitute regulation for markets, with the norm for regulation itself being that of duplicating market results. Equally, if not more, important are the demonstrations that markets fail because of unnecessary political control and regulation, with the implication that removal and/or reduction of control itself will generate desired results. In summary, the policy implications of microeconomics are not themselves overtly interventionist and, if anything, probably tend toward the anti-interventionist pole.

The contrast with macroeconomics in this respect is striking. There is nothing akin to the "well-functioning market" which will produce optimally preferred results, no matter how well embedded in legal and institutional structure. Indeed, the central thrust of the Keynesian message is precisely to deny the existence of such an underlying ideal. "The economy," in the Keynesian paradigm, is afloat without a rudder, and its own internal forces, if left to themselves, are as likely to ground the system on the rocks of deep depression as they are to steer it toward the narrow channels of prosperity. Once this model for an economy is accepted to be analytically descriptive, even if major quibbles over details of interpretation persist, the overall direction of the economy by governmental or political control becomes almost morally imperative. There is a necessary interventionist bias which stems from the analytical basis of macroeconomics, a bias that is inherent in the paradigm itself and which need not be at all related to the ideological persuasion of the economist practitioner.

The New Role for the State

The Keynesian capture of the economists, therefore, carried with it a dramatically modified role for the state in their vision of the world. In this new vision, the state was obliged to take affirmative action toward ensuring that the national economy would remain prosperous, action which could, however, be taken with clearly defined objectives in view. Furthermore, in the initial surges of enthusiasm, few questions of conflict among objectives seemed to present themselves. Who could reject the desirability of

high-level output and employment? Politicians responded quickly, and the effective "economic constitution" was changed to embody an explicit commitment of governmental responsibility for
full employment. The Full Employment Act became law in the
United States in 1946. The President's Council of Economic Advisers was created, reflecting the political recognition of the enhanced role of the economists and of economic theory after
Keynes.

The idealized scenario for the then "New Economics" was relatively straightforward. Economists were required first to make
forecasts about the short- and medium-term movements in the appropriate aggregates—consumption, investment, public spending,
and foreign trade. These forecasts were then to be fed into the suitably constructed model for the working of the national economy.
Out of this, there was to emerge a prediction about equilibrium
levels of output and employment. This prediction was then to be
matched against desired or targeted values. If a shortfall seemed
likely, further estimation was to be made about the required magnitude of adjustment. This result was then to be communicated
to the decision makers, who would, presumably, respond by ma-
nipulating the government budget to accommodate the required
changes.

This scenario, as sketched, encountered rough going early on
when the immediate post–World War II forecasts proved so de-
monstrably in error. Almost from the onset of attempts to put
Keynesian economics into practice, conflicts between the employment and the price-level objectives appeared, dousing the early enthusiasm for the economists' new Jerusalem. Nonetheless, there
was no backtracking on the fundamental reassignment of functions. The responsibility for maintaining prosperity remained
squarely on the shoulders of government. Stabilization policy occupied the minds and hearts of economists, even amidst the developing evidence of broad forecasting error, and despite the
sharpening analytical criticism of the basic Keynesian structure.
The newly acquired faith in macroeconomic policy tools was, in
fact, maintained by the political lags in implementation. While
textbooks spread the simple Keynesian precepts, and while
learned academicians debated sophisticated points in logical anal-

ysis, the politics of policy proceeded much as before the revolution, enabling economists to blame government for observed stabilization failures. The recessions of the 1950s, even if mild by prewar standards, were held to reflect failures of political response. Economists in the academy were preparing the groundwork for the New Frontier, when Keynesian ideas shifted beyond the sanctuaries to capture the minds and hearts of ordinary politicians and the public.

The Scorn for Budget Balance

The old-time fiscal religion was not easy to dislodge. Before the Keynesian challenge, an effective "fiscal constitution" did exist, even if this was not embodied in a written document. This "constitution" included the precept for budget balance, and this rule served as an important constraint on the natural proclivities of politicians. The economists who had absorbed the Keynesian teachings were faced with the challenge of persuading political leaders and the public at large that the old-time fiscal religion was irrelevant in the modern setting. As a sacrosanct principle, budget balance had to be uprooted. Prosperity in the national economy, not any particular rule or state of the government's budget, was promoted as the overriding policy objective. And if the achievement and the maintenance of prosperity required deliberate creation of budget deficits, who should be concerned? Deficits in the government budget, said the Keynesians, were indeed small prices to pay for the blessings of high employment.

A new mythology was born. Since there was no particular virtue in budget balance, per se, there was no particular vice in budget unbalance, per se. The lesson was clear: Budget balance did not matter. There was apparently no normative relationship, even in some remote conceptual sense, between the two sides of the government's fiscal account. The government *was* different from the individual. The Keynesian-oriented textbooks hammered home this message to a continuing sequence of student cohort groups. Is there any wonder that, eventually, the message would be heeded?

The New Precepts for Fiscal Policy

The new rules that were to guide fiscal policy were simple. Budget deficits were to be created when aggregate demand threatened to fall short of that level required to maintain full employment. Conversely, and symmetrically, budget surpluses were to be created when aggregate demand threatened to exceed full-employment targets, generating price inflation. A balanced budget would rationally emerge only when aggregate demand was predicted to be just sufficient to generate full employment without exerting inflationary pressures on prices. Otherwise, unbalanced budgets would be required. In this pure regime of functional finance, a regime in which the government's budget was to be used, and used rationally, as the primary instrument for stabilization, budget deficits or budget surpluses might emerge over some cumulative multiperiod sequence. Those who were most explicit in their advocacy of such a regime expressed little or no concern for the direction of budget unbalance over time. In the wake of the experience of the Great Depression, however, the emphasis was placed on the possible need for a continuing sequence of deficits. The potential application of the new fiscal principles in threatened inflationary periods was discussed largely in hypothetical terms, appended to lend analytical symmetry to the policy models.

Budget Deficits, Public Debt, and Money Creation

The deliberate creation of budget deficits—the explicit decision to spend and not to tax—was the feature of Keynesian policy that ran most squarely in the face of traditional and time-honored norms for fiscal responsibility. But there was no alternative for the Keynesian convert. To increase aggregate demand, total spending in the economy must be increased, and this could only be guaranteed if the private-spending offsets of tax increase could be avoided or swamped. New net spending must emerge, and the creation of budget deficits offered the only apparent escape from economic stagnation.

If, however, the flow of spending was to be increased in this manner, the problem of financing deficits necessarily arose. And at this point, the policy advocate encountered two separate and subsidiary norms in the previously existing "constitution." Deficits could be financed in only one of two ways, either through government borrowing (the issue of public debt) or through the explicit creation of money (available only to central government). But public debt, in the classical theory of public finance, transfers burdens onto the shoulders of future generations. And money creation was associated, historically, with governmental corruption along with the dangers of inflation.

Retrospectively, it remains somewhat surprising that the Keynesians, or most of them, chose to challenge the debt-burden argument of classical public finance theory rather than the money-creation alternative. (By so doing, quite unnecessary intellectual confusion was introduced into an important area of economic theory, confusion that had not, even as late as 1976, been fully eliminated.) Within the strict assumptions of the Keynesian model, and in the deficient-demand setting, the opportunity cost of additional governmental spending is genuinely zero. From this, it follows directly that the creation of money to finance the required deficit involves no net cost; there is no danger of price inflation. In the absence of political-institutional constraints, therefore, the idealized Keynesian policy package for escape from such economic situations is the explicit creation of budget deficits along with the financing of these by pure money issue.

In such a context, any resort to public debt issue, to public borrowing, is a necessary second-best. Why should the government offer any interest return at all to potential lenders of funds, to the purchasers of government debt instruments, when the alternative of printing money at negligible real cost and at zero interest is available? Regardless of the temporal location of the burden of servicing and amortizing public debt, there is no supportable argument for public borrowing in the setting of deficient demand. In trying to work out a supporting argument here, the Keynesian economists were confused, even on their own terms.

Because they unreasonably assumed that deficits were to be financed by public borrowing rather than by money creation, the

Keynesian advocates felt themselves obliged to reduce the sting of the argument concerning the temporal transfer of cost or burden. To accomplish this, they revived in sophisticated form the distinction between the norms for private, personal financial integrity and those for public, governmental financial responsibility. Budget balance did matter for an individual or family; budget balance did not matter for a government. Borrowing for an individual offered a means of postponing payment, of putting off the costs of current spending, which might or might not be desirable. For government, however, there was no such temporal transfer. It was held to be impossible to implement a transfer of cost or burden through time because government included all members of the community, and, so long as public debt was internally owned, "we owe it to ourselves." Debtors and creditors were mutually canceling; hence, in the macroeconomic context, the society could never be "in debt" in any way comparable to that situation in which a person, a family, a firm, a local government, or even a central government that had borrowed from foreigners might find itself.

This argument was deceptively attractive. It did much to remove the charge of fiscal irresponsibility from the deficit-creation position. Politicians and the public might hold fast to the classical theory, in its vulgar or its sophisticated variant, but so long as professional economists could be found to present the plausible counterargument, this flank of the Keynesian intellectual position was amply protected, or so it seemed.

The "new orthodoxy" of public debt stood almost unchallenged among economists during the 1940s and 1950s, despite its glaring logical contradictions. The Keynesian advocates failed to see that, if their theory of debt burden is correct, the benefits of public spending are always available without cost merely by resort to borrowing, and without regard to the phase of the economic cycle. If there is no transfer of cost onto taxpayers in future periods (whether these be the same or different from current taxpayers), and if bond purchasers voluntarily transfer funds to government in exchange for promises of future interest and amortization payments, there is no cost to anyone in society at the time public spending is carried out. Only the benefits of such spending remain. The economic analogue to the perpetual motion machine would have been found.

A central confusion in the whole Keynesian argument lay in its failure to bring policy alternatives down to the level of choices confronted by individual citizens, or confronted for them by their political representatives, and, in turn, to predict the effects of these alternatives on the utilities of individuals. It proved difficult to get at, and to correct, this fundamental confusion because of careless and sloppy usage of institutional description. The Keynesian economist rarely made the careful distinction between money creation and public debt issue that is required as the first step toward logical clarity. Linguistically, he often referred to what amounts to disguised money creation as "public debt," notably in his classification of government "borrowing" from the banking system. He tended to equate the whole defense of deficit financing with his defense of public debt, as a financing instrument, when, as noted above, this need not have been done at all. On his own grounds, the Keynesian economist could have made a much more effective case for deficit financing by direct money creation. Had he done so, perhaps the transmission of his message to the politicians and to the public would have contained within it much stronger built-in safeguards. It is indeed interesting to speculate what might have happened in the post-Keynesian world of fiscal policy if the financing of budget deficits had been restricted to money issues, and if this means of financing had been explicitly acknowledged by all parties.

The Dreams of Camelot

But such was not to be. The Keynesian economists were able to remain within their ivory towers during the 1950s, secure in their own untested confusions and willingly assessing blame upon the mossback attitudes of politicians and the public. In the early 1960s, for a few months in history, all their dreams seemed to become potentially realizable. The "New Economics" had finally moved beyond the elementary textbooks and beyond the halls of the academy. The enlightened would rule the world, or at least the economic aspects of it. But such dreams of Camelot, in economic policy as in other areas, were dashed against the hard realities of democratic politics. Institutional constraints, which seem so commonplace to the observer of the 1970s, were simply overlooked by the Keynesian economists until these emerged so quickly in the 1960s. They faced the rude awakening to the simple fact that their whole analytical structure, its strengths and its weaknesses, had been constructed and elaborated in almost total disregard for the institutional world where decisions are and must be made. The political history of economic policy for the 1960s and 1970s is not a happy one. Can we seriously absolve the academic scribblers from their own share of blame?

THE SPREAD OF THE NEW GOSPEL[4]

Economists do not control political history, despite their desires and dreams. Our narrative summary of the Keynesian revolution cannot, therefore, be limited to the conversion of the economists. We must look at the spreading of the Keynesian gospel to the public, and especially to the political decision makers, if we are to make sense of the situation that we confront in the late 1970s and the 1980s. The old-time fiscal religion was surprisingly strong. The effective fiscal constitution was not amended at one fell swoop, and not without some struggle. But ultimately it did give way; its precepts lost their power of persuasion. The Keynesian revolution began in the classroom and was nurtured there, but ultimately it invaded the citadels of power. The ideas of the Cambridge academic scribbler did modify, and profoundly, the actions of politicians, and with precisely the sort of time lag that Keynes himself noted in the very last paragraph of his book. Since the early 1960s, politicians have become at least half Keynesians, or they have done so in sufficient number to ensure that budget policy proceeds from a half-Keynesian paradigm. We shall discuss the attitudes of modern politicians at length, but we must first complete our narrative.

[4]Reprint of an article by James M. Buchanan and Richard E. Wagner, professors of economics. *Democracy in Deficit: The Political Legacy of Lord Keynes.* pp. 37–53. Academic Press, 1977. Reprinted by permission.

Passive Imbalance

Budget deficits may emerge either as a result of deliberate decisions to spend beyond ordinary revenue constraints or because established flows of spending and taxing react differently to shifts in the aggregate bases of an economy. We may refer to these as "active" and "passive" deficits, respectively. One of the first effects of the Great Depression of the 1930s, which dramatically reduced income, output, and employment in the American economy, was the generation of a deficit in the federal government's budget. From a position of comfortable surplus in 1929, the budget became unbalanced in calendar 1930, largely owing to the dramatic reduction in tax revenues. This revenue shortfall, plus the increase in transfer programs, created an even larger deficit for 1931.

The old-time fiscal religion, which embodied the analogy between private and public finance, dictated revenue-increasing and spending-decreasing actions as countermeasures to the emergence of passive budget deficits. These precepts were dominant in 1932 when, in reaction to the deficits of the two preceding calendar years, along with prospects for even larger deficits, federal taxes were increased substantially. Even this tax increase was apparently not sufficient to stifle political criticism; Franklin D. Roosevelt based his electoral campaign of 1932 on a balanced-budget commitment, and he severely criticized Herbert Hoover for the fiscal irresponsibility that the budget deficits reflected. In a radio address in July 1932, for instance, Roosevelt said, "Let us have the courage to stop borrowing to meet continuing deficits. . . . Revenues must cover expenditures by one means or another. Any government, like any family, can, for a year, spend a little more than it earns. But you and I know that a continuation of that habit means the poorhouse."

The first task for the economists, even in these years before the publication of Keynes' book, seemed to be clear. They tried, or at least many of them did, to convince President Roosevelt, along with other political leaders, that the emerging budget deficits, passively and indirectly created, gave no cause for alarm, and that tax increases and spending cuts could only be counterproductive in the general restoration of prosperity. Once in office, President Roosevelt soon found that, regardless of the old-fashioned precepts discussed in his campaign, expansions in spending programs were politically popular, while tax increases were not. So long as the traditional rules were not widely violated, so long as the times could genuinely be judged extraordinary, and so long as there were economists around to offer plausible reasons for allowing the emerging deficits to go undisturbed, political decision makers were ready to oblige, even if they continued to pay lip service to the old-time principles.

Even before 1936, therefore, the first step on the road toward political implementation of the full Keynesian message was accomplished. During periods of economic distress, when the maintenance of budget balance required explicit action toward increasing taxes and/or reducing governmental outlays, the political weakness inherent in the traditional fiscal constitution was exposed, and the norms were violated with little observable consequence. Until Keynes presented his "General Theory," however, these policy actions (or inactions) were not embedded in a normative analytical framework that elevated the budget itself to a dominant instrumental role in maintaining prosperity. The basic Keynesian innovation lay precisely in such explicit use of the budget for this purpose, one that had scarcely been dreamed of in any pre-Keynesian philosophy. As we have noted, many economists readily accepted the new religion. But the conversion of the politicians encountered unpredicted obstacles.

In the euphoria of victory in World War II, and flush with the observed faith of economists in their new prophet, the Full Employment Act of 1946 became law. Despite the vagueness of its objectives, this act seemed to reflect an acceptance of governmental responsibility for the maintenance of economic prosperity, and it seemed also to offer economists an opportunity to demonstrate their greatly enhanced social productivity. Early expectations were rudely shattered, however, by the abject failure of the Keynesian economic forecasters in the immediate postwar years. The initial bloom of Keynesian hopes faded, and politicians and the public adopted a cautious wait-and-see attitude toward macroeconomic policy planning.

Built-in Flexibility

The late 1940s saw many of the Keynesian economists licking their wounds, resting content with the exposition of the Keynesian message in the elementary textbooks, and taking initial steps toward consolidating the territory staked out in the 1930s. The apparent coolness of the politicians toward the active creation of budget deficits, along with the economists' own forecasting limits, suggested that more effective use might be made of the observed political acquiescence to passive imbalance. Even if budget deficits could not be, or would not be, created explicitly for the attainment of desired macroeconomic objectives, the two sides of the budget might be evaluated, at least in part, according to their by-product effects in furthering these objectives. If the politicians could be brought to this level of economic sophistication, a second major step toward the Keynesian policy mecca would have been taken. The initial assurance against reactions toward curing passive imbalance would now be supplemented by political recognition that the budget deficit, in itself, worked as a major element toward restoring prosperity. For the politicians to deplore the fiscal irresponsibility reflected in observed deficits while passively accepting these and foregoing counterproductive fiscal measures was one thing; for these same politicians to recognize that the observed deficits themselves offered one means of returning the economy toward desired output and employment levels was quite another.

Once the emergence of deficits came to be viewed as a corrective force, and once alternative budgets came to be evaluated by the strength of the corrective potential, only a minor shift in attitude was required to incorporate such potential in the objectives for budget-making itself. The economists quickly inserted "built-in flexibility" as a norm for both the taxing and spending sides of the fiscal account. Other things equal, taxes "should" be levied so as to ensure wide variations in revenue over the business cycle, variations that carry the same sign as those in the underlying economic aggregates, and which are disproportionately larger than the latter. Similarly, for the other side of the budget, spending programs, and notably transfers, "should" be arranged so that variations over the cycle are of the opposing sign to those in the underlying economic aggregates and, ideally, of disproportionate magnitude. These post-Keynesian norms for the internal structure of budget making offered support to those political pressures which would ordinarily support progressive taxation of personal incomes, along with the taxation of corporate income and/or profits, and, on the spending side, the initiation or increase of welfare-type transfers.

Hypothetical Budget Balance

Even with passive imbalance accepted, however, and even with built-in flexibility accorded some place in an array of fiscal norms, a major step in the political conversion to Keynesian economics remained to be accomplished. Balance or imbalance in the budget was still related to income, output, and employment only in some *ex post* sense. The specific relationship between budget balance, per se, and the level of national income was not developed in the early discussions among the fiscal policy economists and surely not in the thinking of political leaders. In its early formulations, Keynesian fiscal policy involved the deliberate usage of the budget to achieve desired levels of income and employment, the use of "functional finance," without regard to the question of balance or imbalance. And, indeed, much of the early discussion implied that a regime of permanent and continuing budget deficits would be required to ensure economic prosperity.

As the predictions of events for 1946 and 1947 turned sour, however, and as inflation rather than stagnation appeared as an unanticipated problem for the American economy, the question of budget balance more or less naturally presented itself. Even the most ardent Keynesian could not legitimately support the creation of budget deficits in periods of full employment and high national income. In other words, the budget "should" attain balance once the macroeconomic objectives desired are attained. This conclusion provided, in its turn, a norm for directly relating the degree of balance or imbalance in the government's budget to the underlying state of the economy.

The limitations on forecasting ability, along with the political-institutional constraints on discretionary budgetary adjustments, turned attention to built-in flexibility. It was suggested that, with such flexibility, the Keynesian policy norms could be applied even in the restrictive setting of passive imbalance. If political decision makers either would not or could not manipulate the two sides of the budget so as to further output and employment objectives directly, the Keynesian precepts still might prove of value in determining long-range targets for budget planning. The economists still might have something to offer. When should the government's budget be balanced? When should planned rates of outlay be fully covered by anticipated revenue streams? The post-Keynesians had clear answers. Both the expenditure and the tax side of the budget should be arranged, on a quasipermanent basis, so that overall balance would be achieved if and when certain output and employment objectives were attained.

Budget balance at some hypothetical level of national income, as opposed to any balance between observed revenue and spending flows, became the norm for quasipermanent changes in taxes and expenditures. Proposals for implementing this notion of hypothetical budget balance were specifically made in 1947 by the Committee for Economic Development. In 1948, the proposal was elaborated in a more sophisticated form by Milton Friedman. Professional economists attained a "remarkable degree of consensus" in support of the norm of hypothetical budget balance in the late 1940s and early 1950s.

Monetary Policy and Inflation

The economists' discussions of built-in flexibility and of budget balance at some hypothetical level of national income stemmed from two separate sources. The first, as noted above, was the recognition that discretionary budget management simply was not within the spirit of the times. The second, and equally important, source of the newfound emphasis lay in the dramatically modified historical setting. Keynesian economics, and the policy precepts it embodied, was developed almost exclusively in application to a depressed national economy, with high unemployment, excess industrial capacity, and little or no upward pressures on prices. But the years after World War II were, by contrast, years of rapidly increasing output, near full employment, and inflationary movements in prices.

The Keynesian elevation of the budget to its position as the dominant instrument for macroeconomic policy, along with the parallel relegation of monetary policy to a subsidiary role, was based, in large part, on the alleged presence of a liquidity trap during periods of deep depression. The basic model was asymmetrical, however, for nothing in Keynesian analysis suggested that monetary controls could not be effectively applied to dampen inflationary threats. Properly interpreted, Keynesian analysis does not imply that money does not matter; it implies that money matters asymmetrically. High interest rates offer, in this analysis, one means of choking off an inflationary boom. But this policy instrument need not be dusted off and utilized if, in fact, fiscal policy precepts are adhered to, in boom times as well as bust.

Immediately after World War II, the Keynesian economists came close to convincing the Truman-era politicians that a permanent regime of low interest rates, of "easy money," could at long last be realized. But the fiscal counterpart to such an "easy money" regime, one that required the accumulation of budgetary surpluses, did not readily come into being. As the inflationary threat seemed to worsen, money and monetary control were rediscovered in practice in 1951, along with the incorporation of a policy asymmetry into the discussions and the textbooks of the time. "You can't push on a string"—this analogy suggested that monetary policy was an appropriate instrument for restricting total spending but inappropriate for expanding it.

This one-sided incorporation of monetary policy instruments makes difficult our attempt to trace the conversion of politicians to Keynesian ideas. Without the dramatic shift in the potential for monetary policy that came with the Treasury–Federal Reserve Accord in 1951, we might simply look at the record for the Eisenhower years to determine the extent to which the Keynesian fiscal policy precepts were honored. But the shift did occur, and there need have been nothing specifically "non-Keynesian" about using the policy instruments asymmetrically over the cycle. A regime with alternating periods of "easy budgets and tight money" suggested a way station between the rhetoric of the old-time fiscal religion and the Keynesian spree of the 1960s and 1970s.

The Rhetoric and the Reality
of the Fifties

How are we to classify the Eisenhower years? Did the fiscal politics of the 1950s fully reflect Keynesian teachings? Politically, should we call these years "pre-Keynesian" or "post-Keynesian"?

The answers must be ambiguous for several reasons. The relatively mild swings in the business cycle offered us no definitive test of political will. There is nothing in the historical record that demonstrates a political willingness to use the budget actively as an instrument for securing and maintaining high-level employment and output. On the other hand, the record does show a willingness to acquiesce in passive budget imbalance, along with repeated commitments for explicit utilization of budgetary instruments in the event of serious economic decline. The political economics of the Eisenhower years was clearly not that of the 1960s, which we can definitely label as "post-Keynesian," but it was far from the economics of the 1920s.

Much of the rhetoric was pre-Keynesian, both with specific reference to budget balance and with reference to other macroeconomic concerns. The conflict between the high-employment and price-level objectives, a conflict that was obscured in the Great Depression only to surface with a vengeance in the late 1940s, divided the most ardent Keynesians and their opponents. The former, almost without exception, tended to place high employment at the top of their priority listing, and to neglect the dangers of inflation. Those who were most reluctant to embrace Keynesian policy norms took the opposing stance and indicated a willingness to accept lower levels of employment in exchange for a more secure throttle on inflation. The Eisenhower administration came into office with an expressed purpose of doing something about the inflation of the postwar years, and also about a parallel policy target, the growth in the rate of federal spending. A modified trade-off among macroeconomic objectives, quite apart from an acceptance and understanding of the Keynesian policy instruments, would have been sufficient to explain the observed behavior of the Eisenhower political leaders. That is to say, the politicians of the 1950s, on the basis of their observed actions alone, cannot be found guilty of pre-Keynesian ignorance. They were, of course, sharply criticized by the "Keynesians"; but this criticism was centered more on the acknowledged value trade-off between the inflation and unemployment targets than the use or misuse of the policy instruments.

At a different level of assessment, however, we must look at the analytical presuppositions of these decision makers. Did they acknowledge the existence of the trade-off between employment and inflation, the trade-off that was almost universally accepted and widely discussed by the economists of the decade? Was the Eisenhower economic policy based on an explicit willingness to tolerate somewhat higher rates of unemployment than might have been possible in exchange for a somewhat more stable level of prices? If the evidence suggests an affirmative answer, we may say that the political conversion to Keynesian economics was instrumentally completed. We are, of course, economists, and it is all too easy to interpret and to explain the events of history "as if" the results emerge from economists' models. It is especially tempting to explain the macroeconomics of the 1950s in such terms and to say that the Eisenhower political leaders were dominated by a fear of inflation while remaining relatively unconcerned about unemployment.

If we look again at the rhetoric of the 1950s, along with the reality, however, and if we try to do so without wearing the economists' blinders, the label "pre-Keynesian" fits the Eisenhower politicians better than does its opposite. The paradigm of the decade was that of an economic system that is inherently stable, provided that taxes are not onerously high and government spending is not out of bounds, and provided that the central bank carries out its appropriate monetary role. There was no political inclination to use the federal budget for achieving some hypothetical and targeted rate of growth in national income. The economics of George Humphrey and Robert Anderson was little different from that of Andrew Mellon, thirty years before. The economics of the economists was, of course, dramatically different. In the 1920s, there was no overt policy conflict between the economists and the politicians of their time. By contrast, the 1950s were years of developing tension between the economists-intellectuals and their political peers, with the Keynesian economists unceasingly berating the effective decision makers for their failure to have learned the Keynesian lessons, for their reactionary adherence to outmoded principles of fiscal rectitude. This discourse laid the groundwork for the policy shift of the 1960s.

But, as noted earlier, there were major differences between the 1920s and the 1950s. Passive deficits were accepted, even if there was extreme reluctance to utilize the budget actively to combat what proved to be relatively mild swings in the aggregate economy. The built-in flexibility embodied in the federal government's budget was both acknowledged and allowed to work. Furthermore, despite the rhetoric that called for the accumulation of budget surpluses during periods of economic recovery, little or no action was taken to ensure that sizeable surpluses did, in fact, occur. The promised increased flow of revenues was matched by commitments for new spending, and the Eisenhower leadership did not effectively forestall this. Public debt was not reduced in any way remotely comparable to the previous postwar periods.

Fiscal Drag

The Eisenhower administration was most severely criticized for its failure to pursue an active fiscal policy during and after the 1958 recession. Political pressures for quick tax reduction were contained in 1958, with the assistance of Democratic leaders in Congress, and attempts were made to convert the massive $12 billion passive deficit of that year into budget surpluses for the recovery years, 1959 and 1960. The rate of growth in federal spending was held down, and a relatively quick turnaround in the impact of the budget on the national economy was achieved, in the face of continuing high levels of unemployment.

It was during these last months of the Eisenhower administration that the notion or concept of "fiscal drag" emerged in the policy discourse of economists, based on an extension and elaboration of the norm for budget balance at some hypothetically defined level of national income and incorporating the recognition that income grows through time. The Eisenhower budgetary policy for the recovery years of 1959 and 1960 was sharply criticized for its apparent concentration on observed rather than potential flows of revenues and outlays. By defining a target "high-employment" level of national income on a projected normal growth path, and then by projecting and estimating the tax revenues and government outlays that would be forthcoming under existing programs at that level of income, a test for hypothetical budget balance could be made. Preliminary tests suggested that the Eisenhower budgetary policies for those years would have generated a surplus at the targeted high-employment level of income. That is to say, although actually observed flows of revenues and outlays need not have indicated a budget surplus, such a surplus would indeed have been created if national income had been generated at the higher and more desired level. However, since observed national income was below this target level, and because the potential for the surplus was already incorporated in the tax-spending structure, the budget instrument itself worked against the prospect that the target level of national income could ever be attained at all. This result seemed to follow directly from the recognition that the budget itself was an important determinant of national income. Before the targeted level of income could be reached, the budget itself would begin to exert a depressing influence on aggregate demand. This "fiscal drag" was something to be avoided.

From this analysis follows the budgetary precept that runs so strongly counter to ordinary common sense. During a period of economic recovery, the deliberate creation of a budget deficit, or the creation of a larger deficit than might already exist, offers a means of securing the achievement of budget surplus at high-employment income. We shall discuss this argument further at a later point. But here we note only that this was the prevailing wisdom among the enlightened economists on the Washington scene in 1960; this, plus the relatively sluggish recovery itself, provided the setting for the politics and the economics of Kennedy's New Frontier.

The Reluctant Politician

In one of his more exuberant moments, President Kennedy may have called himself a Berliner; but during the early months of his administration, he could scarcely have called himself a Keynesian. As Herbert Stein suggested, "Kennedy's fiscal thinking was conventional. He believed in budget-balancing. While he was aware of circumstances in which the budget could not or should not be balanced, he preferred a balanced budget, being in this respect like most other people but unlike modern economists." But President Kennedy's economic advisers were, to a man, solidly Keynesian, in both the instrumental and the valuational meaning of this term. They were willing to recommend the usage of the full array of budgetary instruments to secure high employment and economic growth, and they were relatively unconcerned about the inflationary danger that such policies might produce. The trade-off between employment and inflation was explicitly incorporated in their models of economic process, and they were willing to accept the relatively limited inflation that these models seemed to suggest as the price for higher employment.

But these advisers were also Galbraithian, in that they preferred to increase demand through expansions in federal spending rather than through tax reductions. Furthermore, they were strongly supportive of "easy money," a policy of low interest rates designed to stimulate domestic investment. These patterns of adjustment were closely attuned with the standard political pressures upon the Democratic administration. Hence, in 1961 and early 1962, there was little or no discussion of tax reduction, despite the continuing sluggishness of the national economy, sluggishness that was still blamed on the follies of the previous Eisenhower leadership. Balance-of-payments difficulties prevented the adoption of the monetary policy that the Keynesians desired, and dramatic proposals for large increases in federal spending would surely have run squarely in the face of congressional opposition, a fact that President Kennedy fully recognized. Stimulation of the economy was, therefore, limited in total, despite the arguments of the president's advisers.

66 The Reference Shelf

Political Keynesianism:
The Tax Cut of 1964

The principles of the old-fashioned fiscal religion did not remain inviolate up until the early 1960s only to collapse under the renewed onslaught of the modern economists. The foundations had been eroded, gradually and inexorably, since the conversion of the economists in the 1940s. And the political resistance to an activist fiscal policy was steadily weakened throughout the 1950s, despite much rhetoric to the contrary. But if a single event must be chosen to mark the full political acceptance of the Keynesian policy gospel, the tax cut of 1964 stands alone. Initially discussed in 1962, actively proposed and debated throughout 1963, and finally enacted in early 1964, this tax reduction demonstrated that political decision makers could act, and did act, to use the federal budget in an effort to achieve a hypothetical target for national income. Tax rates were reduced, and substantially so, despite the presence of an existing budget deficit, and despite the absence of economic recession. The argument for this unprecedented step was almost purely Keynesian. There was little recourse to the Mellon-Taft-Humphrey view that lowered tax rates, whenever and however implemented, offered the sure path to prosperity. Instead, taxes were to be reduced because national income was not being generated at a level that was potentially attainable, given the resource capacities of the nation. The economy was growing, but not nearly fast enough, and the increased deficit resulting from the tax cut was to be the instrument that moved the economy to its growth path. There was no parallel reformist argument for expenditure increase, and the tax reduction in itself was not wildly redistributionist. The objective was clean and simple: the restoration of the national economy to its full growth potential.

Should we not have predicted that the economists would be highly pleased in their newly established positions? The "New Economics" had, at long last, arrived; the politicians had finally been converted; the Keynesian revolution had become reality; its principles were henceforward to be enshrined in the conventional political wisdom. These were truly the economists' halcyon days.

But days they were, or perhaps months. How can they (we) have been so naive? This question must have emerged to plague those who were most enthusiastic, and it must have done so soon after 1965. Could the fiscal politics of the next decade, 1965–1975, and beyond, not have been foreseen, predicted, and possibly forestalled? Or did the economists in Camelot dream of a future in which democratic fiscal politics were to be replaced, once and for all, by the fiscal gospel of Lord Keynes, as amended? We shall discuss such questions in depth, but for now we emphasize only the results of this conversion of the politicians to the Keynesian norms. As we have pointed out, this conversion was a gradual one, extending over the several decades, but 1964–1965 offers the historical watershed. Before this date, the fiscal politics of America was at least partially "pre-Keynesian" in both rhetoric and reality. After 1965, the fiscal politics became definitely "post-Keynesian" in reality, although elements of the old-time religion remained in the political argument.

The results are on record for all to see. After 1964, the United States embarked on a course of fiscal irresponsibility matched by no other period in its two-century history. A record-setting deficit of $25 billion in 1968 generated a temporary obeisance to the old-fashioned verities in 1969, the first Nixon year. But following this, the federal government's budget swept onward and upward toward explosive heights, financed increasingly and disproportionately by deficits. Deficits of more than $23 billion were recorded in each of the 1971 and 1972 fiscal years. This provided the setting for Nixon's putative 1974 "battle of the budget," his last pre–Watergate scandal effort to bring spending into line with revenues. Fiscal 1973 saw the deficit reduced to plausibly acceptable limits, only to become dangerously large in fiscal 1975 and 1976, when a two-year deficit of more than $100 billion was accumulated. Who can look into our fiscal future without trepidation, regardless of his own political or ideological persuasion?

The mystery lies not in the fact of the fiscal record, but in the failure of social scientists, and economists in particular, to predict the results of the eclipse of the old rules for fiscal responsibility. Once democratically elected politicians, and behind them their constituents in the voting public, were finally convinced that budget balance carried little or no normative weight, what was there left to restrain the ever-present spending pressures? The results are, and should have been, predictable at the most naive level of behavioral analysis. After the 1964 tax reduction, the "price" of public goods and services seemed lower. Should we not have foreseen efforts to "purchase" larger quantities? Should we not have predicted the Great Society–Viet Nam spending explosion of the late 1960s?

Economists, Politicians, and the Public

The Keynesian economists are ready with responses to such questions. They fall back on the symmetrical applicability of the basic Keynesian policy precepts, and they lay the fiscal-monetary irresponsibility squarely on the politicians. If the political decision makers of the 1960s and 1970s, exemplified particularly in Lyndon Johnson and Richard Nixon (both of whom remain forever villains in the liberal intellectuals' lexicon), had listened to the advice of their economist advisers, as did their counterparts in Camelot, the economic disasters need not have emerged. After all, or so the argument of the Keynesian economists proceeds, the precepts are wholly symmetrical. Budget surpluses may be desired at certain times. Enlightened political leadership would have imposed higher taxes after 1965, as their economist advisers recommended, and efforts would have been made to hold down rates of growth in federal domestic spending to offset Viet Nam outlays.

In such attempts to evade their own share of the responsibility for the post-1965 fiscal history, the economists rarely note the politician's place in a democratic society. From Roosevelt's New Deal onward, elected politicians have lived with the demonstrated relationship between favorable election returns and expansion in public spending programs. Can anyone seriously expect the ordinary persons who are elected to office to act differently from the rest of us? The only effective constraint on the spending proclivities of elected politicians from the 1930s onward has been the heritage of our historical "fiscal constitution," a set of rules that did include the balancing of outlays with revenues. But once this constraint was eliminated, why should the elected politician behave differently from the way we have observed him to behave after 1965? Could we have expected the president and the Congress, Democratic or Republican, to propose and to enact significant tax rate increases during a period of economic prosperity? In Camelot, the politicians followed the economists' advice because such advice coincided directly with the naturally emergent political pressures. Why did the economists fail to see that a setting in which the appropriate Keynesian policy would run directly counter to these natural pressures might generate quite different results?

Functional Finance and
Hypothetical Budget Balance

In retrospect, it may be argued that damage was done to the basic Keynesian cause by the attempts to provide substitutes for the balanced-budget rule, and most notably by the rule that the government's budget "should" be balanced at some hypothetical level of national income, a level that describes full capacity or full-employment output. In the pristine simplicity of their early formulation, most clearly exposited by Abba Lerner, the Keynesian policy precepts contained no substitute for the balanced budget. Functional finance required no such rule at all; taxes were to be levied, not for the purpose of financing public outlays, but for the sole purpose of forestalling and preventing inflation. It is indeed interesting to speculate on "what might have been" had the Keynesian economists followed Lerner's lead. The "education" of political leaders, and ultimately of the public, would have been quite different. The principles for policy would have been much simpler, and it is scarcely beyond the realm of plausibility to suggest that the required lessons might have been learned, that a politically viable regime of *responsible* functional finance might have emerged.

But such was not to be. Even the Keynesian economists seemed unwilling to jettison the time-honored notion that the extension and the makeup of the public sector, of governmental outlays, must somehow be related to the willingness of persons to pay for public goods and services, as expressed indirectly through the activities of legislatures in imposing taxes. But how was this tie-in between the two sides of the fiscal account to be reconciled with the basic Keynesian thrust which called for the abandonment of the balanced-budget rule? We have already traced the developments that reflected this tension, from the initial acquiescence in passive imbalance on the presupposition that balance would somehow be achieved over the business cycle, to the more sophisticated notion that a rule of budget balance might be restored, but balance this time at some hypothetically determined level of national income. But we must now look somewhat more closely and carefully at the burden that this new norm places on the political decision maker. He is told by his economists that budget balance at high employment is desirable, and that both outlay and revenue adjustments should be made on the "as if" assumption that the targeted level of income is generated. Once this exercise is completed, he is told, he may then acquiesce in the deficits or surpluses produced by the flow of economic events secure in the knowledge that all is well. This is a deceptively attractive scenario until we recognize that it offers an open-ended invitation to strictly judgmental decisions on what is, in fact, "high-employment" income. Furthermore, it tends to "build in" a presumed trade-off between unemployment and inflation, which may or may not exist.

What is the hypothetical level of income to be chosen for budget balance?—or, if desired, for some overbalance? There may be no uniquely determined level of high-employment income, and economists will surely continue to argue about the degree and extent of genuinely structural unemployment that might be present at any time. Additional definitiveness might be introduced by stipulating that the target income is that which could be generated without inflation. But, if structural unemployment is pervasive, this sort of budgetary norm may suggest balance between revenues and outlays in the face of observed rates of unemployment that are higher than those considered to be politically acceptable. In such a setting, imagine the pressures on the politicians who attempt to justify the absence of a budget deficit, after forty years of the Keynesian teachings.

An additional difficulty arises in the division of responsibility between the fiscal and monetary instruments. With the budget-balance-at-hypothetical-income norm, the tendency may be to place the restrictive burden on the monetary authorities and instruments while adding to this burden by the manipulation of budgetary-fiscal instruments applied to unattainable targets. Consider, for example, the setting in 1975, when we observed *both* unemployment and inflation rates of roughly 8 percent. The balance-at-hypothetical-income norm could have been, and indeed was, used by economists and politicians to justify the budget deficits observed in that year, and to argue for increases in these deficits. The inflation was, in turn, "explained" either by structural elements (administered prices) or by the failures of the monetary authorities to restrain demand. In this latter sense, the monetarists tended to support the Keynesians indirectly because of their emphasis on the purely monetary sources of inflation. This emphasis allows the politicians to expand the budget deficit in putative adherence to the balance-at-high-employment norm, bloating the size of the public sector in the process. To the extent that the responsibility for inflation can be placed on the monetary authorities, the restrictive role for fiscal policy is politically weakened regardless of the budgetary norm that is accepted. Neither the monetarists nor the Keynesians can have it both ways. "Easy money" cannot explain inflation and "fiscal drag" unemployment. Yet this is precisely the explanation mix that was translated directly into policy in 1975, generating the tax-reduction pressures on the one hand and the relatively mixed monetary policy actions on the other.

II. THE DEFICITS OF THE 1980S:
A GROWING AND COMPLEX BURDEN

EDITOR'S INTRODUCTION

Budget deficits became a dominant national preoccupation only in the 1980s. In his first major economic address after taking office, the first selection in this section, President Reagan criticized deficit spending and the ballooning national debt, but saved by far his choicest ammunition for inflation, excessive taxation, and costly government regulation.

In the second article, James R. Barth and Stephen O. Morrell outline the immediate background to today's deficits, and suggest good reasons for widespread concern. J. Peter Grace, head of President Reagan's Private Sector Survey on Cost Control, defends in the third article the president's drive against any growth in federal spending, citing numerous examples of flagrant governmental bloating, waste, and inefficiency.

George P. Brockway, in the fourth article, advances the idea that the economic recovery of 1983–84 has been heavily subsidized by the trillion-dollar military buildup undertaken by the Reagan administration and discusses the interrelationship of the deficit and interest rates. The fifth article, an advertisement paid for by a bi-partisan group of former federal cabinet secretaries, expresses extreme alarm at the size and intractability of the present deficits, and urges budget cuts as the only practicable way to reduce them.

Presidential candidate Walter Mondale suggested a plan to cut the "Reagan" deficits by reducing military spending and raising taxes. Business leaders were skeptical, and the fact that many of the suggested tax increases fell on the middle class was considered a political blunder. Jonathan Fuerbringer, in the final article of this section, discusses the Mondale plan with specific reference to its impact on the middle class.

THE STATE OF THE NATION'S ECONOMY:
WE ARE OUT OF TIME[1]

I am speaking to you tonight to give you a report on the state of our nation's economy. I regret to say that we are in the worst economic mess since the Great Depression. A few days ago I was presented with a report I had asked for—a comprehensive audit if you will—of our economic condition. You won't like it, I didn't like it, but we have to face the truth and then go to work to turn things around. And make no mistake about it, we can turn them around.

I'm not going to subject you to the jumble of charts, figures, and economic jargon of the audit but rather will try to explain where we are, how we got there, and how we can get back.

First, however, let me just give a few "attention getters" from the audit. The Federal budget is out of control and we face runaway deficits, of almost $80 billion for this budget year that ends Sept. 30. That deficit is larger than the entire Federal budget in 1957 and so is the almost $80 billion we will pay in interest this year on the national debt.

Twenty years ago in 1960 our Federal Government payroll was less than $13 billion. Today it is $75 billion. During these 20 years, our population has only increased by 23.3 percent. The Federal budget has gone up 528 percent.

We have just had two years of back-to-back double digit inflation—13.3 percent in 1979, 12.4 percent last year. The last time this happened was in World War I.

In 1960 mortgage interest rates averaged about 6 percent. They are two and a half times as high now, 15.4 percent. The percentage of your earnings the Federal Government took in taxes in 1960 has almost doubled. And finally there are seven million Americans caught up in the personal indignity and human tragedy of unemployment. If they stood in a line—allowing three feet

[1]Reprint of an address to the American people by President Ronald Reagan, delivered from the White House, F. 5, '81. From *Vital Speeches of the Day* 47:290–3. Reprinted with permission.

for each person—the line would reach from the coast of Maine to California.

Well, so much for the audit itself. Let me try to put this in personal terms. Here is a dollar such as you earned, spent or saved in 1960. Here is a quarter, a dime and a penny—36 cents. Thirty-six cents is what this 1960 dollar is worth today. And if the present inflation rate should continue three more years, the dollar of 1960 will be worth a quarter. What incentive is there to save? And if we don't save we are short of the investment capital needed for business and industry expansion. Workers in Japan and West Germany save several times the percentage of their income than Americans do.

What has happened to that American dream of owning a home? Only 10 years ago a family could buy a home and the monthly payment averaged little more than a quarter—27 cents out of each dollar earned. Today it takes 42 cents out of every dollar of income. So, fewer than one out of 11 families can afford to buy their first new home.

Regulations adopted by Government with the best of intentions have added $666 to the cost of an automobile. It is estimated that altogether regulations of every kind, on shopkeepers, farmers and major industries, add $100 billion to the cost of the goods and services we buy. And then another $20 billion is spent by Government handling the paperwork created by those regulations.

I'm sure you are getting the idea that the audit presented to me found Government policies of the last few decades responsible for our economic troubles. We forgot or just overlooked the fact that Government—any Government—has a built-in tendency to grow. We all had a hand in looking to Government for benefits as if Government had some sources of revenue other than our earnings. Many if not most of the things we thought of or that Government offered to us seemed attractive.

In the years following the second world war it was easy (for a while at least) to overlook the price tag. Our income more than doubled in the 25 years after the war. We increased our take-home pay in those 25 years by more than we had amassed in all the preceding 150 years put together. Yes, there was some inflation, 1 or $1\frac{1}{2}$ percent a year, that didn't bother us. But if we look back at those golden years we recall that even then voices had been raised warning that inflation, like radioactivity, was cumulative and that once started it could get out of control. Some Government programs seemed so worthwhile that borrowing to fund them didn't bother us.

By 1960 our national debt stood at $284 billion. Congress in 1971 decided to put a ceiling of $400 billion on our ability to borrow. Today the debt is $934 billion. So-called temporary increases or extensions in the debt ceiling have been allowed 21 times in these 10 years and now I have been forced to ask for another increase in the debt ceiling or the Government will be unable to function past the middle of February, and I've only been here 16 days. Before we reach the day when we can reduce the debt ceiling we may in spite of our best efforts see a national debt in excess of a trillion dollars. This is a figure literally beyond our comprehension.

We know now that inflation results from all that deficit spending. Government has only two ways of getting money other than raising taxes. It can go into the money market and borrow, competing with its own citizens and driving up interest rates, which it has done, or it can print money, and it's done that. Both methods are inflationary.

We're victims of language, the very word "inflation" leads us to think of it as high prices. Then, of course, we resent the person who puts on the price tags forgetting that he or she is also a victim of inflation. Inflation is not just high prices; it is a reduction in the value of our money. When the money supply is increased but the goods and services available for buying are not, we have too much money chasing too few goods.

Wars are usually accompanied by inflation. Everyone is working or fighting but production is of weapons and munitions, not things we can buy and use.

One way out would be to raise taxes so that Government need not borrow or print money. But in all these years of Government growth we've reached—indeed surpassed—the limit of our people's tolerance or ability to bear an increase in the tax burden.

Prior to World War II, taxes were such that on the average we only had to work about two and a half months each year to pay our total Federal, state and local tax bill. Today we have to work about five months to pay that bill.

Some say shift the tax burden to business and industry, but business doesn't pay taxes. Oh, don't get the wrong idea, business is being taxed—so much so that we are being priced out of the world market. But business must pass its costs of operation, and that includes taxes, onto the customer in the price of the product. Only people pay taxes—all the taxes.

Government first uses business in a kind of sneaky way to help collect the taxes. They are hidden in the price and we aren't aware of how much tax we actually pay. Today, this once great industrial giant of ours has the lowest rate of gain in productivity of virtually all the industrial nations with whom we must compete in the world market. We can't even hold our own market here in America against foreign automobiles, steel and a number of other products.

Japanese production of automobiles is almost twice as great per worker as it is in America. Japanese steelworkers out-produce their American counterparts by about 25 percent.

This isn't because they are better workers. I'll match the American working man or woman against anyone in the world. But we have to give them the modern tools and equipment that workers in the other industrial nations have.

We invented the assembly line and mass production, but punitive tax policies and excessive and unnecessary regulations plus Government borrowing have stifled our ability to update plant and equipment. When capital investment is made it is too often for some unproductive alterations demanded by Government to meet various of its regulations.

Excessive taxation of individuals has robbed us of incentive and made overtime unprofitable.

We once produced about 40 percent of the world's steel. We now produce 19 percent.

We were once the greatest producer of automobiles, producing more than all the rest of the world combined. That is no longer true, and, in addition, the big three, the major auto companies, in our land have sustained tremendous losses in the past year and have been forced to lay off thousands of workers.

All of you who are working know that even with cost-of-living pay raises you can't keep up with inflation. In our progressive tax system as you increase the number of dollars you earn you find yourself moved up into higher tax brackets, paying a higher tax rate just for trying to hold your own. The result? Your standard of living is going down.

Over the past decades we've talked of curtailing Government spending so that we can then lower the tax burden. Sometimes we've even taken a run at doing that. But there were always those who told us taxes couldn't be cut until spending was reduced. Well, we can lecture our children about extravagance until we run out of voice and breath. Or we can cure their extravagance simply by reducing their allowance.

It is time to recognize that we have come to a turning point. We are threatened with an economic calamity of tremendous proportions and the old business as usual treatment can't save us.

Together, we must chart a different course. We must increase productivity. That means making it possible for industry to modernize and make use of the technology which we ourselves invented: that means putting Americans back to work. And that means above all bringing Government spending back within Government revenues, which is the only way, together with increased productivity, that we can reduce and, yes, eliminate inflation.

In the past we've tried to fight inflation one year and then when unemployment increased turn the next year to fighting unemployment with more deficit spending as a pump primer. So again, up goes inflation. It hasn't worked. We don't have to choose between inflation and unemployment—they go hand in hand. It's time to try something different and that's what we're going to do.

I've already placed a freeze on hiring replacements for those who retire or leave Government service. I have ordered a cut in Government travel, the number of consultants to the Government, and the buying of office equipment and other items. I have put a freeze on pending regulations and set up a task force under Vice President Bush to review regulations with an eye toward getting rid of as many as possible. I have decontrolled oil, which should result in more domestic production and less dependence on foreign oil. And I am eliminating the ineffective wage and price program of the Council on Wage and Price Stability.

But it will take more, much more and we must realize there is no quick fix. At the same time, however, we cannot delay in implementing an economic program aimed at both reducing tax rates to stimulate productivity and reducing the growth in Government spending to reduce unemployment and inflation.

On Feb. 18, I will present in detail an economic program to Congress embodying the features I have just stated. It will propose budget cuts in virtually every department of Government. It is my belief that these actual budget cuts will only be part of the savings. As our Cabinet Secretaries take charge of their departments, they will search out areas of waste, extravagance and costly administrative overhead which could yield additional and substantial reductions.

At the same time we are doing this, we must go forward with a tax relief package. I shall ask for a 10 percent reduction across the board in the personal income tax rates for each of the next three years. Proposals will also be submitted for accelerated depreciation allowances for business to provide necessary capital so as to create jobs.

Now here again, in saying this, I know that language, as I said earlier, can get in the way of a clear understanding of what our program is intended to do. Budget cuts can sound as if we are going to reduce government spending to a lower level than was spent the year before.

This is not the case. The budgets will increase as our population increases and each year we'll see spending increases to match that growth. Government revenues will increase as the economy grows, but the burden will be lighter for each individual because the economic base will have been expanded by reason of the reduced rates.

Let me show you a chart I've had drawn to illustrate how this can be. Here you see two trend lines. The bottom line shows the increase in tax revenues. The red line on top is the increase in Government spending. Both lines turn upward reflecting the giant tax increase already built into the system for this year 1981, and the increases in spending built into the '81 and '82 budgets and on into the future.

As you can see, the spending line rises at a steeper slant than the revenue line. That gap between those lines illustrates the increasing deficits we've been running, including this year's $80 billion deficit.

Now, in the second chart, the lines represent the positive effects when Congress accepts our economic program. Both lines continue to rise allowing for necessary growth but the gap narrows as spending cuts continue over the next few years, until finally the two lines come together meaning a balanced budget.

I am confident that my Administration can achieve that. At that point, tax revenues, in spite of rate reductions, will be increasing faster than spending, which means we can look forward to further reductions in the tax rates.

In all of this we will of course work closely with the Federal Reserve System toward the objective of a stable monetary policy.

Our spending cuts will not be at the expense of the truly needy. We will, however, seek to eliminate benefits to those who are not really qualified by reason of need.

As I've said before, on Feb. 18 I will present this economic package of budget reductions and tax reform to a joint session of Congress and to you in full detail.

Our basic system is sound. We can, with compassion, continue to meet our responsibility to those who through no fault of their own need our help. We can meet fully the other legitimate responsibilities of Government. We cannot continue any longer our wasteful ways at the expense of the workers of this land or our children.

Since 1960 our Government has spent $5.1 trillion; our debt has grown by $648 billion. Prices have exploded by 178 percent. How much better off are we for it all? We all know, we are very much worse off.

When we measure how harshly these years of inflation, lower productivity, and uncontrolled Government growth have affected our lives, we know we must act and act now.

We must not be timid.

We will restore the freedom of all men and women to excell and to create. We will unleash the energy and genius of the American people—traits which have never failed us.

To the Congress of the United States, I extend my hand in co-operation and I believe we can go forward in a bipartisan manner.

I have found a real willingness to cooperate on the part of Democrats and members of my own party.

To my colleagues in the executive branch of Government and to all Federal employees I ask that we work in the spirit of service.

I urge those great institutions in America—business and labor—to be guided by the national interest and I'm confident they will. The only special interest we will serve is the interest of the people.

We can create the incentives which take advantage of the genius of our economic system—a system, as Walter Lippmann observed more than 40 years ago, which for the first time in history gave men "a way of producing wealth in which the good fortune of others multiplied their own."

Our aim is to increase our national wealth so all will have more, not just redistribute what we already have, which is just a sharing of scarcity. We can begin to reward hard work and risk-taking, by forcing this Government to live within its means.

Over the years we have let negative economic forces run out of control. We have stalled the judgment day. We no longer have that luxury. We are out of time.

And to you my fellow citizens, let us join in a new determination to rebuild the foundations of our society; to work together to act responsibly. Let us do so with the most profound respect for that which must be preserved as well as with sensitive understanding and compassion for those who must be protected.

We can leave our children with an unrepayable massive debt and a shattered economy or we can leave them liberty in a land where every individual has the opportunity to be whatever God intended us to be. All it takes is a little common sense and recognition of our own ability. Together we can forge a new beginning for America.

Thank you and good night.

A PRIMER ON BUDGET DEFICITS[2]

During the past 20 years, the federal government budget has been in deficit 19 times, the only budget surplus occurring in 1969. Most current projections indicate that this trend will continue in the years ahead. In response to this situation, 31 state legislatures have already approved resolutions petitioning for a constitutional convention that would require an annually balanced budget. Similar resolutions are currently being considered by other state legislatures, with only three more needed to force the Congress to organize a constitutional convention to consider a balanced-budget amendment. Recently, President Reagan endorsed the idea of such an amendment. One amendment approved by the Senate early this month would permit a budget deficit only in wartime or when authorized by a three-fifths majority of the House and Senate.

This article is a primer on budget deficits. Section I defines what is meant by a budget deficit, how deficits are measured, and what is not included in conventional measures of the deficit. In Section II, we'll examine the U.S. budgetary record from the beginning of the Republic in 1789 to the present. Section III relates current concerns about budget deficits to parallel concerns expressed during the Great Depression—a period marked by significant changes in thinking about the effects of deficits. Section IV examines the major points of controversy about the economic impact of deficits.

What Is a Budget Deficit?

In any discussion of budget deficits, one must be sure to understand exactly what this term means. Most of the concern focuses on federal deficits, not the aggregate budgetary positions of local, state and federal governments. For this reason, we will consider only federal budgetary deficits here. At the federal level, the government collects taxes (T) out of which it spends on goods and ser-

[2]Reprint of an article by James R. Barth and Stephen O. Morrell, economists, in the *Federal Reserve Bank of Atlanta Economic Review*. 67:6–17. Ag. '82.

vices and provides for transfer payments (G) as well as pays interest on its outstanding debt (iB) (where i is the nominal interest rate and B is federal government debt outstanding). In recent years, government expenditures frequently have exceeded receipts, resulting in deficits. A deficit therefore occurs whenever expenditures exceed receipts and the size of the deficit is measured by the amount by which expenditures exceed receipts. Symbolically, this situation may be expressed as:

(1) Deficit = G + iB − T.

Of course, government spending does not always exceed revenue. When the reverse is the case, the government budget is said to be in surplus. A balanced budget occurs whenever expenditures are exactly matched by receipts.

Naturally, deficits must be financed. There are two principal ways in which this is done, both of which involve an increase in government liabilities. One way to finance deficits is through the sale of federal government securities to the public (both domestic and foreign) while the other way is through the sale of securities to the Federal Reserve. The Federal Reserve purchases securities, not directly from the Treasury Department, but rather through open market operations conducted through security dealers in the New York financial markets. When the Federal Reserve buys securities, it results in an increase in its monetary liabilities, specifically reserves of commercial banks and thrift institutions plus coin and currency, or an increase in the monetary base. Since an increase in the monetary base typically increases the money supply, the sale of securities to the Federal Reserve to finance deficits is commonly referred to as money-financed deficits. Sales of securities to the public, on the other hand, are commonly referred to as bond-financed deficits.

Equation (1) may now be written as:

(2) Deficit = $\Delta B + \Delta M$ = G + iB − T

where ΔB represents the positive change in bonds held by the public and ΔM represents the positive change in bonds held by the Federal Reserve. This equation states that when government spending exceeds revenues, the resulting deficit must be bond-

and/or money-financed. Most discussions of the federal deficit are based upon equation (2), which represents the nominal federal budget deficit. It should be noted that the widely reported figures on deficits in newspapers, magazines, and other news media are based upon the unified budget concept, not the national income accounts concept. The essential difference between the two concepts is that the former is on a cash basis, whereas the latter is on an accrual basis.

An Alternative Measure of the Budget Deficit

The budget deficit as measured by equation (2) is not the only or, for that matter, the most appropriate measure available. An alternative measure that merits special attention is the real or inflation-adjusted deficit. This measure of the deficit is given by:

(3) Real Deficit $= \Delta(B/P) + \Delta(M/P) = G/P + rB/P - \pi M/P - T/P$.

where P is the price level, r is the real rate of interest $(i - \pi)$, and π is the inflation rate. This equation states that the amount by which real federal government expenditures exceed real revenues is financed by changes in the real value of government bonds and monetary liabilities.

A few comments about this measure of the deficit are appropriate. First, when there is no inflation $(\pi = 0)$, one simply multiplies equation (3) by the price level (P) to obtain equation (2). Second, real interest payments on the federal debt are given by rB/P. This means that if inflation is fully anticipated and thus completely embodied in the nominal interest rate that the Treasury Department pays on federal government debt, then a higher inflation rate need not affect the real deficit. But, for this to happen, the nominal debt must increase along with the price level. Inflation would, therefore, increase the nominal deficit (see equation (2)) due to increased interest payments on debt outstanding (iB). Third, the real return on M/P is minus the inflation rate $(-\pi)$, since the nominal rate of return on M is zero. Fourth, money-financed deficits that persist over time would continually increase the nominal deficit but could decrease the real deficit so long as M and P move together. Fifth, and most importantly, inflation essentially acts as a tax on the government's monetary liabilities whether it is anticipated or not; it also constitutes a tax on bond liabilities to the extent that the inflation is unanticipated. For this reason we should examine both nominal and real deficits, especially during periods of chronic inflation.

To illustrate the importance of adjusting for inflation, consider that the nominal deficit was nearly $60 billion in fiscal year 1980. Given that B was equal to $594 billion and M was equal to $157 billion in that year and that the inflation rate was 9 percent, one would have to subtract about $68 billion from the nominal deficit to obtain an inflation-adjusted deficit. Doing this, the result is that the fiscal year 1980 deficit becomes an $8 billion surplus.

Finally, rather than simply considering the size of federal deficits in isolation, it is frequently more informative to measure deficits relative to gross national product (GNP). In other words, it is useful to consider deficits (or surpluses) as a share of GNP. To illustrate the information this approach yields, consider the years 1968 and 1979. In the earlier year, the deficit was $25.2 billion, nearly the same as the 1979 deficit of $27.7 billion. When measured as a share of GNP, however, the situation is quite different. In 1968, the deficit amounted to 3 percent of GNP, whereas in 1979 the corresponding amount was only 1.2 percent. These figures demonstrate that financing the same size deficits may have far different implications depending upon the level of overall economic activity. Furthermore, as will be shown in the next section, the level of economic activity will significantly affect the size of the deficit. In short, to better understand deficits it is important to put them into perspective by expressing the deficits as a share of GNP.

WHAT THE BUDGET DEFICIT DOESN'T MEASURE

It is important when discussing federal deficits to realize what they do not measure. Certainly, federal deficits as commonly known do not measure the change in the net worth of the federal government. In other words, although it may be conceptually sound to be interested ultimately in the federal government's net worth (assets less liabilities), such a measurement is extremely difficult to obtain. Valuing equipment, buildings, land, social security obligations, retirement benefits, and loan guarantees, to mention just a few assets and liabilities, would require a herculean effort. One could even ask whether monetary liabilities actually exist, since there is no presumption that base money (reserves plus currency) will ever be retired. In any event, deficits should not be equated with dis-saving in the sense that the federal government's net worth is necessarily declining by the same amounts. The widely reported measures of the budget deficit are far narrower in scope.

Another factor is that the federal deficit does not include the activities of off-budget federal entities such as the Federal Financing Bank, Synthetic Fuels Corporation, and the Postal Service fund. Off-budget entity activities do not show up in the unified budget spending and thus the deficit figures. This means, of course, that off-budget spending does not go through the normal congressional process. In 1973, when off-budget federal entity outlays began, the federal deficit was $14.9 billion when these entities were included. Excluding them reduced the deficit only to $14.8 billion. However, by 1981, the situation was vastly different. The federal deficit was $57.9 billion excluding these entities. But it jumps to $78.9 billion when they are included. Clearly, the exclusion of off-budget entities understates the size of the deficit and thus the magnitude of borrowing undertaken by the federal government.

In addition, almost all of the talk about budget deficits refers to the federal deficit, yet not all government borrowing in the credit markets is done by the federal government. State and local governments also borrow in the credit markets. They may also, of course, purchase federal government securities. Thus, when assessing the impact of government borrowing on the competition for loanable funds between the public and private sectors, one should properly consider total borrowing (net of intergovernmental transactions) by all levels of government, not just federal borrowing.

The Federal Budgetary Record

To put the concern over budget deficits into better perspective, it is useful to review the federal budgetary record. From the establishment of the U.S. Treasury in 1789 through 1981, there have been 191 budgets. During this long period, the record shows that there have been 88 deficits and 103 surpluses.

Such a long period, however, may obscure important changes in budgeting behavior. The period is therefore broken down into two subperiods, 1789 to 1930 and 1931 to 1981. The reason for this particular split is that, as Lewis Kimmel has stated, " . . . at no time prior to the 1930s were public expenditures used deliberately and consciously as a balancing factor; there was little or no evidence of a conscious fiscal policy in the modern sense of the term." Subsequent to the 1930s, however, fiscal policy became increasingly viewed as a tool for smoothing cyclical fluctuations in economic activity.

During the 140 years from 1789 to 1930, there were 45 deficits. This means, of course, that there were 95 surpluses. In short, during the first 140 years of U.S. history the budget was in the red 32 percent of the time. The budgetary record for the more recent 1931 to 1981 subperiod, however, is quite different. In almost one-third fewer years (51), there were nearly as many deficits (43). Surpluses occurred only eight times. In other words, the past half century saw deficits 84 percent of the time.

The situation for the past 32 years is even more striking. Since 1950, there have been 27 deficits and only five surpluses, the most recent one in 1969. The largest deficit on record occurred during this period—$66.4 **billion** in 1976. This compares to the first budget deficit of $1.4 **million** in 1792.

The entire budgetary record shows that there are clearly periods in which deficits as a share of GNP have tended to skyrocket. What is striking, however, is that the largest deficits always have occurred during war periods. In fact, the record is that of the 88 deficits during the past 191 years, 30 of these occurred during war years. Omitting war years, then, one finds that there were 103 surpluses versus 58 deficits since the first U.S. budget. Of course, depressions and recessions, by reducing revenues and stimulating expenditures, also are associated with deficits. The largest peace-time deficit occurred during the Great Depression of the 1930s.

Given that there were so many surpluses during U.S. history, it is important to understand their purpose. Basically, surpluses are intended to reduce, and ultimately to retire, federal debt out-standing. This goal has been largely accomplished. Wars caused federal debt as a share of GNP to rise sharply. However, after the wars, federal debt fell rather steadily. The same pattern emerged for severe recessions, such as the Great Depression of the 1930s. Also, the federal debt was essentially eliminated during the 1830s.

Contrary to what people may believe, the federal debt has not grown without limit. On the basis of the historical record, there was every reason to believe that eventually it would be paid off. Only in the last few years has the federal debt leveled off. What will happen in future years, of course, is very uncertain. This un-certainty, in turn, affects financial markets in ways that are not fully understood. More will be said about this in subsequent sec-tions.

Budget Deficits and the Great Depression

The current concern about federal deficits is reminiscent of the concern expressed during the Great Depression. Prior to the 1930s it was widely believed that a balanced budget was "the prin-cipal test of sound fiscal management." As the previous section demonstrated, surpluses were the rule, not the exception. When deficits did occur, it was mainly due to wars. But following the wars, surpluses were typically accumulated so that outstanding federal debt could be retired. During the 1930s, however, some-thing quite different happened. For the first time in U.S. history, the nation incurred 10 successive peacetime deficits.

On December 2, 1929, approximately six weeks after the col-lapse of the stock market, President Hoover submitted his budget for 1931 to the Congress. There was no indication in this budget nor any direct admission during the following year that large and continual deficits were looming. Indeed, "even the 1932 budget re-leased in December 1930 indicated surpluses for the fiscal years

1931 and 1932." This situation did not last long, however. "As the depression deepened, it became apparent that the budget estimates had been far too optimistic and that the Treasury would soon be faced with larger deficits than any previously incurred in time of peace."

Despite the depression, a balanced budget was considered to be an essential condition for recovery. "A balanced budget was regarded as a prerequisite for a revival of business confidence." Moreover, "federal borrowing was viewed as competitive with business and other private borrowing; interest rates were higher because of federal competition for loan funds." Lastly, an "unbalanced federal budget was equated with inflation." Thus, it is no surprise that in the early 1930s "the President (Hoover), officials of the executive branch, and the leadership of both parties in Congress" united in "making a balanced budget the primary policy goal."

Interestingly enough, throughout the early years of the depression, it was frequently asserted that heavy or excessive tax burdens were a major reason for, if not the sole cause of, the "unsatisfactory economic situation." Despite this view, however, tax reductions were not regarded as a viable option. Instead, a balanced budget achieved primarily through rigorous expenditure control was the primary goal.

During the 1932 presidential campaign, "the Democratic party became the self-appointed champion of what was accepted as fiscal conservatism." In this role, the Democrats "made the most of the 'recklessness' of those who would tolerate continued unbalance in the federal accounts." With the election of President Roosevelt, however, the campaign rhetoric faded fast. By the time of the budget message of January 5, 1937, in contrast to the first budget message "which promised a balanced budget in the third year of recovery," " . . . a fully balanced budget was now assured only in the indefinite but apparently not-too-distant future." Instead of balancing the budget, very early on in the Roosevelt administration "restoring the economy, which above all else required a reduction in unemployment to a reasonable minimum, became a primary objective of public policy." Indeed, "on numerous occasions the President stated that government was responsible for providing for the unemployed and the needy." While doing this, however, "it was held that these and other governmental expenditures would contribute to rising income levels and increases in private employment."

The above quotations from the period of the Great Depression support the view that economic views often repeat themselves. Much of the current controversy and concern over budget deficits is remarkably similar to that which surfaced a half century ago. Apart from this, the Great Depression demonstrated to many individuals that sharp contractions in economic activity can cause huge deficits. Eventually, this realization led to the development of the concept of a full employment budget deficit. Rather than simply relying only on the reported federal deficit figures the notion was that one should calculate what the budget deficit (or surplus) would be if the economy were operating at full or a high level of employment. On a full employment basis, for example, during the spring and summer of 1981, the federal budget was in surplus, not in deficit. Some interpret this as a sign that fiscal policy was, if anything, contractionary during this recessionary period.

Why All the Concern over Budget Deficits?

Why is there such widespread concern over federal budgetary deficits? Or, more to the point, do budget deficits really matter? Unfortunately, determining the economic impact of deficits is very controversial. It is an area where there are widely differing points of view. Some economists, for example, state that "bigger deficits, if allowed to accumulate, have evil consequences of their own; either more inflation, or more government borrowing from private lenders, which in turn means less chance for private firms to borrow funds needed for capital improvements and expansion." Others say "an increase in the budget deficit . . . does not necessarily mean either a crowding out of private investment or an accentuation of inflationary pressure." To understand the potential economic impact of budget deficits, we will discuss the rationale underlying such different views.

As discussed earlier, federal deficits may be bond-financed and/or money-financed. There is broad agreement that money-financed deficits do indeed increase aggregate demand, push prices higher, and drive up the nominal, if not real, rate of interest. The monetization of deficits, in other words, is generally considered to be inflationary. To the extent that the inflation is anticipated, nominal interest rates, in turn, will be higher insofar as they embody an inflation premium, particulary long-term rates of interest. As far as crowding out (that is, the decline in interest-sensitive private investment and durable goods spending due to big deficits) is concerned, there should be none. Money-financed deficits are likely to leave the real rate of interest unaffected or, if affected, cause it to decline.

But how can one be sure that budget deficits will not be money-financed? Since the Federal Reserve is independent of the Treasury Department, there is no requirement that it purchase federal securities whenever there is a deficit. If the Federal Reserve so decides, deficits may be completely bond-financed. Historically, this has not been the case. On the other hand, the record does not demonstrate that deficits are completely money-financed either. What appears to be the case is that the Federal Reserve monetizes a varying fraction of budget deficits. Even when the Federal Reserve monetizes a portion of the deficit, however, it doesn't necessarily mean that the money stock increases one-for-one with the deficit. For example, the deficit was $3.8 billion in 1962. This deficit became a surplus of $0.7 billion in 1963. At the same time money growth (M1) more than doubled, from a rate of 1.8 percent in 1962 to 4.0 percent in 1963. An even more striking example occurred during the 1974–75 period. In 1974, the deficit was $4.7 billion. The deficit ballooned to $63.8 billion in 1975. Money growth, however, remained relatively constant, growing at a rate of 4.9 percent in 1975 as compared to a rate of 4.7 percent in 1974.

In general, movements in money do not track movements in budget deficits one-for-one. Whether the movements are much closer once we adjust for the level of economic activity (so as to distinguish between "passive" and "active" deficits) is another matter. The evidence relating to whether deficits in the past have led to faster money growth and, thus, inflation appears to be somewhat mixed. In any event, regardless of what has happened in the past, the Federal Reserve is in a strong position to prevent future deficits from becoming inflationary.

More controversial is the case of bond-financed deficits, in which deficits are financed through the sale of securities to the public. The crucial issue here is whether the bonds that are sold increase aggregate demand and thus drive up prices as well as increase the real rate of interest. Output effects may also occur which, via an "acceleration mechanism," can temporarily offset any reduction in interest-sensitive components of real aggregate demand. Some economists contend that government bonds are properly considered as a component of private wealth. According to this view, bond-financed deficits will therefore increase wealth which, in turn, will stimulate consumption and the demand for money. Increased consumption and money demand will lead to a higher real rate of interest. This, they argue, will generate crowding out as investment in plant and equipment and purchases of consumer durables decline due to higher real interest rates. If interest rates rise sufficiently, there will be complete crowding out, which means that the bond-financed deficit will not increase aggregate demand and thus prices. Although the defictis will not be inflationary in this more extreme situation, they will still drive up real interest rates and thus generate crowding out.

Other economists disagree with this scenario. They contend that government bonds do not represent net wealth. According to this view, there are no wealth effects associated with bond-financed deficits. Proponents argue that people realize the bonds issued will pay interest and will eventually be retired. This means that issuance of bonds implies an offsetting future tax liability to cover the interest payments and principal. To meet this future tax liability, the public will save more. This means that the federal deficit (government dis-saving) will be matched exactly by an increase in private saving. In this case, there will be no increase in aggregate demand and thus no increase in prices. Furthermore, the increase in private saving to match the budget deficit means that the deficit will not siphon funds away from private investment. In short, real interest rates will be unaffected and, as a result, there will be no crowding out.

Still another view of bond-financed deficits maintains that cuts in tax rates (particularly marginal tax rates), will increase the after-tax rate of return to saving. As a result, it is argued that tax-induced deficits will stimulate a greater amount of saving. If stimulated sufficiently, this additional saving will be available to purchase the government bonds that are sold to finance the deficit. In this way, there need not be any crowding out or increased inflationary pressure. The increase in saving will prevent aggregate demand from rising and will provide the additional funds to keep real interest rates from moving upward.

We can probably safely draw the following conclusions. First, if anything, deficits caused by increased federal spending are likely to be more inflationary and generate more crowding out than those caused by cuts in marginal tax rates. Second, money-financed deficits are more likely to be inflationary but less likely to generate crowding out than are bond-financed deficits. Third, deficits that persist and grow (both absolutely and as a share of GNP) during peacetime, nonrecessionary periods are more likely to be inflationary and lead to crowding out, regardless of how they are financed. Fifth, as should perhaps now be clear, attempting to predict the impacts of government spending and tax rate changes on the economy is an extremely difficult task, especially if it is not clear whether the changes are temporary or permanent. For this and related reasons, a sensible budget policy may be to set government spending and tax rates so as to balance the budget not every year but over the course of a business cycle. In this way, deficits could occur with wars and recessions, while surpluses could occur during cyclically expansionary periods.

The Budgetary Bottom Line

Despite the fact that budget deficits may not always be painful economically, they always seem to be painful politically. This is a case in which perceptions may be more important than reality. So whether the economic issues as discussed above are fully understood or not, in such a situation, deficits do indeed matter. If the Congress perceives that federal deficits are harmful—politically and/or economically—it surely will take steps to eliminate them.

The issue then becomes whether the resulting actions are more harmful to the economy than the deficits would have been.

THE PROBLEM OF BIG GOVERNMENT: ARE WE LOSING OUR MARBLES?[3]

Today I'd like to share with you some facts and figures about what I believe is the single, most critical issue facing our nation today: namely, the proper size and role of government.

1789 was the first year of the federal government. The original Articles of Confederation, established after independence from the British in 1776, had been thrown out, and the new Constitution that replaced it made possible, among other things, a common federal currency and a central national government with the power to tax and spend, and, along with it, to borrow or even mint or print money.

State and local governments, the non-central governments, were the "big spenders" at that time, and state and local government spending in 1789 totalled $8 million. Federal spending was a relatively scant $2 million—these are millions (with an "M" and not a big "B" soon to be a gigantic "T").

Now, if you adjust that $2 million for inflation assuming a 2 percent compound annual rate over the 194 years since then, an historically accurate figure, it's worth about $93 million today. But we know that the federal government alone, at its current spending rate of $800 billion a year, spends $93 million in about an hour. So we know that government spending is far greater in real terms today—mind-bogglingly so—than our Founding Fathers ever could have imagined.

In fact, most of the growth involved is very recent.

To illustrate what has happened, I want to take a break here for what we used to call a "brainteaser" when I was studying at

[3]Reprint of a speech by J. Peter Grace, chairman and chief executive officer of W. R. Grace & Company, delivered at Business and Economics Week, Chautauqua, New York, Jl. 12, '83. Reprinted from *Vital Speeches of the Day*, 49:701–4, S. 1, '83, with permission.

Yale. Here's one of my favorites: suppose someone had a very large jar with one marble in it. And he said, "The number of marbles in this jar doubles every minute, and at the end of one hour, the jar is completely full of marbles." Easy so far, right?

Okay, then, here's the question: when is the jar only half-full if it takes an hour to fill completely with the number of marbles doubling every minute? To repeat, one jar; one marble; doubles every minute, jar is full after one hour. When is the jar half-full? Any volunteers? Don't be bashful—it's only a brainteaser, and it's stumped some fairly sharp people (some of whom *used* to be with our Company).

I heard a couple of correct answers out there. Now, how many (show of hands, please) said 30 minutes?

Quite a few, I see.

Okay, now think about it. If the jar is half-full after 30 minutes and the number of marbles doubles every minute, wouldn't that mean the marbles would double again after the 31st minute and fill the jar?

So, the correct answer, after all this dialogue, is 59 minutes. In the last minute the marbles double and the jar is full after one hour like we said in the first place.

Okay, so what's the point?

The point is that if federal spending was $2 million in 1789, how did it get to $800 billion (with a "B") today?

The answer is in the marbles.

It took *155* years after 1789, until 1944, for federal spending to reach $95 billion. 155 years.

Then, just *21* years after that, in 1965, the amount of federal spending had risen only another $24 billion, roughly, to $118 billion.

Then, just *ten years later*—1975—and federal spending had almost tripled, from $118 billion in '65 to $324 billion in '75. Ten years.

But what happened after that? In the seven or eight short years since 1975, federal spending more than *doubled* again to $805 billion. A far cry from the $2 *million* (with an "M") in 1789 that we said was worth about what the federal government spends in an hour today if you adjust for inflation.

This is what geometric growth rates do. Like the marbles, most of the action in any given time-frame occurs at the tail end. It means we can expect our government spending situation to get worse because the doubling period is still getting shorter.

It means that the federal *deficit* alone—that's the amount we run in the red *each year,* not the total debt—will be upwards of $2 trillion by fiscal year 2000, and since the spending rate keeps increasing, it may happen sooner. This isn't alarmist rhetoric; this is straight from the "garden variety" pocket calculator.

But it is a serious, dangerous situation. Now here's the real brainteaser: what do we do about it?

Logic dictates we must do one of three things. Raise taxes, cut spending, or some combination of both.

Let's go through them one at a time.

Nowadays, with the deficits running as high as they are and no end in sight, the voices advocating that our government "soak the rich" have become more vocal and are getting renewed attention. Soaking the rich is a noble-sounding idea, and all of us have heard from time to time about Americans with seven-figure incomes who paid little or no tax to the federal government.

My question is this: would raising taxes on the rich narrow the deficits significantly? To answer that question, we need to look at which tax brackets produce the most absolute revenues. Surprising to many, it's the middle-income levels. Fully 90 percent of all the taxable personal income in the U.S. flows through brackets under $35,000 annually. That's 90 percent of *taxable personal income.*

As for actual *personal-income taxes raised,* 90 percent of that sum comes from the brackets under $40,000. That's not the rich either.

In fact, if you could take *all* the taxable income above $75,000—the whole pile—you'd raise enough extra money to cover *only 4.1 percent* of total federal expenditures. And that's if you took it all.

If your Congressman is part of the "soak the rich" crowd, try this out on him. I've tried it. I've said, "Congressman so-and-so, how are you going to 'soak the rich' and get a balanced budget if you take *everything* above $75,000, when that increases revenues only enough to cover 4.1 percent of expenditures?" I guarantee you he'll change the subject.

Now, what this means is that balancing the budget requires cuts in spending, because there aren't enough rich people and the middle-class is already on its knees even with the Reagan tax cuts which have only partially offset the accumulated bracket creep so far.

Well, when you say "cut spending," immediately numerous fingers point to the defense budget, and the same people that tell you Reagan is a warmonger and a friend of the rich will tell you that he's taking money from the social programs to put into military weapons. In fact, I would say that most Americans believe defense spending is the largest part of the budget.

The facts suggest otherwise. Spending under Reagan on defense takes up 26.2 percent of the total. Spending on human resources, meanwhile, takes up 53.2 percent of total spending; twice as much, about $240 billion vs. a little over $110 billion on defense. Spending on human resources is now 11.6 percent of our GNP vs. 5 percent on defense.

But Reagan is called the big scrooge, the warmonger.

Remember John Kennedy and Camelot? He's the symbol when they talk about the compassion Reagan supposedly lacks. Under Kennedy in 1962 defense was *47.8 percent* of the budget and *9.0 percent* of GNP. So things have changed, and the images are just the opposite of the facts.

As a businessman, I can tell you there is nothing unusual about having to cut budgets in order to remain profitable or cut your losses. We cut some of our budgets more than twice during this recession, which is still going on for the chemical industry, and this is nothing new.

When businessmen go after a budget, they look for the biggest and fastest-growing areas, because if you cut a budget that's only a small part of your overall spending, or one that isn't growing much, you can't make much difference at the bottom line.

Clearly, the largest portions of federal spending are in the human resource/transfer payment categories. The *percentage increases* in this area—payments to individuals from government coffers, meaning taxpayers—are actually larger under the Reagan

Administration—at far higher levels of spending—than any Administration's from 1962 to the present.

Most of these programs are tied to increases in the cost of living, so the increases are automatic. Congress calls these "uncontrollables"; read, "hot potatoes." They won't touch them, and now they're more than three-fourths of the budget.

The increases in these programs over just the past 10 years range from the astonishing to the astronomical. Veterans benefits had the lowest increase—in the past ten years it's up "only" 114 percent. The average increase is 283 percent or nearly triple.

Food stamps went up 489 percent. Housing assistance by 636 percent or nearly 6½ times. Ask yourself, if you're a taxpayer, if your income went up by 6½ times in the past 10 years. You're paying for all this.

Food stamps, by the way, were $10 million in 1962. Today it's $11.2 billion, a 112,000 percent increase in two decades. Carter wanted it to go to $14 billion, but Reagan proposed scaling that back to $12 billion and everybody objected. So this is a very serious problem with tremendous political implications one would never have to deal with in running a business that has to remain solvent or go under.

Okay, you might say, we know that deficits can't be cut much by raising taxes on the rich, and we know that social programs take up twice as much money as defense. What else?

Well, as I alluded to before when I said taxpayers should ask whether their incomes have risen as fast as these social programs, the fact is that government spending is growing faster than our economy—that, in fact, is precisely how deficits happen. And all of us are forking over more of our incomes to the government, and still the deficits grow.

What does bigger and bigger government mean?

As a businessman, I think of government as an overhead cost of our economy as a whole. By that I mean that in a corporation, you have profit centers that earn money, like our chemicals, natural resources and consumer operations. But you also have to turn on the lights, pay your rent and so on. That's the overhead. Now, as your operations grow and earn more the overhead part remains relatively constant, and so it goes *down* as a percent of the total.

Government's legitimate overhead functions include defense, streets, sewers, bridges, roads, tunnels, police, etc., all the things people need a central organization to provide conveniently. Things individuals by themselves *can't* do.

But once government goes beyond these overhead functions and tries to provide everything—student loans, food stamps, etc.— you have a political and eventually a fiscal problem. It's no more complicated than the company that has no profits to pay the rent or the electric bill.

So big government isn't just spending gone wild, it's that government as a percentage of our total economy is growing when it should be declining. It's overhead consuming what pays for overhead. And it's now 25 percent of GNP, and in the last quarter of last year it was 26.3 percent. Remember that's more than one-quarter of all economic activity. It's less than 10 percent in Japan.

That's why President Reagan asked me to lead the President's Private Sector Survey on Cost Control, which is a group of top executives whose job it is to look at every agency and function in the federal government to see how wasteful spending can be identified and reduced. The idea is to cut the unnecessary spending without cutting the quality of services.

More than 160 executives like myself chaired 36 task forces, 24 of which were devoted to department/agency analyses; the other 12 looked into "cross-cutting" government functions like data processing, personnel practices, asset management and other things that could be applied across-the-board. Each of the 160 executives volunteered other top executives from their companies for the field work, making the total team about 1600 strong. We've been at this more than a year now with about $65 million in donated time and cash—not one tax dollar was involved—and we've learned a very great deal.

Here are a few examples of areas we've identified for cost savings that wouldn't cut service levels and which have nothing to do with hurting the truly needy:

—Our task force examining the operations of the U.S. Department of Agriculture found that 70 percent of the borrowers loaned money by the Farmers Home Administration were not farmers. The delinquency rate among these non-farm borrowers is 26 percent, more than seven times the private-sector average of 3 percent–4 percent. And the average interest rate on all these loans is 2.7 percent. This program is supposed to help people who couldn't otherwise get financing; then, when they're financially "on their feet" they're supposed to "graduate" to non-government lending sources. But because of the interest subsidies, they seldom do. As a result this program has grown from $6.5 billion in outstanding loans in 1970 to $58 billion in 1982.

—The Patent and Trademark office receives 20,000 pieces of mail a day. Guess what? They're processed by an all-paper, hand-file and routing system. The backlog is two years.

—Our Department of Education Task Force looked into the Student Loan program. The total value of loans in default is now $2.2 billion, including those to some fairly wealthy doctors and lawyers. Some of the debt has been on the books 10 years.

—Our task force investigating the Department of Energy found that this department, inexplicably, has twice as many supervisors for its size than the federal government as a whole, one supervisor for every three employees vs. one supervisor for every seven employees government-wide.

—Our Task Force on federal construction projects found that it costs 15 percent–20 percent more to build a federal facility than a private-sector building. The reason is "standard federal specifications" which spell out exact materials. The private sector uses "performance specifications" to maintain materials flexibility and control costs. With federal construction contracts of $20 billion that means $4 billion is pure waste. By the way, the federal government owns $2.6 billion square feet of building space, equivalent to the floor space of 1,040 Empire State Buildings.

—We set up an Asset Management Task Force. They found that U.S. government collections and disbursements total almost $1 billion per working hour. Nevertheless, the government can't even centrally determine the aging of $35 billion in delinquent debt, or 16 percent of total receivables of $219 billion.

—Our task force examining Social Security found that this program has made $14.6 billion in erroneous payments just from 1980–1982.

—Our task force on Health and Human Services looked at this monster's operations. For fiscal 1983, HHS has a budgeted authority of $274 billion, or two of every five federal tax dollars.

Outlays have multiplied by 55 times over the past 30 years, and HHS now accounts for a third of the total budget. Now, if you're caught in that monster and want to write HHS to ask a question, keep your fingers crossed that a reply doesn't require the signature of the HHS Secretary. If it does, 55–60 people will have to get into the act, and it will take almost a month and a half.

—When the VA processes a claim, the processing alone costs an average $100–$140. Private insurance and fiscal intermediaries spend $3–$6 per claim for processing.

—You might well ask why the government has so many delinquent loans outstanding? Well, one reason is that when you're lending someone else's money the incentive isn't there to keep track of it. Our task force on the Housing and Urban Development Agency (HUD) found that HUD makes only three attempts to collect charged-off loans compared with an average 24–36 such attempts in the private sector where there is an incentive.

If HUD used collection agencies who would have an incentive to earn a fee, we estimate at least $19 million in one-time revenue enhancements on delinquent loans.

—Our Low Income Standards and Benefits task force looked into some of the fraud and abuse in Food Stamps. The Food and Nutrition Service, which administers the program, admits that overpayments of food stamps totalled $1 billion in fiscal 1981 or 10 percent of the whole program. Now who's lacking in compassion? The Reagan Administration or the food stamp cheats who take food out of the mouths of the poor? The amount of food-stamp fraud totally undetected must be mind-boggling, since undercover agents managed to use $60,000 worth of food stamps in Tampa, Florida, to buy a car, a motorcycle, television sets, refrigerators and $40,000 in drugs.

That also means that the merchants who are authorized to redeem food stamps are in on it too, and that is very disturbing when we talk about compassion.

—Our Personnel Management Task Force studied the Civil Service Retirement System (CSRS). Our conservative estimate of this system's unfunded liability is $499 billion. More likely it's $600 billion. Now, the law requires private-sector pensions to amortize liability over 40 years. If CSRS had to do this, the liability involved would amount to 85 percent of payroll costs vs. the private sector's 14 percent.

—A lot of this is due to COLA provisions. From 1973 to 1979 inflation measured by the CPI (which in itself overstates inflation) moved up 60 percent. But federal pensions increased 84 percent. Only 3 percent of private-sector employees have COLAs in their pensions.

—Now, we didn't spare the Defense Department. Our procurement task force looked at weapons purchases and found all kinds of abuse in the contracting system, with under-bidding used to get a contract, then negotiating for more on subsequent contracts.

—If the Defense Department used some of its own ordering systems properly instead of ignoring them, we estimate one-time savings of $3.5 billion plus three-year savings of $1 billion just on proper weapons inventory control. So, we haven't overlooked Defense. And we're not talking about cutbacks in service there either.

—Imagine keeping track of the government's records the way they try to do it: 37 million cubic feet of stored records growing at the rate of 400,000 cubic feet a year. Government files occupy the equivalent of 60 acres of storage space stacked 14 feet high. Well, this is your government, and all of the foregoing are just random, tip-of-the-iceberg examples. Our 36 task forces have detailed hundreds and hundreds of others and made an equivalent number of recommendations to try to make a dent in some of this unbelievable waste.

The important thing to remember is that America is basically broke, and if these recommendations were followed, we could be saving billions of dollars without a big debate about how to further tax the working people of this country. We also wouldn't be distracting ourselves with a lot of rhetoric about compassion, because none of the savings we're talking about has anything to do with service levels—only the waste. In fact, if you cut out the waste, fraud and abuse you'll get better service, so we think this is the most practical form of compassion and not just the lip-service.

Now, President Reagan did a very courageous thing to get us looking into these matters, because he has risked a great deal of political capital in the process. This kind of unprecedented investigation stirs up all the special interest groups, and they run the country, and some of them don't like what they think we're doing, even though most of that is based on rumor. If they had the facts we've gathered they'd know that waste is waste and that's that, and there's nothing political about it.

Congress, on the other hand, doesn't do anything without considering the politics, and that's why the spending has gone up as fast under Reagan as before him. Congress had 40 committees in the early 1960s, and now they have a couple of hundred, all of which serve their constituent special interests very effectively with lots of goodies you taxpayers provide. Meanwhile, you don't have a Congressional committee looking after you or an office on "K" Street in Washington following up. They do. Lot's of them.

As a religious man, let me say something about compassion. The Chautauqua Institution's earliest history is deeply rooted in religious conviction, and many of you here know that the root word "passion" means "suffering" and is derived from Jesus's predictions to his Disciples about His eventual torture and crucifixion. It is interesting that the New Testament makes special note of the Disciples' failure to grasp the meaning of Jesus's predictions; He eventually taught them, of course, the difference between death and life—the hard way—and *then* they understood.

As a patriotic man, my heart is heavy with the realization that our country's history—some say Divinely inspired—has so many similarities.

In 200 years:

—From bondage to spiritual faith.
—From spiritual faith to great courage.
—From courage to liberty.
—From liberty to abundance.
—From abundance to selfishness.
—From selfishness to complacency.
—From complacency to apathy.
—From apathy to dependency.

The last step, of course, is from dependency back to bondage, and when that happens—when the State has it all—maybe then your Congressman will finally say you had some compassion. So there is a great deal of difference between real compassion and Washington's brand of compassion by proxy.

Compassion by proxy—taking what's yours, giving it to someone else, then asking for more—works only in two places. In Heaven, where it is not needed; and in Hell, where they already have it.

Well, my friends, 100 percent of your income taxes are already spent on all these social programs and interest on the debt alone, leaving nothing for the functions of government. That's why the deficit is going to be $600 billion in 1990. That's why it will be more than $2 trillion in 2000. Per year. And that's at current rates, but the rates keep increasing, and these enormous deficits will probably come sooner.

A lot of people who should know better are looking at that jar with the marbles in the 59th minute and telling you "no problem—it's only half-full."

Watch out, because those people are your elected officials.

Have they already lost *their* marbles?

Thank you very much.

ALL YOU NEED TO KNOW ABOUT THE DEFICIT[4]

Now, about that deficit: Ronald Reagan was quite correct, during the first Presidential debate, in insisting that there is no connection between the deficit and the interest rate. If he had been more precise, he would have said that there is no invariant connection between the two. Walter Mondale, too, was quite correct in insisting that the deficit presents a threat to the economy, to the nation and to the peace of the world, although again there is no

[4]Reprint of an article by George P. Brockway, economics columnist. *The New Leader*. 67:9–10. O. 29, '84. Reprinted with permission of The New Leader. Copyright © the American Labor Conference on International Affairs, Inc.

invariant connection. There are, in fact, few (if any) invariant connections in economics, but it would be lèse majesté to expect Mr. Reagan or Mr. Mondale to understand that, especially since most economists don't either.

There are few (if any) invariant connections in economics, because every economics question has to do with money. As I said in this space last time ("'Trust Funds,'" NL, October 15), without money you have physiology and engineering and so on (all necessary parts of our life), but you don't have economics (also a part of life, like it or not). And as I said here two and a half years ago ("Let's Put Indexing on the Index," NL, April 5, 1982), there is no invariant connection between any good or service and money. The mere fact of inflation is enough to settle that question, even if there were not sound metaphysical considerations (which you may not take so seriously as I do) on the same side.

So we seem to have a dilemma. Reagan and Mondale are both right, and they're both wrong. At the root of the dilemma is money—well known to be at the bottom of much else. At the root of money is the banking system, and in the United States the Federal Reserve Board is at the root of the banking system. Since neither Reagan nor Mondale dared or cared to mention the Federal Reserve Board, there was an air of irrelevance to their debate.

Before digging to the root of the matter, let's consider the causes for and the effects of the exponential surge in the deficit. The principal causes are not in dispute: a tremendous increase in military spending, the vast and varied tax cuts of 1981 and the high interest rates. Of these, the military spending had a positive effect on the business recovery, the tax cuts were neutral and the interest rates were negative.

The economic virtue of military spending is that there is no end to it. In a famous example of his irony, Keynes writes: "Ancient Egypt was doubly fortunate . . . in that it possessed *two* activities, namely, pyramid building as well as the search for precious metals, the fruits of which, since they could not serve the needs of man by being consumed, did not stale with abundance. The Middle Ages built cathedrals and sang dirges. Two pyramids, two masses for the dead, are twice as good as one, but not so two railways from London to York."

Military hardware likewise does not "serve the needs of many by being consumed," so it can be added to forever. And like pyramid building it increases aggregate demand. Demand is what stimulates business activity. Businesses produce things if they foresee a demand for them. Any expenditure is stimulative, yet government expenditure, being both large and highly visible, is especially stimulative. As Keynes suggests, building housing would be as stimulative as building pyramids or armaments. Or as John Ruskin (a better economist than you may have realized) exclaims, "What an absurd idea it seems, put fairly in words, that the wealth of the capitalists of civilized nations should ever come to support literature instead of war!" It would, in short, not be difficult to conjure up better uses for our money, and hence better ways of stimulating the economy; nonetheless, the military build-up—foolishness, highmindedness, viciousness, waste, and all—has in fact been the motive power behind the recent business recovery.

The tax cuts were, as I say, essentially neutral. If you wisely keep a file of *The New Leader,* you will find the reasons set forth in the issue of March 8, 1982 ("Why Deficits Matter"). For those who can't lay their hands on back issues, I'll summarize the reasons briefly. The tax cuts were, you will remember, intended to stimulate the supply side, on the theory that saving is the cause of investment. The theory is fallacious. Not even Representative Jack Kemp (R.-N.Y.) can imagine that the industrial half of President Eisenhower's Military-Industrial Complex would build a factory to produce cruise missiles before the military half placed an order.

The supply-side theory turned out to be fallacious in still another way. In accordance with its logic, the 1981 personal income tax favored the rich, and the corporate tax favored the prosperous, the hope being that those who didn't need the money would save it. This hope was disappointed, and for a simple reason. Since the Federal budget was already in deficit, the tax cuts necessarily increased that deficit. The increased deficit had to be funded; that is, bonds to cover it had to be sold. To whom were they sold? To those who had money to pay for them, of course, and they were, in general, the people who had benefited from the tax cuts. The upshot was that the rich and prosperous were given money to buy government bonds. In effect, they were given the bonds. The maneuver accomplished as extraordinary a transfer of wealth—albeit to the wealthy—as America had seen.

But if this transfer had any effect on the Gross National Product, it was merely a distortion of priorities. The disadvantaged were somewhat what less able to buy food and housing, and the fall-off was balanced by a surge in the sale of Cadillacs and Lincolns. Aggregate demand, and hence aggregate production, were not substantially affected one way or the other. (Do you wonder why I'm disrespectful of the GNP?)

The third factor in the deficit, the high interest rates, was of course a drag on the business recovery. Mind-boggling though the fact is, that was *intended* to be a drag. The idiocy of the intention is not, however, what interests me at the moment. It is the effectiveness of the intention that gets to the root of the matter, for the policies of the Federal Reserve Board are thus demonstrated to be not irrelevant.

Empirically, Reagan was perfectly right. In 1980 the deficit was much lower than today's, but the interest rate was much higher. How, then, can one claim that the deficit is the cause of high interest rates? But Mondale was perfectly right, too. The present deficit is indeed the cause of the present high interest rates, and these in turn contribute to continuing high unemployment, the strength of the dollar, the decline in exports, and the increasing trade gap.

The reason why the deficit is the cause of high interest rates is very simple: The Federal Reserve Board says it is. On this subject Board Chairman Paul A. Volcker is a cracked record, going around and around, saying the same thing endlessly.

To be sure, it is not literally what the Federal Reserve Board *says* that is of consequence. Persuasive though he is, Volcker does not run the rates up or down simply by jawboning. His speeches have an impact on the rates only to the extent that they are taken as hints of what the Board will do. It is what the Board *does* that matters. For the Board controls the rates, partly by setting the rediscount rate, partly by determining margin requirements, and mainly by controlling the money supply. Money earns interest in rough proportion to its scarcity, and for a third of a century now the Federal Reserve has been making money scarcer and scarcer. It has been doing this under the misapprehension that it was thereby containing inflation. It obviously wasn't. The record is clear here, but that is another story.

Whether the deficit causes the high interest rates directly by scaring Wall Street or indirectly by scaring the Federal Reserve Board, there is no doubt that the high rates increase the deficit. The bonds that were sold to finance the 1981 tax cuts and are now sold to finance the deficit offer a fantastic return—12–14 per cent or more. I have some that will pay me 14 per cent yearly until November 15, 2011. I should live so long.

Interest payable on the Federal debt is an incubus of daunting weight that will smother the economy for generations to come. Even now, as Senator Daniel P. Moynihan (D.-N.Y.) has shown, the annual interest payments are approximately equal to the annual deficit, and the compoundng of that interest will more than offset any savings that might be made elsewhere in the budget.

The compounding, moreover, is not of the ordinary sort. Thirty-year bonds that were sold in 1954, paying an average rate of 2.4 per cent, must be paid off today with money raised by selling bonds paying more than five times the old rate. Look at this another way: If the old rates were still in force, the deficit would be less than one fifth of what it is.

Continuing the observation, we see that the world according to Volcker is upside down. He says it would be fine to have low interest rates, if only the deficit could be reduced to manageable size. But the deficit would have been manageable if the Federal Reserve Board had kept interest rates low. The interest rates have no life of their own, any more that the deficit has. Even on Volcker's theory, it would appear that high interest rates swelled the deficit, and not the other way around.

As things are, the only way to reduce the deficit—the Federal Reserve Board's price for lowering the interest rates—is to raise taxes. That is what Mondale promised to do. But Reagan (good Keynesian *malgré lui*) said raising taxes threatens to send the economy into a new depression, because increased taxes mean a reduction in aggregate demand, and a reduction in demand is followed by a depression as surely as an increase in demand is followed by a boom.

This dilemma could have been avoided if the tax cuts had gone to those who would spend them. It could have been avoided if the Treasury and the Federal Reserve Board had cooperated in holding down the interest rates, as they did during World War II. As it happened, both fiscal and monetary policies were fatefully misdirected. If the President does not look good in the history books, the reason may be that he did not have the wit—and we did not give him the power—to beat some sense into the Federal Reserve Board.

TO THE PRESIDENT AND CONGRESS: A BI-PARTISAN APPEAL TO RESOLVE THE BUDGET CRISIS[5]

The federal budget is now out of control. It is primed to generate immense deficits, year after year, for decades ahead—deficits far larger than any in our history. This fiscal course is senseless. It threatens to lock the economy in stagnation for the remainder of this century. Massive deficits would absorb savings urgently needed for investment in plant and equipment, infrastructure and R&D. Productivity would sag and inflation resurface. Interest-sensitive industries would be smothered and exports would dwindle. The result would be a period of gradual decline, punctuated by high unemployment and social conflict and culminating in an America that is permanently poorer and weaker.

The Nation cannot afford to leave the budget to politics as usual. It is time to set aside differences of party, region and ideology. We appeal to you, our leaders, to display true leadership in the spirit of national unity, to resolve the current crisis. Only if you

[5]Excerpted from an advertisement by The Bi-Partisan Budget Appeal, an organization whose founding members are former Treasury secretaries W. Michael Blumenthal, John B. Connally, C. Douglas Dillon, Henry H. Fowler, and William E. Simon and former Commerce secretary Peter G. Peterson. *The Wall Street Journal,* January 25, 1983, pp. 40–1.

do so can the balance of this century yet be a time of prosperity and growth, of new jobs and higher standards of living. And only if it is, can we leave future generations with a richer and stronger America.

The Budget Disaster

Despite the budget actions of 1981 and 1982, the deficit has just topped 100 billion dollars for the first time in history and will rise beyond 200 billion dollars—5% to 6% or more of GNP—by the mid-1980s. After 1985, the deficit outlook actually worsens.

We are rapidly moving into uncharted fiscal territory. Deficits now in prospect have no precedent in our peacetime history, either in periods of sturdy growth or recession.

Further, it is now widely realized that the solvency of the Social Security system is clearly threatened. It is now acknowledged that from 1983 to 1990, the Social Security system alone will run cumulative deficits approaching 200 billion dollars. By the year 2000, the system's annual deficit, including Medicare, could reach over 350 billion dollars, in spite of significant increases in Social Security taxes between now and 1990.

The Sources of Disaster

Today's deficit is partly caused by the recession, reflecting a shortfall in tax revenue caused by today's weak economy. The present recession has clearly been aggravated by a collision between tight money and loose budget. Recovery requires a better balance between the two policies. Making the budgets even looser will make such a balance and thus a healthy recovery virtually impossible.

The crux of the budget problem resides not in 1983 but in the ensuing years. The startling growth in the deficits projected for the mid-1980s and beyond is not recession-related. These immense, structural deficits will take place even on the happy assumption that economic recovery commences immediately and proceeds at a sustained, healthy pace. We cannot "grow out of" this deficit shadow. Even if real GNP grows at a buoyant annual rate of 5% over the next 3 years, the 1985 deficit still will be about 200 billion dollars. On the other hand, if economic recovery is partial or halting (a more likely case, because massive federal borrowing will itself retard the recovery) the 1985 deficit could reach 250 to 300 billion dollars.

The growth in tomorrow's deficits arises not from today's economic recession but from yesterday's government policies. Recent tax legislation will keep relatively constant the share of national income going to federal taxes over the next several years. But federal spending, already authorized or announced, will be rising as a share of national income.

Federal spending no longer fluctuates in parallel with national needs. It no longer rises and falls much due to emergency defense programs to meet temporary crises, or due to cyclical outlays designed to counter recession, such as unemployment compensation or jobs programs. Rather, 75% of the budget now flows into open-ended social entitlement programs, contractual interest expenses, and long-term defense modernization, and by 1985 this proportion would grow to over 80%. These long-term commitments have enormous momentum. They are scheduled to grow rapidly—in absolute terms, as a share of the budget, and as a share of GNP—for as far as we can project. That is why, as now structured, the federal budget would never achieve balance, but would sink deeper into the red with each passing year.

Thus, we face a basic mismatch of tax and spending policies:

• Recent tax cuts will keep total federal revenues fixed at 18% to 20% of GNP over the 1980s.

• By contrast, the growth in total spending has not been reduced. Quite the contrary. Without further budget cutting, spending in 1985 is projected to equal 25% or more of GNP, up from 22.4% in 1980—an increase of about 380 billion dollars.

• This spending growth comes from three sources: social *entitlement programs* unrelated to means tests, such as Social Security, Medicare, and federal pensions, the *defense* buildup; and *interest* on the debt.

• Under current laws, these non-means-tested social "entitlement" programs would grow by over 150 billion dollars—from 227 billion dollars in 1980 to 380 billion dollars in 1985—

rising from 8.8% to about 9.9% of GNP. (By contrast, social programs targeted to the poor will decline relative to the economy, from 2.2% to about 2% of GNP. Budget actions to date have reduced the growth in these means-tested programs by more than twice as much on a percentage basis as non-means-tested programs.)

• Defense spending, under the currently planned buildup, will increase by 150 billion dollars, a real (after inflation) increase of about 9% a year--over 15% per year in hardware items—lifting defense (not including military retirement) from 4.8% in 1980 to about 7.1% of GNP in 1985. (By contrast, public investment, grants to state and local governments, and federal operating expenses will actually decline from about 4.6% to about 2.9% of GNP.)

The Consequences

Huge-deficits—and high real interest rates, with few precedents in modern history—risk denying too many Americans any chance at sustained jobs and prosperity in the new decade, after a decade in which real median income per worker showed little or no increase and unemployment rose to higher levels.

• Recovery from today's recession could be feeble and temporary as a result. Depression conditions now prevail in most industries which sell their product on long-term credit: housing, automobile, construction, durable goods and the like.

• High long-term interest rates, largely attributable to concern over future government policy, would remain abnormally high, holding back new investment, which in recent years has been the lowest of any industrial country and is now declining still further. High short-term real interest rates would threaten to push thousands of small businesses and farms into bankruptcy—to say nothing of the adverse effects on the fragile economies of the developing world as well as on the global financial system.

• Dollar exchange rates—now at lofty levels that have already crushed our export industries, overwhelmed our manufacturers in practically every international market, and have cost us an estimated one to two million job opportunities in the current period—

would remain artificially high; they would continue to choke off American exports, suck in imports, destroy U.S. jobs, and could make the temptation of full-scale protectionism irresistible.

• As a result, capital formation and job creation would continue to stagnate, making unacceptably high unemployment a fixed feature of the industrial landscape.

Thus, tomorrow's big deficits, and the high long-term real interest rates that will accompany them, are already doing serious damage now and will wreak even more havoc in the coming decade and beyond. Without savings available to fuel productive investments, the economy will face nearly perpetual stagnation.

In short, by losing control of the budget, we are sacrificing the jobs and prosperity of our children and grandchildren, and shrinking America's stature and influence in the world.

Principles for Budget Reform

Budget crisis transcends conventional politics. No solution is possible through partisan maneuver. We, the undersigned, believe Americans must now rally around three basic principles of budget reform:

1. **Focus on the Long-Term**. Financial markets, and the American people, are worried by today's deficits, but much more by the huge deficits now in prospect for the mid-1980s and beyond. Today's government action must commit to a *sustantial, progressive scaling down of those outyear deficits*. The reforms must be large, structural, and permanent—equal to the size and duration of the problem itself. Temporary, one-shot actions won't do any good.

2. **Fairness**. Balancing the budget on the back of just one group or one set of programs is not feasible, and trying to do so would not be fair. So far in 1981 and 1982, the budget cuts have focused on the means-tested programs, through reductions in Medicaid, AFDC, food stamps, legal services and the like. The much larger programs which have been barely touched are those social programs that confer a large part of their benefits on middle and upper income groups (such as Social Security and federal pensions) and the military defense programs. Together, such pro-

grams in 1985 would amount to over 650 billion dollars in spending or 68% of the budget (interest on the national debt would be another 12%). *It is now time for a wider sharing of the burden.*

3. **Focus on Investment**. The chief vice of uncontrolled spending and deficits is that they rob the future, by absorbing investment capital needed to build up productive jobs and real income for tomorrow. (Beginning in 1983, budget deficits will amount to a stunning and unprecedented 100% of the net savings generated by individuals and families in the U.S.) The 1980s should be a decade of investment, not a decade of red ink. Cutting deficits by measures that would simultaneously reduce savings and productive investment would make no sense. Budget reform should protect the future. As we squeeze the share of GNP taken up by federal spending—which we must—*we should concentrate on programs that subsidize consumption* (e.g., the social entitlement programs) and spare programs of public investment (e.g., R&D and economically sound public works). When increasing revenues, we must focus our new taxes on private consumption and not on private savings and investment.

The Goal

We must put the budget on a multi-year path toward balance.

To achieve credibility in long-term financial markets, a project of fiscal reform must aim, at a minimum, *to cut the projected 1985 deficit by about 175 billion dollars*. This would bring the 1985 deficit to the 75 billion dollar range. Also, specific actions taken in 1983 should assure budget balance within a few years thereafter. If we do less than this, future deficits will likely remain well above 2% of GNP for years to come, which would make the nation's financial and investment situation in the 1980s even worse than in the 1970s. The last decade was bad enough for the nation's economic performance. To invite a further drop in our economic performance would be totally irresponsible.

We recognize that this budget reform is not the only action necessary to achieve long-term economic recovery. Many who signed this statement also favor other changes, such as in monetary policy, in the structure of the Social Security and federal pension systems to assure their long-term affordability and financial integrity, in support for research and development, in tax incentives for savings and capital investment, in manpower retraining, in rebuilding public infrastructure, in reformed exchange rate systems, in export policies, etc. But we are firmly united in our conviction that such measures will not prove effective without basic and major changes in budget policies.

A Program for Immediate Action

We can remake the budget without gutting our military security, without starving private savings and investment, and without putting harsh burdens on the poor. But we will have to address head-on each of the three major sources of runaway deficit: the growth of large social entitlement programs, the growth of defense spending, and the inadequacy of tax revenues. If any of these areas is placed "out-of-bounds," no fair or effective solution to the problem is possible.

We, the undersigned, rarely stand together on political and economic issues. But we believe Americans must rally to the common cause of fiscal responsibility. We support this plan as a fair, realistic, and bi-partisan approach toward regaining mastery over our economic destiny, and we commend it to you for early action:

1. **Entitlements and Other Non-Defense Programs**. *We should now slow down the growth in non-defense spending so as to reduce the deficit by about 60 billion dollars in 1985.* The best way to begin is with a one-year freeze in the growth of benefit levels of cash payments flowing from the large, non-means-tested entitlement programs: Social Security, veteran's benefits, civil service and military retirement, and other non-defense subsidies and payments that are not means-tested. Thereafter, there should be limits on the automatic inflation indexing of benefits (e.g., by capping inflation adjustments at 60% of the CPI, or at 4% per year, or by providing adjustments only for the amount of inflation in excess of 3% per year). *However difficult politically, controlling the budget requires controls on the large entitlement programs and on the inflation indexing process that drives the cost of those programs upward. If those programs are instead placed off-limits, it*

will be impossible to make budget savings now necessary for financial stability. Similar restraint is required on all transfers, subsidies, and programs other than those essential to the needy.

These measures can be carried out in ways to protect those citizens truly in need.

2. **Defense**. *The defense budget increases now planned should be moderated so as to save about 25 billion dollars in FY 1985.* This would still provide for a major and sustained defense buildup, an overall increase in real terms between 1981 and 1985 of about 7% and an increase in hardware purchases of about 11% per annum. It would encourage more explicit planning for that buildup and lead to wider, sustained public support for a strong defense posture.

3. **Taxes**. Revenues should be increased by about 60 billion dollars in FY 1985. The principal source of these increases in revenue should be from *consumption-based* taxes, and by imposing user fees for the government's commercially valuable services. Modifying, delaying, or stretching out the income tax cut for 1983 has the unanimous approval of the undersigned members *only* in the context of a prior agreement on the kind and magnitude of spending cuts referred to in parts 1 and 2 of this program.

These steps, if undertaken now, would cut the FY 1985 deficit by about 145 billion dollars. This in turn could lead, through less federal borrowing, to a further deficit reduction of about 30 billion dollars in lower interest payments. We would then meet the overall target of about 175 billion dollars in FY 1985 deficit reductions.

Leadership

The program we suggest would require tangible sacrifices from many middle and upper income citizens. But the sacrifices would not be severe, and they are simply necessary to avoid economic chaos and stagnation. Inaction would exact enormous and unnecessary sacrifices from every American.

The budget crisis is a national crisis. Only a united leadership in Washington, extending across both parties and embracing liberals and conservatives alike, can avert a fiscal disaster. Let us work together, as Americans, to rescue the future of our economy . . . and our country.

STATEMENT ON DEFICIT REDUCTION PROGRAM[6]

Today, I challenge Ronald Reagan to respond to the most important economic problem facing our country. I'm putting my plan on the table. Mr. President, where's yours?

Listening to Mr. Reagan, you'd never know that our economy faces a crisis. In fact, the economic Dunkirk Mr. Reagan once warned of has arrived—and on his watch.

The truth is that Government hasn't shrunk under Mr. Reagan; it has expanded. Last year, the Federal budget consumed almost a quarter of our gross national product. That breaks all peacetime records.

The deficit hasn't shrunk under Mr. Reagan either; it has tripled, to a world record of nearly $200 billion.

Mr. Reagan's response is to duck. If America ducks, the deficit will reach $263 billion by 1989. That will double the national debt; raise interest on the debt by $100 billion a year; hike interest rates, choke off investment, and clobber trade even more; destroy rural America; attack entire industries; kill more jobs; and shrink our future.

Mr. Reagan's deficit has bought him a temporary, unbalanced election-year recovery—and a happy talk campaign. The price will be a postelection catastrophe for us and our children. It's tough to face the raw truth—but then, Americans don't elect leaders to turn their backs on reality.

Today, I'm leveling with the American people. And I'm answering the question Mr. Reagan fears most: Who will pay for the Reagan deficit? He fears it because his answer is so unfair to Americans of average income. Mine isn't.

Let me make a few points about my plan to cut the Reagan deficit by two-thirds.

[6]Reprint of a statement on the deficit by Walter Mondale, Democratic candidate for president. *New York Times*. S. 10, '84. Copyright © 1984 by The New York Times Company. Reprinted by permission.

First, my budget is a lift for our future. By chopping down the deficit, we will reduce interest rates, improve trade and make possible the steady growth we need to provide jobs.

Second, my budget is practical. It is based on the best, most independent evidence and advice. It's a hard realistic plan—not a wish list.

Third, my budget is tough. It sets up a deficit reduction trust fund. By law every penny of new revenues will go into that fund to be used for reducing the deficit—not for new spending or new programs. And it rests on the principle of "pay as you go." There will be no new spending without an earmarked new source of revenue.

Fourth, my budget insures a strong defense. Meeting the Soviet challenge requires a steady, sustainable increase in defense support. That's not the Reagan binge—but it's not free, either.

Fifth, my budget invests in the future. Education, science, high technology, training, infrastructure; supporting these today will pay off for decades. Mr. Reagan may think they're a waste of money; I think they're a gold mine of opportunity for our children.

Sixth, my budget is fair.

A budget is an X-ray of our values. It says what kind of people we are. My budget is fair to the most vulnerable people in our society who bore the brunt of Mr. Reagan's budget cuts. And it is fair to average income families who got no relief from Mr. Reagan's tax cuts.

Refusal to Cut Benefits

I refuse to cut Social Security and Medicare so that wealthy Americans can pay less taxes. And I refuse to make average Americans pay a national sales tax so that big corporations can pay nothing at all.

Presenting this budget reflects my view of our democratic system. This is the most detailed and specific plan any candidate for President has ever advanced. I'm offering it now, well before the election, because I believe the American people have a right to know how I plan to lead our country—and I trust the American people.

I challenge Mr. Reagan to stop avoiding the deficit issue and start telling you what he intends to do about it. Mr. Reagan, all my cards are on the table—face up. Americans are calling your hand.

Enough is Enough, Mr. President. You can't hide your red ink with blue smoke and mirrors. Let's tell the truth about the future. And then you, the American people, can make your choice.

MONDALE'S PLAN:
THE MIDDLE CLASS IS NOT EXEMPT[7]

Washington, Sept. 10—Walter F. Mondale, who announced his plan today for reducing the Federal budget deficit, had to reach down into the middle class with his tax increases to come up with the final results he had promised.

His fiscal package also includes an assumption that a tighter fiscal policy would not bring on recession because the Federal Reserve Board would agree to give him lower interest rates in exchange for smaller deficits. Whether any President could get such a commitment from the central bank that prizes its independence is in doubt.

The Mondale budget program relies mostly on tax increases, military spending reductions and moderately optimistic economic assumptions to reach the promised goal of cutting by two-thirds the projected 1989 Federal budget deficit of $263 billion. That deficit figure was calculated by the nonpartisan Congressional Budget Office and accepted by the Mondale campaign as a point of departure.

The candidate's insistence on preserving his own spending increases totaling $30 billion in 1989, including more for education and nutrition, and his earlier, relatively restrained proposals for domestic spending reductions left him with tax increases as the key element of deficit reduction.

[7]Reprint of a newspaper article by Jonathan Fuerbringer, staff reporter. *New York Times*. p. A25. S. 11, '84. Copyright © 1984 by The New York Times Company. Reprinted by permission.

Difficulties in Selling Plan

Apart from uncertanties about whether the economy would perform as assumed, the question inherent in the Mondale fiscal strategy is whether the voters are worried about the Federal deficit enough to prefer his "first resort" of tax increases to President Reagan's "last resort" tax increase. In addition, Mr. Mondale runs the risk that some other proposals he announced today may make his selling job difficult.

On the other hand, he hopes his specificity will contrast favorably with what he portrays as Mr. Reagan's vagueness on where he would reduce spending.

Mr. Mondale's proposed tax increases, raising $85 billion in 1989, do not fall solely on the rich, who Mr. Mondale has said are Mr. Reagan's friends.

Families of four with adjusted gross income exceeding $25,000 would face a tax increase because of Mr. Mondale's proposed delay in the linking of tax brackets to the rate of inflation, now scheduled to be effective next Jan. 1. Single taxpayers with adjusted gross incomes exceeding $45,000 and couples with more than $60,000 would find their taxes raised because of the repeal of part of the third stage of the Reagan tax cut enacted in 1981, what the Democrats call an income cap on the third year.

Plan Hits Some Harder

Some middle-class families, especially with two incomes, would be hit by both the delay in linking brackets to inflation and the cap on the third year. Families with incomes exceeding $100,000 would be hit by a third increase, a 10 percent surcharge on the taxes they owe on their income beyond $100,000.

While the Mondale campaign did not have a detailed analysis of the tax increases, aids said a family of four with an adjusted gross income of $100,000 would pay $2,600 more in taxes in 1989. The tax increase for a family of four in the income range of $25,000 to $35,000 would be $95 in 1989, and it would be $200 for a family in the range of $35,000 to $45,000. The candidate's advisers said that 75 percent of the tax increases would be borne by families with incomes of $60,000 and more.

Families with incomes of $60,000 these days usually regard themselves as middle income, not rich, especially where there are two earners.

The reason Mr. Mondale must go so far down the income scale is that he seeks to raise a lot of revenue, more than can plausibly be raised from the very rich alone. As the treasury has told Presidents time and again, the middle class is where the revenue is.

The Mondale gamble is that the voters are worried enough about the deficit to vote for the candidate who promises higher taxes and to reject the candidate, Mr. Reagan, who says he hopes to cut taxes again. In a poll by The New York Times in August, 52 percent of those surveyed said taxes must be raised to reduce deficits and 75 percent said they expected whoever was President next year to propose tax increases.

The deficit-reducing program, if approved, would be the largest since that became a major issue in 1981.

One of Mr. Mondale's important assumptions is that the Federal Reserve Board would loosen monetary policy and assure that interest rates decline if the deficit is reduced. Mr. Mondale and some of his economic advisers have talked of a specific "accord" with the Federal Reserve to guarantee the decline in interest rates. This could prove to be an explosive issue. The central bank has kept a discreet silence but is known to be fiercely protective of its independence and is thought likely to resist any such pact.

Mondale economists say that without an easing by the Federal Reserve, the increases in taxes proposed and the net spending cuts could throw the economy into a recession.

Tilting toward Optimism

Like the economic program Mr. Reagan presented in the 1980 campaign, which projected a balanced budget in 1983, and like all Presidential budgets, the projections hang on economic assumptions that tilt toward optimism. If they are wrong, the deficit projections would not work. In addition, the program announced today is couched largely in general proposals, making it difficult to assess the effects of spending cuts, spending increases and tax increases.

Many economists and others are likely to be skeptical of the projections, partly because of the economic assumptions and partly because they will contend that some of the program will not be enacted. An erroneous projection of the interest rate could push the Mondale projected deficit in 1989 above $100 billion. There also will be questions, as there have been of similar Reagan Adminstration proposals, of the savings from managing spending better and the added tax revenue from tougher compliance and closing of loopholes.

Many of the country's leading economic forecasters have argued that a combination of underlying economic trends and political attitudes in Congress will leave annual budget deficits at the $200 billion level for the rest of the decade, regardless of who is President.

Neither Mr. Mondale nor Mr. Reagan grapples with the broad questions of programs such as Social Security and Medicare where benefits are determined by law, or with the reductions in spending in those programs that many budget analysts and economists argue are necessary to reduce the deficit. For example, there is no mention of curbing cost-of-living increases in Social Security benefits and pensions for civil service and military personnel.

Mr. Mondale's main savings would come through the assumed $51 billion saving in interest costs in 1989 because of lower interest rates and a lower deficit. This assumes that short-term interest rates, now just above 10 percent, decline to 7.5 percent in 1989. In addition, Mr. Mondale assumes there would be slightly stronger economic growth than that forecast by the Congressional Budget Office, producing additional savings of $17 billion. Together, this accounts for more than one-third of $177 billion deficit reduction in 1989.

III. DO DEFICITS REALLY MATTER?

EDITOR'S INTRODUCTION

The question of whether the current federal budget deficits "matter"—whether, that is, they harm the economy—was one of the most contentious of the early 1980s. The first article in this section offers the opinions of a number of policy and opinion makers, both conservative and liberal. Paul Davidson, in the second article, argues for an updating of the traditional Keynesian attitude toward deficits—that they lead to capital formation, consumer expenditure, and eventually full employment. In the third article, George P. Brockway, after reviewing the arguments that deficits are stimulative, finds such arguments do not hold in the present economic climate.

In the fourth article, Robert Heilbroner considers the history of more modest federal deficits, and concludes that the real danger of the current deficits lies in their size. M. S. Forbes Jr., in the fifth article, contends that the economic revival that set in after the recession of 1981–82 will eventually tame the deficit by increasing tax revenues. This view is reinforced in the sixth article, by Eric Gelman, who suggests that the supply-side economists may have been right in their expectations that a booming economy would shrink the deficit with no need for a tax increase.

The final article expresses the progressive-liberal opinion that only the transformation of the economy's structure will restore the nation to economic health.

DO $200-BILLION DEFICITS REALLY MATTER?[1]

It's a dispute that is fast becoming the key issue in shaping Uncle Sam's economic policy: How dangerous is the flood of red ink the government is running?

The battle over 200-billion-dollar-a-year deficits already has split the Reagan administration. Martin Feldstein, chairman of the Council of Economic Advisers, warns that the deficits help cause high interest rates and threaten to slow the recovery. Treasury Secretary Donald Regan says that isn't necessarily so.

What top economists and lawmakers say—

No "Danger" of Aborting Recovery

Our studies at the Treasury fail to confirm a strong systematic relationship between changes in deficits and interest rates. I'm not saying there is absolutely no connection, but our studies yield ambiguous results. Clearly, in many periods of recession, they show interest rates falling when deficits are rising. But even when business-cycle factors are adjusted for, statistical research fails to establish a consistent positive relationship.

Obviously, if you run excessive deficits indefinitely, intution tells you that would ultimately put upward pressure on interest rates. Yet its magnitude is debatable. One study concludes that every 10 percent increase in the total public debt held by the private sector—or a rise of about 100 billion dollars nowadays—pushes long-term interest rates up by an average of only two tenths of 1 percent.

Therefore, even if you accept the findings of the studies that demonstrate an impact of deficits on interest rates, don't think there's any danger of the recovery being aborted by the current 200-billion-dollar deficits. The deficit is a normal response to the recession we went through in 1981–82. As the recovery continues, the deficit will fall as the Treasury gains revenues and government spending declines.

[1]Reprint of an article from U. S. News & World Report. 95:33–4. O. 17, '83. Copyright 1983, U. S. News & World Report, Inc.

On the other hand, many studies do show a systematic link between federal spending and high interest rates. Because government pre-empts available resources for its programs, expanding federal spending tends to push prices and interest rates up, thus diverting funds from private consumption and investment.

Raising taxes also takes funds out of private hands, just as government borrowing does. That's why increasing taxes substantially, especially now when the recovery is young, would be a misguided policy that might well produce unwanted results. Rather, to deal with the deficits, we ought to rely on the one policy that on the evidence from the professional literature, we know will moderate interest rates and improve the economy—we should cut federal spending.

—Manuel Johnson
Assistant Secretary of the Treasury
for Economic Policy

We Could Be Headed for Disaster

Persistent high deficits really do matter. The Treasury studies that say there is no cause-and-effect relationship between high deficits and high interest rates are generally recognized as flawed because they don't relate the level of deficits to the supply of available capital.

First, as long as we as a nation continue to soak up more than three fourths of total net private savings to pay for the deficits, we are shortchanging what should be going into capital formation and private investment. We cannot sustain economic competitiveness and growth that way.

Second, as the recovery continues, the growing private need for credit to finance expansion will clash with the federal borrowing requirement. That will push interest rates up. When? Probably between mid-1984 and mid-1985.

We can't wait until after the November, 1984 election to deal with the deficits. By then it may be too late. Peter Grace, chairman of the President's Survey on Cost Control, says such a delay will add 200 billion dollars to the problem.

We must act now on the deficits in a fair way. We must cut the growth of spending for entitlements and defense. Then we will need to raise some revenues, probably by limiting the indexation of the tax code against inflation and by adopting President Reagan's proposed temporary 5 percent income-tax surcharge.

Unless we do something soon, we could be headed for disaster. By that I mean a repeat of the 1981–82 recession.

—Representative James Jones
Democrat of Oklahoma

Don't Be "Scared into a Tax Increase"

The real issue is not between those who say deficits don't matter—because chronic deficits do matter—and those who say that deficits are the sole cause of high interest rates. The real issue is between those who want to force a tax increase on the American people and those who believe that rapid economic growth and spending cuts will do more to get these deficits down than anything else.

With inflation as low as it is—and commodity prices falling again—the Federal Reserve Board has room to lower interest rates right now. That would help insure a sustained recovery. Economic growth and lower unemployment, in turn, would reduce the deficit in two ways: Tax receipts would rise, and costs for social programs and interest would drop. This is no pipe dream: Treasury Secretary Regan says the pace of recovery will lower the 1985 deficit to about 100 billion from the 170-billion forecast in July.

Robert Mundell of Columbia University figures the economy is operating at about 500 billion dollars below capacity. If it were running at full potential that would raise the Treasury's revenues by some 125 billion dollars, leaving a fiscal 1984 deficit of 60 to 70 billion dollars. That would look awfully good in a 4-trillion-dollar economy. The deficit could be sliced even further by selective spending cuts.

So the national choice boils down to this: Are we going to be scared into a tax increase and austerity measures to reduce the deficit? Or are we going to rely on expansion and lower unemployment to bring it down?

—Representative Jack Kemp
Republican of New York

Prospect of Higher Interest Rates

Chronic deficits of the 200-billion-dollar-a-year magnitude do matter because they create the worrisome prospect of higher interest rates that "crowd out" private borrowers, make U.S. goods less competitive internationally and worsen the problem of less-developed-country debt.

Current deficits are not at issue. In fact , they have helped pull the economy out of recession. But as the recovery proceeds, you will get increasing competition for funds.

That will leave the Federal Reserve with only two policy choices. Theoretically, it could decide to finance both expanding private borrowing and federal deficits by holding interest rates down. That might prolong the economic expansion for the short run—and I emphasize the phrase *short run*—but would raise the risk of renewed inflation.

The other policy choice—one that seems more probable to me—is that the Fed would decide not to give up the fight against inflation by accommodating the expanding private and public borrowing requirements. That, by definition, would bring higher interest rates.

Inevitably, rising interest rates would pose a clear and present danger to the expansion itself. In my judgment, if the deficits are not reduced, the risk that the recovery will abort will become very real, beginning as early as 1985.

—Bruce MacLaury
President, Brookings Institution

Precious Little for Private Borrowers

Saying that deficits don't cause rising interest rates is like saying that hospitals do cause ill health. The logic is the same. People confined to hospitals are not as healthy as those outside. That's a fact, but that doesn't mean hospitals cause poor health.

Interest rates tend to be low when deficits are high. That's a fact, but that doesn't mean deficits cause low interest rates. All that correlation tells you is that interest rates tend to go down during recessions, when deficits tend to expand because federal receipts fall off and spending increases.

To see the true effect of big deficits—and by that I mean a string of them, not just one or two in recession years—you must look to the government claim on available credit. As recently as the decade of the 1970s, the Treasury was borrowing about one fifth of the credit supply. Now its claim is up to about 40 percent. With the projected deficits, the Treasury will be absorbing more than half of all available credit before long. Add in the credit needs of government-sponsored agencies and the figure could rise well above 60 percent.

That leaves precious little for private borrowers and puts upward pressure on interest rates. I don't buy the argument that rising revenues from a maturing recovery will solve our deficit problem. A hard-core deficit of at least 100 billion dollars a year will remain even if Treasury receipts do improve.

Fundamental budget therapy is needed. Something will have to be done both to cut spending further and to raise more money from taxes. The nation cannot afford to have the White House and the Congress crouching behind ramparts glaring at each other.

Waiting until 1985 to solve the budget problem is a very high-risk strategy.

—Paul McCracken
Professor of Business
University of Michigan

"It's Congress's Turn" to Cut Costs

I'm in the middle. Deficits do contribute to higher interest rates, but the question is how much. We in this organization figure that every 100 billion dollars of increased federal debt raises interest rates by about six tenths of 1 percent. That's small.

But that does not mean that deficits are unimportant. By preempting the pool of credit available to private investors, they are a cancer on capital formation. Deficits, therefore, have a crippling effect on healthy, long-term economic growth, which, after all should be our overriding objective.

If that, indeed is our goal, then we should be careful about how we go about reducing the deficits. A lot of politicians are using the big deficits as an excuse for wanting to raise taxes. In effect, they say that because deficits cause high interest rates, which, in turn, prevent the economy from growing, we need to raise taxes to sustain the recovery. That's an absurd argument.

All that would do is put more money in the hands of the guys who love to spend it. Their motives are not snow-white. The fact is that runaway spending, not too little taxes, is the reason we have these big deficits.

Sooner or later we must bring spending under control. Politically, the checkreins are beginning to bite on Congress's profligacy.

The easy way to attack the deficits is to give our representatives more money to spend. The tough way is to tell them to start spending less. Consumers and businesses have had to cut costs severely over the past three years. Now I say, it's Congress's turn.

—John Rutledge
President,
Claremont Economics Institute

WHY DEFICITS HARDLY MATTER[2]

The conventional economic wisdom being dispensed this election year by Democrats and Republicans alike is that the current size of the Federal deficit is ruining our nation's economic health. In the past deficits might have been useful, we are told, but in 1984 our rising debt is "bad governmental policy" because:

1. We are approaching full production capacity (even with 7.5 per cent unemployment?).

2. It is being financed by excessive monetary expansion and is therefore inflationary.

3. It is absorbing half of net savings and hence is reducing productive capital formation.

4. The resulting high interest rates are necessary to shield the economy from inflation.

[2]Reprint of an article by Paul Davidson, professor of economics at Rutgers University and editor of the *Journal of Post Keynesian Economics*. *The New Leader*. 67:3–5. Ag. 20, '84. Reprinted with permission of The New Leader. Copyright © the American Labor Conference on International Affairs, Inc.

5. Foreigners who buy U.S. Treasury bonds are laying claim to future American wealth.

Thus the conventional wisdom maintains that eliminating the deficit is a top national priority. Blind acceptance of this 19th-century sophistry has caused many liberal economists and politicians to docilely concur that entitlement programs designed to alleviate poverty must be trimmed, and that the U.S. is too poor a country to afford the public works needed to rebuild its decaying cities, bridges, highways, and waterways. Moreover, it is often argued that any additional taxes levied have to be earmarked for deficit reductions so that they will not be diverted to providing useful public goods and services for our citizens.

In truth, a shortage of leadership and will inherited from the Carter Administration, not a shortage of resources, has prevented the U.S. from completing the New Deal, Fair Deal and Great Society reforms of the last 50 years. The seeming "success" of Reaganomics in limiting inflation and restoring economic growth has deflected the media from critically analyzing the benefits and costs of the conservative counterrevolution engineered by Ronald Reagan and Federal Reserve Board Chairman Paul Volcker, contributing to the image of the man in the White House as a Teflon President.

Stripped of its rhetoric and jingoism, Reaganomics has always had as its basic objective a reversal of the trend over the past half-century toward an expanding government service sector and a more progressive tax and expenditure structure. In the 1980 campaign Reagan was fond of asking, "Why should the government do a better job of spending your income than you?" Simply by raising the question he was suggesting that individuals had no social responsibility to contribute to the investment in education and community institutions, to aid those in ill health or poverty, beyond what they deemed to be in their own interests.

The popularity of Reaganomics is readily explainable, for it appeals to those unpleasant yet ubiquitous human traits, selfishness and greed. We prefer to imagine the possibility of getting rich, rather than face the reality that, without the help of the community, most of us will remain relatively poor.

Domestically, the New Deal, Fair Deal and Great Society programs—and, internationally, the Marshall Plan, Aid to Developing Nations, etc.—appealed to our sense of cooperation. In so doing, these undertakings enriched everyone spiritually as well as economically. The historical record indicates that when people join together out of a feeling of kinship and compassion, growth and prosperity for all inevitably follow. Reaganomics, by contrast, has caused a greater disparity between the rich and the poor, and has reduced community services at a pace that, if allowed to continue for the next four years, may result in their regressing to levels where the middle class will virtually disappear.

The ability of Reaganomics to tame inflation is not very difficult to understand either once one abandons conventional wisdom's clichés. Despite the rapid growth of the money supply during the past few years, inflation has not heated up, as Milton Friedman and his fellow Monetary economists had warned. This is due to the Reagan-Volcker 19th-century-type "incomes policies," which create slack markets and high unemployment to limit the power of labor and others to force wage and price increases onto buyers. These ancient tactics, based on a philosophy that New York's Governor Mario Cuomo in his keynote address to the Democratic Convention aptly called "Social Darwinism," have involved the deliberate reduction of aggregate demand to create the worst worldwide recession in a half-century, plus direct union bashing (remember the air traffic controllers).

But no one should pursue low inflation at the price of high unemployment. What is required is the kind of incomes policy Sidney Weintraub advocated in the pages of this magazine during the five years prior to his death in June 1983—specifically, a tax-based incomes policy, or TIP, that would control production costs and hold down inflation while preventing unemployment. With such a civilized incomes policy, there would be no need for high interest rates to protect us from inflation. The rates could then drop dramatically, reducing the cost of servicing the national debt and consequently helping somewhat to bring down the deficit.

As for the current recovery, it is being sparked by traditional Keynesian maneuvers to stimulate the components of aggregate demand. The first year of the Reagan tax cut (starting in July 1981) was largely offset by higher Social Security and other levies, but the second and third stages of the tax cut raised real incomes (except for those with very low earnings), stimulating consumer spending and retail sales. Lower business taxes since 1981 increased the after-tax profitability on these additional sales, encouraging more investment. Additional purchases of goods by the government, especially for the military, began to come on stream in significant volume by 1982.

Although still quite high compared with past history, the lower interest rates of the last two years are the result of the Federal Reserve, in its "lender of last resort" function, deliberately abandoning its Monetarist experiment and rapidly expanding the money supply to avoid an impending Debt Crisis. The decline in interest rates since August 1982 has added to the value of the expected discounted cash flow from new investments, thereby reviving investment expenditures. The present surge in investment spending from its depressed levels of 1979–81 is directly attributable to the August 1982 reversal of monetary policy just as the Reagan tax cuts were finally improving the after-tax income of employed middle- and upper-income families.

The belief that today's huge government deficits are absorbing too much savings and therefore squeezing out productive investment that otherwise would be occurring might have some validity if the United States, and the rest of the industrialized world, were already at full employment and businessmen were clamoring for more capital goods. Further, only at that point could government deficits be throttled with the hope that private spending would immediately pick up the ensuing slack. Increasing taxes before that state of bliss is achieved would merely slide us back into recession. The extent of the backward slide would be directly related to the amount of tax increase earmarked for deficit reduction.

In these uncertain times, the desire for liquidity is quite high, and net investment is still constrained by the existence of some unused capacity as well as by concern about the profitability of added capital outlays. The problem is not that there has been no increase in investment and consumption since 1982, it is that the stimulating Keynesian policies have not stepped up capital formation and consumer expenditures sufficiently to generate full employment in the U.S. and simultaneously act as the engine for creating full employment abroad. New taxes now would adversely affect any drive toward worldwide full employment.

In sum, the unprecedented deficit is not a symptom of illness in the economy. Quite the contrary, it is the medicine that promoted the robust recovery of 1982–84 and lifted profits from the terrible depths induced by the 1979–82 Volcker Monetarist experiment.

Preachers of the conventional wisdom about the danger of deficits forget George Santayana's warning that those who do not study history are doomed to repeat its mistakes. A half-century ago, the conventional wisdom had it that the unprecedented New Deal deficits would bankrupt this country. In the election year of 1936, the government, bending to the warnings, moved vigorously to improve the situation—mainly by (shades of Ronald Reagan) reducing "unnecessary" government spending. The result was a drastic nine-month plunge in GNP in 1937, matching the rates of decline experienced during the Hoover era.

In this election year of 1984, many prestigious economists are providing similar counsel and suggesting programs for an immediate reduction in the deficit to head off economic disaster. If followed, however, these prescriptions could make the 1982–85 period a replay of the 1933–37 years.

We would do well to remember that after 1937 (admittedly under the threat of war) the admonitions of conventional wisdom were ignored. By 1945 the annual deficit was approximately 25 per cent of GNP and government spending was roughly 40 per cent of GNP. Even though much of the deficit-financed expenditures were for the wholly unconsumable war materials, the fact is that between the mid-'30 and the mid-'40s the U.S. economy was transformed from its depressed condition to a modern cornucopia. The long-term growth in living standards (from the '40s through the '60s) was born in the huge deficits of the New Deal and World War II. Why must it take calamities like a great depression or a world war to force us to dispense with the conventional wisdom and recognize some obvious economic fundamentals?

Part of the problem may be that because we have not adopted a civilized incomes policy, such as TIP, the high interest rates used to shield us from inflation in tandem with the rapid growth of the deficit have had undesirable side effects on domestic and international income distribution. The great interest cost on government borrowing has fattened the purses of wealthy residents and foreigners who hold Treasury debt obligations at the expense of middle-and low-income taxpayers. This redistributive effect is not surprising, though, given the Reagan philosophy of "survival of the wealthiest."

In any case, despite the huge deficits from 1981 on, the heavens have not fallen. Nor will they fall if we overthrow the conventional wisdom that Federal deficits are inherently bad and moves toward a balanced governmental budget are necessarily good.

President Reagan, who pays homage to that notion and goes so far as to support a balanced budget amendment (which would not take effect until after 1988), has ignored the conventional view in his economic policies aimed at rewarding the rich and starving the public sector, except for the military. As a result, he is the first incumbent since 1964 to face an electorate where the majority appears satisfied with the recent progress of the economy. Indeed, the public's complacency regarding the large government deficit suggests that the average citizen is instinctively more sensible than many politicians running for office, let alone the conventional wisdom of their economic advisers.

WHY DEFICITS MATTER[3]

My head is spinning—which is not surprising, for I have been reading a circular argument. If you read much economics, you encounter a good many circular arguments. This one is a dandy.

[3]Reprint of an article by George P. Brockway, economics columnist. *The New Leader*. 65:12–13. Mr. 8, '82. Reprinted with permission of The New Leader. Copyright © the American Labor Conference on International Affairs, Inc.

I refer you to the "Annual Report of the Council of Economic Advisers." It is said to be a document of 357 pages, but all I know of it is what was printed in the New York *Times,* which is enough. In the section headlined "Why Deficits Matter" we find the following:

"Financing a budget deficit may draw on private saving and foreign capital inflows that otherwise would be available to the private sector. . . . Weak and marginal borrowers may be 'rationed' out of the market by higher interest rates unless saving flows are adequate. . . . During a recession—as now exists—the borrowing requirements of business and consumers tend to be relatively small. At such a time a given deficit can be financed with less pressure on interest rates than during a period of growth. . . . Much of the Adminstration's tax program is designed to increase the private saving of the nation. As a consequence, both public and private borrowing will be accommodated more easily."

What (if anything) is being said here? Restating the argument, it goes like this: First, the Adminstration's tax cuts are a net addition to an already existing deficit. Second, government borrowing will have to go up to cover the raised deficit. Third, there will be no trouble with the increased borrowing, provided the recession continues (or deepens)—and the people who receive the tax cuts lend the money back to the government.

In short, at the end of the circular maneuver—assuming it works as it is intended to—the recession will be just what it was, and sizable transfer payments will have been made to people judged not to need them. In fact, they have been chosen to get the money precisely because they don't need it. Also (incidentally) the deficit will be increased, and interest at 14 per cent or so will have to be paid on that. It adds up to real money, and it's crazy, no matter how you look at it.

Let's imagine (as I've remarked before, economists have to have good imaginations) that we had a Republican adminstration that knew something about finance. It would occur to such an imaginary adminstration that it would be simpler to keep the tax money it has, instead of returning part of it to rich people in the hope that they will lend it back to the government. Not only simpler but, of course, cheaper. Not only cheaper but, of course, less disruptive of the economy. Not only less disruptive of the economy but, of course, more equitable.

I don't know what I'd do if I were a supply-side economist (my imagination isn't lively enough for that). The supply-sider's game plan is to put money into the hands of producers, who will invest it in new plant, which will eventually improve our productivity and make possible a higher standard of living for us all. He'd have to be blind not to see that, in general, producers are richer than other people. Thus to get money to them, he cuts taxes for the rich rather than for the poor or even for the middle class. He's playing for the trickle down. Fair enough.

He recognizes that when taxes are cut faster than expenditures, the Federal deficit (not to mention the state and local deficits) rises. The Laffer Curve doesn't say there won't be an initial deficit rise; it merely promises, as President Hoover did, that prosperity is around the corner. So Jack Kemp isn't worried about the deficit; he's going for the long ball.

Nevertheless, the deficits have to be monetized or funded. Monetizing the debt means just printing money to pay the bills, and supply-siders are afraid to do that. The deficits therefore have to be funded. That is, bonds have to be issued to cover them. But one doesn't simply issue bonds, one sells them. To whom? Why, naturally, to the rich. No one else has the money to buy them. Unfortunately, the money the rich use to buy the bonds is the money they were supposed to invest on the supply side.

Try as he will, the supply-sider can't get money into the hands of producers. This is not because of the conspicuous consumption of the rich or the notorious perversity of Wall Street. Even when everyone is doing his best to cooperate, the scheme can't work. The supply-sider's tax cuts go to the rich, all right; but the recipients have to lend the money right back to the government to cover the deficits. No more money becomes available for productive investment than there was before the game started.

Actually, even less is available, because the pressure of the deficits pushes up interest rates. This doesn't *have* to happen, yet it *will* happen as long as the Federal Reserve Board clings to its monetarist doctrine of restricting the money supply (if it could only figure out what money is). You may be sure that the Fed will depress both the supply side and the demand side if it can. The resulting high interest rates will increase the cost of government borrowing and add to the deficits in what is now a pretty tight upward spiral. But that's not the end. High interest rates inhibit investment. Businesses that used to borrow money to expand in the good old-fashioned capitalist way can't afford to pay 15–20 per cent for their money and have to cut back in order to survive.

Hence the supply-side tax cuts, with the best will in the world, will *reduce* the amount of money available for investment. You will note that I say "available," because I don't for a minute believe much of that tax windfall would go into productive investment even if it could. Almost all of its earmarked for speculation. No goods will be produced as a result of it, nor any services rendered. But the rich will be richer.

To show what I mean about speculation, let me call your attention to some figures the *Times* printed a couple of weeks ago about Merrill Lynch, Treasury Secretary Regan's old firm and, breeding apart, the very model of a modern "investment" house. It turns out that by far the biggest part of Merrill Lynch's income comes from interest its clients pay on margin accounts. Margin accounts are nothing if they are not speculations, and interest on them is 45.4 per cent of Merrill Lynch's income. Next we have commissions, which amount to 22.8 per cent of their income, and the transactions the commissions were earned on were also speculations, buying and selling securities, without a penny of all those billions going into new productive enterprise.

Then comes "investment banking," 8.6 per cent of income. That sounds more like it. Well, it sounds more like it until you hear what the small print says. Then you learn that "investment banking" includes "municipal and corporate underwriting and merger and acquisition advice." Of this, the only part (and we don't know how large it is) that *might* concern productive investment is the corporate underwriting, but even that is unlikely, coming in close conjunction, as it does, with "merger and acquisition advice." Was Merrill Lynch involved in the $3 billion US Steel borrowed to buy Marathon Oil, or the $4 billion DuPont borrowed to buy Conoco? I don't know, but I do know that transactions like that are speculations, not productive investments. No more oil is refined—no more anything is produced—as a result of them.

Yet this is the sort of thing—and the only sort of thing—that is encouraged by the supply-side tax breaks. Don't get me wrong. I'm in favor of producers; after all, I'm sort of one myself. The late Professor John William Miller used to say that an entrepreneur is an economic surd: there's no accounting for him, but you don't have any economic activity at all unless some willful character says that, come hell or high water, there's going to be this herenow business. Such types should be encouraged. I'm willing to believe that at least some supply-siders *want* to encourage them. But I'm here to declare that Reganomics is going to encourage only those whose principal activity is clipping coupons.

Let me, as the fellow said, make myself perfectly clear. I'm not arguing against a deficit or against tax cuts, or for them. All I'm saying is that *unless the government is running a surplus, there is no way for tax cuts to be a direct stimulus to productive investment.* Tax cuts can be an indirect stimulus: By giving some people more money to buy things, they can eventuate in producers producing more. But that is the *demand* side, *not* the supply side.

To be sure, Reagonomics has its demand side: the military buildup. Because of its specialized nature, this is not the most efficient stimulus the economy could have; it produces comparatively few jobs for a buck. Moreover, it cannot continue to stimulate the economy even as much as it does unless the arms race speeds up. (That may rate as a suitably dismal thought.)

If you really want to stimulate the demand side (which you really ought to want to do), you will give tax breaks to people who will spend their windfalls, not "save" them. In short, you will start cutting taxes at the bottom (Social Security taxes, for example) and work tentatively upward. This is the precise contrary of Reaganomics, but it makes precise sense.

REFLECTIONS: THE DEFICIT[4]

The federal deficit for 1984 is estimated to amount to a hundred and eighty-five billion dollars. This is one of those imagination-defying sums that call out for illustration, like the old-fashioned drawings that defined the length of ocean liners by picturing them upended next to the Woolworth Building. A deficit, which is a kind of negative quantity, is hard to depict as an ocean liner, so artists usually draw the national debt instead—the outstanding bonds and notes by which the present and past deficits have been financed. This is often shown as a great bag on the shoulders of John Q. Public, or sometimes as a stack of dollar bills. Early in 1981, when President Reagan was much exercised about the size of the debt, he said such a stack, made up of thousand-dollar bills, would be sixty-seven miles high. Today, one could add another stack labelled "Probable Addition to the Debt during the Next Five Years." By the Administration's estimates, this second stack is already higher than the first.

Such images help explain the present mood of alarm and concern about the deficit and the debt. A two-page "Bipartisan Budget Appeal" advertisement in the *Times* this May, organized by five former Secretaries of the Treasury and a former Secretary of Commerce and signed by six hundred business, foundation, academic, and public figures, called on the President, the Presidential candidates, and Congress to take "major action" to reduce the federal deficits, warning that unless this was done we Americans would be risking "the recovery, our economic future and our country." And it is not only national leaders who are worried about the deficit and the debt. In 1979, despite widespread support for tax reductions, nearly two-thirds of those interviewed in a Gallup poll declared that they would willingly forgo a tax cut if that would help the federal government avoid incurring a larger deficit. Since most people are quick to admit that they find the whole issue of debts and deficits quite incomprehensible, it seems

    [4]Reprint of an article by Robert Heilbroner, economist. *The New Yorker.* pp. 47–55. Jl. 30, '84. Reprinted by permission: © 1984 Robert Heilbroner.

probable that much of the public abhorrence of them stems from the thrall exerted by vast numbers. We might feel less alarmed about the current deficit if we were told that it was about five per cent of our annual output. Similarly, our national debt of one trillion five hundred billion dollars would lose a good deal of its paralyzing immensity if we were reminded that it, like everything else, must be corrected for inflation. Our national debt today comes to about six thousand dollars per person; Robert Eiser and Paul Pieper have recently shown, in the *American Economic Review,* that our per-capita debt in 1946 was three times as large as that of 1980, in dollars of equivalent purchasing power. Despite the growth in the debt since 1980, the real per-capita debt today is still far below that of 1946.

Mainly, however, I think that the public's concern about the debt and the deficit arises from our tendency to picture both in terms of a household's finances. We invoke Micawber's adage that happiness is the consequence of income exceeding outgo by sixpence, and misery the consequence of things being the other way around; we see the government as a very large family suffering the latter consequence, and although we cannot exactly specify the symptoms of the misery, we all feel that the direction in which these deficits are driving us is one of household bankruptcy on a globe-shaking scale. The problem here is not the thralldom of numbers but the miscomprehensions that arise when imagery suitable for one set of problems and relationships is applied to another. Economists constantly have to do battle with such misconceptions. Banks, for example—common sense to the contrary— are not warehouses stuffed with money but institutions that create purchasing power, of which ordinary currency constitutes only a small part. The stock market does not speak to us as an omniscient presence but serves as an echo chamber in which we hear pretty much what we want to hear. And the government is not a body perched above the economy, the way the Capitol is perched above the Mall, but a set of institutions and agencies that are inextricably interwoven with the activities of production and payment we call economic life. As part of its function in the economy, the government usually runs deficits—not like a household experiencing pinch but as a kind of national banking operation that adds to the flow of income that government siphons into households and businesses. Finally, cartoonists' drawings notwithstanding, the debt is not a vast burden borne on the backs of our citizenry but a varied portfolio of Treasury and other federal obligations, most of them held by American households and institutions, which consider them the safest and surest of their investments.

There are, I should hasten to say, very important problems with respect to the deficit, but the misconceptions raised by the words "debt" and "deficit," and the fearsome images associated with them, tend to make us worry about imaginary dangers rather than the real ones. Before we come to the real problems, we should disabuse ourselves of the unreal ones. A good place to start is in the corporate world, where activities very similar to those carried on by the government are clothed in the respectability of private enterprise. It always comes as a shock to people to learn that corporations also normally run "deficits"; that is, that the corporations pay out more money for various purposes than they receive from their sales, and cover the difference by borrowing money or floating stock or issuing bonds. In 1960, for example, the total debt owed by manufacturing corporations came to about forty billion dollars. In 1983 it was roughly ten times that. Just as with the figures that represent the national debt, these numbers have to be trimmed substantially to adjust for the shrinking value of the dollar, but even if we subtract two-thirds of the increase to allow for inflation it is still the case that corporate debt, adjusted for rising prices, has virtually tripled over the last twenty-odd years.

The idea that corporations are continuously accumulating debts seems at odds with the fact that they are making profits. But this is because the corporate world is very careful to separate expenditures made on current account and those made on capital account. Precisely like a household, a business is expected to cover its current expenses for payroll and materials and the like from its current income from selling its products or services, and any company that borrows money to pay its regular work force would soon be as hopelessly bankrupt as a family that tries to get bank financing for its grocery bills. But a quite different set of normal operating procedures applies to the financing of capital projects, such as the construction of a plant or the purchase of durable equipment. In much the same way that a household that lacks the ready cash turns to the bank to finance its purchase of a car or a house, a corporation without sufficient accumulated earnings turns to the capital markets or to banks to pay for additions to its assets. These expenditures, which typically increase the debt or equity of companies, are not, however, charged against current income. If they were, profitable companies would suddenly appear to be less profitable or even in the red just because they had undertaken large capital-building projects. Curiously, this distinction is not applied to the activities of the federal government, even though a not unimportant fraction of government expenditures creates exactly the same kinds of capital goods that are created by private business. Where General Motors puts up plants to build automobiles, the government builds roads and bridges to run them on; where private business erects office buildings, public business erects dams. In fiscal 1983, the Office of Management and Budget estimated that a hundred and eighty-two billion dollars in federal expenditures went for investments of this sort. This amount was roughly the size of the deficit, but, unlike those of a private corporation, these capital expenditures became part of the deficit for that year.

A second aspect of the corporate world which throws an unexpected light on deficits involves the question of paying the debt back. Every household knows that it must pay its debts when they come due or face the consequences—which used to be debtors' prison and are still the unpleasantness of bankruptcy proceedings. What we as householders do not ordinarily consider is that the requirement to pay debts applies to each individual evidence of indebtedness—each promisory note or in the case of a corporation, each particular bond—but not to the collective debt of borrowers as a whole. Looking at the larger economy, we can quickly see that no such total redemption takes place: in the household sector, A's mortgage is repaid, but B takes out a new one; in the corporate world, A.T. & T.'s bond issue dated September, 1984, is repaid, but another company floats an issue of the same or a larger amount more or less simultaneously. The reason that the total volume of private debt steadily increases is that debt's opposite face consists of the houses, automobiles, machinery, and structures that the debt has paid for. Behind the increase in the value of mortgages—up from four hundred and seventy-four billion dollars in 1970 to one trillion seven hundred billion dollars in 1983—is not merely an increase in the price of houses but an increase in their number. Behind the rise in corporate indebtedness is a similar rise in wealth, embodied in steel and glass and cement. It follows that as long as these houses and factories and machines retain their economic usefulness or profitability, their paper counterparts can continue in existence, establishing the individuals who own, or who have claims against, the structure of wealth for which their bonds or stocks are birth certificates.

Years ago, when I taught these ideas to my economics classes, I used to invoke the image of A.T. & T.—this was the *old* telephone company—borrowing a million dollars for ten years at ten per cent to put up a thousand telephone poles at one thousand dollars each. Presumably, the poles generated sufficient business so that A.T. & T., which paying interest to the individuals or banks from whom it borrowed the money, could accrue on its books a depreciation cost that would cover the annual wear and tear suffered by the poles. At the end of ten years (in this classroom example), a great act of renewal would take place. All at the same moment, the poles would come to the end of their useful life and have to be replaced, while the original bond issue would arrive at its moment of redemption and have to be paid back. But—lo and behold!—it all worked out perfectly. The phone company would enter the capital markets to borrow another million dollars, which it would use to pay back the first million dollars, now due. At the same time, it would use its depreciation allowance to buy a million dollars' worth of new telephone poles to replace those that had come to the end of their days. If we forget about technological change, inflation, and the other troublesome realities of business life, we can see how the example illustrates that indebtedness does not have to be paid back as long as its underlying real asset is still economically productive. This is, in fact, exactly what we find in the case of the real A.T. & T. In 1929, the phone company owed a billion dollars in debts of differing kinds and dates. In 1983, its debt total was approximately forty-five billion dollars. As with the phone company, so with the business world as a whole: panics and depressions aside, its debts never decline, any more than do those of householders taken as a collectivity.

This is not to say, of course, that individuals or businesses cannot ruin themselves with debt. Ruin is the outcome when borrowers miscalulate their ability to earn the income needed to make interest payments or to retain their creditworthiness. In the economy taken as an entirety, however, this has been the exception rather than the rule. There have certainly been periods of unsustainable debt creation—the early nineteen-eighties was one such—but over the long run the growing volume of output and incomes has worked to sustain the ability of individual borrowers to make good on their individual debts and to accumulate more debt as the financial side of their long-term accumulation of real wealth. This continuing expansion of debt, moreover, plays a vital role in the expansion process of the economy itself. Debt is not only a claim held by one party against the wealth owned by another but a vital channel through which the great river of expenditure and income is kept moving and growing. The act of buying someone's promissory note, whether that of a friend or a corporation, takes money that is sitting unused at the moment—if it were not unused it would not be available for lending—and returns it to the stream of payments from which we earn our incomes. "The great wheel of circulation," as Adam Smith called it, would lose its momentum if recipients of income did not fairly quickly return all of it to the circuit. Since some portion of the receipts of households and businesses is regularly held back from expenditures because it is put aside as savings, whether for a rainy day or an unusually propitious one, we need a mechanism to reintroduce these savings into the income flow. The mechanism is the act of capital investment by which our savings are put back into circulation; and the act of investment usually requires, in turn, the issuance of debt or equity, making available to business money that would otherwise fail to reenter the wheel of circulation. The growth in the volume of household and corporate debt can be seen as evidence that borrowers have been fulfilling the essential function of renewing the income stream. If debts or equities fail to grow, it means not only that the process of creating real wealth is faltering but that the regeneration of income via expenditure has been disrupted, so that workers or capitalists fail to become beneficiaries of a rising volume of national business and may become instead the victims of a stagnant or contracting one.

It is the regeneration of income that makes the deficits of national economies more closely akin to a banking operation than to the operations of a household. When the government borrows and spends funds, it is creating incomes for those who receive its disbursements, exactly as happens when business spends money on capital expansion. The difference is that business is necessarily interested in the profitability of the capital undertakings it has financed. If this were not the case, we would think it perfectly all right for A.T. & T. to borrow funds not to put up telephone poles but to send a refund to its customers. The government is often vitally concerned with the general level of income enjoyed by its citizens; and deficit spending—that is, borrowing funds and spending them—is one manner in which it can attempt to raise that general level. This is the rationale for the government's going into debt when the economy is sluggish or when unemployment reaches threatening levels. Of course, it makes a great deal of difference whether the channels that the government uses to disburse income are those of warfare or those of welfare, for different groups will be recipients of different programs, and different programs will exert different pressures on prices and bring different social results. Just the same, from the viewpoint of increasing the general flow of expenditure these differences are submerged beneath the common consequences of a stimulus to the economy.

The continuous renewal and normal expansion of public debt have an obvious parallel in the continous renewal and expansion of the private debt, but there are important differences between the two. One difference is that there has never been a default on any item of the federal government's obligation; that is why the credit rating of the government is the standard against which all others are measured. This extraordinary safety of government bonds rests on two foundation stones, and these, while incomparably more solid than those of any individual enterprise, are nonetheless ultimately frail, as all human institutions must be. The first foundation stone is the fact that the government's debt is normally held by individuals and institutions that are within the taxing power of the government, for this means that it is always possible to pay interest on the debt—or, in a pinch, to repay the debt itself—simply by commandeering the money capital that dwells under the aegis of government. Nothing like this is available to even the strongest issuer of private debt. To revert to the example of A.T. & T., the phone compnay has no way of simply seizing some portion of the incomes of the public to service its company debt. It must trust to the continued willingness of the public to buy its services—a trust that may disappear into thin air if the wrong technology suddenly appears, such as the long-imagined wrist radio. Thus, the phone company disburses its current and capital expenditures, wooing the needed inflow of dollars by whatever means it can. With the federal government, things are crucially different. Like the phone company, the government dissolves its expenditures in the river of national purchasing power, but, unlike the company, it does not have to win the customers to produce the income it needs to cover those expenditures. The money that the government spends enters the stream of national income over which it exercises the sovereign power of taxation, so that it can be reasonably certain of recapturing whatever revenues it needs. I say "reasonably certain" because ill-advised tax policies can drive capital abroad or cause transactions to take place under the table, beyond the taxing hand. And, of course, poorly constructed taxes will not yield the revenues that the government expects. Nonetheless, the "internality" of the government's financial structure—the fact that the government generally borrows from the same community over which it has taxing powers—puts the federal debt in an entirely different position from private debt. As the saying goes, we owe the money to ourselves—and, if one forgets for a moment about the eleven or twelve per cent of the debt which is held by foreigners, the saying is true and very important. A lack of internality of debt explains why states or localites, such as New York City, cannot issue debt with the impunity of a federal government: only a small part—perhaps none at all—of the money they disburse will remain within their taxing reach. The same is true of governments like Israel's or Brazil's or Argentina's, which owe interest payments to foreign individuals or institutions from which they cannot collect taxes in return.

The second reason federal debts enjoy a degree of safety that cannot be duplicated in the private sector is that the government has a monopoly on the legal creation of money. In the old days, this meant that a national governments alone could authorize or operate the presses that printed up the national currency or the mints that struck off its coin. Nowadays, it means that national governments alone determine the size of the nation's money supply, mainly by the actions of central banks in loosening or tightening the ability of their member banks to make loans to the public. At least in theory, the capacity of a national government for increasing the money supply is unlimited, so that it could always pay off a debt of astronomical proportions by creating an equivalent amount of money. In point of fact, of course, no government would resort to such action unless its economy was already in ruins. In that case, the government could print up wheelbarrowfuls of currency, but usually the consequence would be to worsen the very crisis that it wished to mend. Even in this terrible instance, however, it would remain true that the government could always redeem its debts by creating the requisite number of dollars or marks or pesos needed to buy its bonds at their face value—although at God knows what value in real terms.

Thus, the ironic fact is that the very power of money creation which is the ultimate source of the financial impregnability of governments is also the source of their potential undoing. It is, in all likelihood, the lurking spectre of such a debauch of the currency that constitutes in the public's mind one of the objections to deficit spending. Deficit spending is often described as "spending money we don't have"—a phrase that does indeed sound inflationary— rather than as "spending money that has been borrowed from the public," which does not sound so dangerous. The crux of the debauchery problem, as these objectors see it, is that the Federal Reserve System will find itself impelled to expand the money supply to enable its member banks to buy the Treasury obligations by which the deficit is financed, and this loosening of credit will lead, sooner or later, to the wheelbarrow syndrome. It is, to be sure, possible that the government would deliberately plan expenditure programs that hugely exceed its tax receipts, or that the Federal Reserve would wantonly apply its money-creating powers, which would result in a debacle of the entire financial structure. But this is to assume that Congress is a wastrel institution, made up of members without a care for the country's future and devoid of the cautionary promptings that are so powerful within its constituents, and that the Federal Reserve System is run by economic dolts or scoundrels. These institutions are sometimes described that way by some of the more extreme groups in the country, but it is not the way I see either of them. In the main, our deficits arise despite, and not because of, reckless congressional attitudes; and the Federal Reserve System, under the chairmanship of Paul Volcker, has steered a course that has erred in the minds of most observers toward overstringency, not overindulgence. It is beyond question that inflation is a chronic condition of our country, as it is of all modern capitalisms, but it seems implausible that the ultimate cause of inflation lies in the financing of deficits. During the late nineteen-seventies, while the inflation rate was heating up from six per cent a year to eleven per cent, our deficits were running at only two or three per cent of the gross national product. (It is noteworthy that the newspaper appeal of the six former Secretaries, which does not stint on unpleasant possibilities, makes no mention of inflation among the various ills for which the current and prospective deficit can be blamed.)

There is one last pseudo problem conjured up by the debt—that heavy bag on our shoulders, the sixty-seven-mile stack under which we totter. Such depictions of the burden of the debt fail to indicate that the government's debt, like all others, is a claim against income, or wealth. What is burdensome about a debt is the necessity of the issuer to live up to the terms of its claim—paying interest when it is due and redeeming the debt when it comes full term. The issuer's burdens are, however, sources of income and pleasure to the recipients of interest payments and bond redemptions. Thus, if the one trillion five hundred billion dollars of government debt were to vanish overnight from the safe-deposit boxes of the country, the government might heave a sign of relief, but many millions of bondholders would utter cries of woe. The bondholders, of course, would be relieved of the burden of paying

the portion of their taxes that results from the need to pay almost
a hundred billion dollars a year in interest—a sum that may rise
to two hundred billion dollars by the end of the decade if the debt
keeps on growing at current rates. On the other hand, those same
taxpayers would also be relieved of the pleasure of opening the
Treasury envelopes that contained their interest checks. To take
the point a step further, let us suppose that by some extraordinary
stroke of fortune it became possible for the government to pay back
the national debt in its entirety, without taxing anyone a penny.
At a stroke, the government would be rid of a huge liability—but
the public would lose the possibility of investing its funds in Treasury securities. Presumably, individuals would put their money
in the next-best thing—perhaps in securities of states and locali-
ties or of foreign governments, or in corporate stocks and bonds.
Evidently, these are the *next*-best thing, not the *best* thing, or capital would not have been put into Treasuries in the first place. In
other words, there would be, in the absence of the particular advantages of securities backed by the federal government, a general
rearrangement of portfolios, each investor trying to achieve a distribution of risks and returns that suited him or her. Would the
nation be better off? Would investors be better off? The question
is very hard to answer in the absence of some kind of before-and-
after questionnaire assessing the state of mind of investors.
Strangely, however, there is no other meaning that we can attach
to the burden of the debt.

Until a few years ago, government deficits were regarded, at
least by the majority of the economics profession, with a relatively
benign eye, just because they *were* seen as a supplementary banking operation—a means of creating additional incomes when the
normal operations of the business sector failed to give us high employment. The idea that the government could stimulate the economy by putting savings or credit into circulation was the child of
the Depression decade and of the Keynesian economics that grew
out of that period. In fact, the Roosevelt Administration was never
able to muster the political nerve to run a peacetime deficit of more
than four or five per cent of the G.N.P. During the war, deficits
of more than twenty-five per cent of the G.N.P. were incurred as

war spending financed by bonds displaced private investment. A very large stimulus was thereby imparted to the economy, but the deficits were excused in the name of national sacrifice—not recognized as the application on a major scale of a program that the Administration had been politically unable to mount in the previous decade.

Deficit spending as a deliberate tool of national policy awaited the Kennedy Administration, which was the first that openly espoused a Keynesian approach to managing the economy. Faced with a threatening undertow of recession in 1963, President Kennedy agreed to follow the advice of his economic counsellors, chief among them Walter Heller, the articulate and intelligent Chairman of the Council of Economic Advisers, and cut taxes in order to deliberately incur a stimulative deficit. Keynesian economists like myself were enthralled at the prospect of a sophisticated economic policy, run right out of the best university economics departments, and we did all we could to advance the idea against the chorus of Philistines who claimed that governments that lived "beyond their means" would suffer the same fate as families that did so. Voices from Congress and elsewhere warned that government debts would lead to bankruptcy, saddle future generations with intolerable burdens, and irreparably ruin our moral fibre.

We do not know what might have happened to the proposed Kennedy tax cut had he not been assassinated, because in the wake of the tragedy all factions rallied around President Johnson in support of his program, including the tax cut. Meanwhile, however, the spontaneous forces of the economy had already begun to reverse the recession, so that the deficit as a matter of national policy became much less urgent. By 1965, the deficit was a trifling one billion six hundred million dollars—less than one-quarter of one per cent of the G.N.P. Thereafter, under the impact of the Vietnam War, the passage of Medicare and Medicaid, and a series of further, gradual tax reductions, deficits began to mount, jumping about from year to year as economic conditions changed but moving into the forty- and fifty- and sixty-billion-dollar range by the last half of the nineteen-seventies. As a result, the national debt also rose, from less than three hundred billion dollars in 1960 to over nine hundred billion dollars in 1980. Nonetheless, few economists were much alarmed. All of them were aware of the arguments I have sketched out concerning the internality of the debt and its largely nonexistent burdensomeness. In any case, output was rising fast enough so that the debt as a proportion of the gross national product actually fell. In 1960, our debt of two hundred and ninety-one billion dollars was equal to over half our G.N.P. By 1980, our debt stood at nine hundred and fourteen billion dollars but was only a third of the G.N.P. In addition, economists were aware that the deficit was in large part a matter of accounting practice, not only as regards the failure to separate current from capital expenditures but also in the fact that the federal government regularly picked up the tab for heavy state and local expenditures. Just as an instance, in 1965 the federal government gave 10.9 billion dollars in aid to state and local governments, mainly for public welfare, construction, and education. This showed up as part of federal expenditures and as part of state and local income. If the books had been kept differently, the federal government would have shown a surplus of 9.3 billion dollars instead of a deficit of 1.6 billion dollars, and the states and municipalities, taken together, would have been 10.9 billion dollars in the red instead of enjoying balanced budgets. It is interesing to note that from 1973 to 1983 the total transfer of funds to states and cities was roughly equal to three-quarters of the increase in federal debt over that period.

These general misunderstandings concerning the deficit and the debt set the stage for the general alarm that has been sounded by the Bipartisan Budget Appeal. Lashing out against the deficit has become standard rhetoric for politicians who speak to the public's fear of large numbers or national bankruptcy. But the danger that stirs the appeal's signatories—at least the more knowledgeable among them—is not these false problems but a new, real problem that has arisen as a consequence of the present Administration's fiscal policies. Normally, deficits diminish and surpluses tend to appear as the gross national product rises. The reason is that tax revenues typically increase as the volume of national expenditure grows, while certain kinds of expenditure, such as outlays for food stamps and for income support in general, tend to fall. Thus, the budget naturally moves toward a balanced condition as employment and output rise. The alarming aspect of the current budget situation is that this normal relationship has come apart. The huge Reagan tax cuts have reduced federal claims against income by a third. These cuts were undertaken not as a means of deliberately creating a deficit but in the hope that their buoyant effect on private spending would be so great that actual tax revenues would remain unchanged or even rise. When this hope of "supply side" economics failed to materialize, we were left with a tax structure that had reduced the inflow of funds to the government from its 1980 level, of just over twenty per cent of the G.N.P., to the very low figure of 18.6 per cent. In 1984, this seemingly trifling fall of one and a half percentage points will mean a loss of over fifty billion dollars in revenue.

At the same time, expenditures rose, partly because military appropriations were increased from a hundred and forty-six billion dollars in 1980 to two hundred and sixty-five billion dollars in 1984 and partly because indexed Social Security payments and soaring Medicare costs overrode reductions that had been gained by slashing away at welfare. The result was the first monster deficit, of a hundred and eleven billion dollars, in fiscal 1982; a second, larger deficit, of a hundred and ninety-five billion dollars, in fiscal 1983; and the probable deficit of a hundred and eighty-five billion dollars this year.

What is upsetting about these deficits is not their size—West Germany and Japan have run deficits as large or larger in relation to their G.N.P.—but their "structural" nature. That is, the current tax and expenditure schedules do not converge in the normal fashion. Instead, even at high levels of output, the structural gap between income and outgo is now estimated in the President's Economic Report to reach a hundred and thirty-eight billion dollars this fiscal year, and the report predicts that it will rise to a hundred and ninety-seven billion dollars by fiscal 1989. The only way to get rid of these deficits is to radically change the taxing and spending programs from which they stem.

In view of the generally benign effects of deficit spending in previous years, why not let the structural deficit stand? The answer has to do with an aspect of the budget known as "crowding out." Crowding out means that the necessity of financing the very large prospective deficits that will remain even at high levels of output will cause a competition between government and business for access to available funds—a competition that the federal government is certain to win. The government is certain to win because the Treasury will price its new bond issues, or adjust their interest rates, to whatever levels are needed to tempt households, banks, and businesses to buy its bonds. The consequences are twofold: First, the absorption of funds by the federal government will leave that much less available for other uses, whether private or state and local. Second, the struggle among borrowers for the nation's savings will raise interest rates. The fear is that federal deficits will absorb up to seventy per cent of all private savings over the next few years and, if the deficits continue to mount, will absorb all of them. In that event, interest rates could again become prohibitive, as they were in the last years of the Carter regime. Sky-high interest rates deal hammer blows to the economy, as many businesses and households learned during that last money squeeze. They also serve as magnets for foreign funds, which pour into the United States to take advantage of high yields. The continuing demand for dollars on the part of foreign investors keeps the dollar exchange rate high, and that, in turn, makes American goods expensive on world markets and foreign goods cheap on American markets. This year, we anticipate our first hundred-billion-dollar trade deficit, as a result of a boom in imports and a lag in exports attributable in considerable measure to the very high price of dollars against marks, francs, yen, and the like. Last, and certainly not least, high American interest rates add to the already impossible burden of debt repayment by the underdeveloped world. Much of the interest that these nations owe on their six hundred billion dollars of debt—a good deal of it happily sold to them by some of the same people who are now signatories of the Bipartisan Appeal—is tied to American interest rates, so that every time the prime rate goes up one percentage point, the underdeveloped nations have to hand over about four billion dollars more in interest and debt payments. This is more than they can take, as well as more than they can give, and the prospect of chaos—meaning repudiation of international debt—still troubles the international credit markets.

The core of the deficit problem thus comes down to the unpleasant, and even dangerous, prospect of murderous interest rates—the inevitable outcome of a demand for money which the supply cannot meet. Moreover, the Federal Reserve cannot avert this unpleasant prospect by increasing the supply of money to satisfy the demand for it. This is because crowding out, for all the haze of monetary considerations that hangs over it, is ultimately a "real" phenomenon, not just a matter of money. What the deficit signifies in these real terms is that we want to give the government more spending power than it could command by using its tax receipts alone. But the government is not the only sector that wants to go into debt to stretch its economic reach. Consumers are today evidencing a willingness to spend almost as high a fraction of their incomes on installment purchases as they did in the record year of 1979. Mortgage indebtedness is also growing at record rates—a hundred billion dollars a year. Business borrowing has leaped upward, as industry seeks to replenish inventory and catch up with investment plans that were deferred during the recent very severe recession. If all of this spending would give rise to more production, then there would be no crowding out but a gathering in, as the borrowing-and-spending process vitalized economic activity that would have lain dormant without it. But that is not the way the economic world works these days. Although we still have eight million unemployed and considerable idle plant capacity—about eighteen per cent by the Federal Reserve's measurements—we seem to have reached the threshold at which more spending by any one sector results primarily in higher prices rather than in higher output. Hence, increasing the supply of money will send up prices much more than production, and the competition for funds will not be alleviated. It cannot be alleviated as long as the public and private sectors together want to exercise more claims against the nation's immediately available production than is realistically possible. This is a situation in which something has to give, if we are to avoid the kind of scramble for funds that will send interest rates through the roof.

There is an obvious way out of this squeeze. It is to cut back
the need for the federal government to enter the capital markets
in such volume that interest rates have nowhere to go but up. That
step is what the House and Senate and White House have been
seeking to achieve as a "down payment" against the day when the
federal budget will again be in balance. It is a down payment rather than payment in full because pressures from all sides make the
quick attainment of a balanced budget impossible. Such a quick
solution would require that the Reagan Administration reverse its
commitment to a low level of taxation as essential for economic
growth, or relax its fervid insistence on a rapid military buildup
as the sin qua non of national security. Neither of these turnabouts
is apt to materalize. Very large cutbacks in Social Security and
Medicare would also be required, and, for obvious reasons, neither Congress nor the Administration can endorse that. Hence, the
down payment consists of marginal increases in such taxes as li-
quor excises, and in the closing of the more egregious tax loopholes, the elimination of some military extravagances, and the
trimming of Medicare costs. These changes are not large enough
to restore the inflow of tax revenues to pre-Reagan levels or bring
a halt to the upward-tilting course of military spending. All told,
the down payment is likely to amount to around a hundred and
forty billion dollars over three years. No one pretends that this
sum will cure the deficit problem or the danger of crowding out.
Presumably, the down payment will have to be followed by much
larger spending cuts or tax increases in the future, but no one is
talking about these, especially in an election year.

The Bipartisan Appeal charts a more ambitious course. It
urges a greater scaling down of military expenditures than the Administration wants, although not enough of a change so that military spending will decline as a proportion of the G.N.P. It calls
for a "substantial" enlargement of the federal tax base, but does
not go so far as to urge a return to the level of taxation that existed
before the Reagan Presidency. And it proposes a drastic cut in entitlement spending, recommending, in addition to a one-or-two
year freeze on cost-of-living adjustments, a ceiling on these adjustments thereafter at sixty per cent of the rises in the cost of living,
with no upward adjustments at all if living costs rise by less than
three per cent a year.

These proposals go much further than any existing down-payment plan in getting us out of our present bind. There is, how-ever, one fundamental issue that is slighted by the six ex-Secretaries and the six hundred national figures. It is whether the contest for funds in the nation's credit markets *should* be resolved at the expense of the public sector. For myself, looking out at the spectacle of the United States, this seems a Procrustean solution. It strikes me that the gravest weaknesses in our economy may lie not in the corporate world or in the middle and upper layers of our household well-being but in our public realm. I am appalled that so much of urban America has the look of an underdeveloped country. I am ashamed of the nation's treatment of the old and worried by its neglect of the young. I blame a good deal of America's laggard economic performance on its rotting infrastructure—by which I mean not only its miserable roads and bridges and harbors but its second-rate education and training. These failings will not be repaired unless we are willing to increase the size of the public sector to at least its previous share of the G.N.P., and pref-erably to the larger share found throughout European capitalist societies. The trouble with the Bipartisan Budget Appeal, as I see it, is its lack of courage—not only in comparing one sector as a whole with another but in weighing the activities that need funds within each sector. The Appeal speaks of the need for credit to modernize industry, but ignores the use of credit to finance lever-aged buy-outs and mergers—activities that are estimated to have absorbed thirty-five billion dollars of credit in the first five months of this year. In similar fashion, the Appeal makes no distinction between the importance of credit for first homes and automobiles as opposed to that for second homes and powerboats. Despite some acknowledgment of the productive role of public expenditures in supporting economic growth, there is a bland and uncritical en-dorsement of the private sector's right to a first claim on funds.

Bolder plans are around for reducing military expenditures, for restructuring the Social Security program, for reforming our Byzantine system of taxation, for preventing wastage of the na-tion's supply of credit. In the present political climate, however, such far-reaching proposals are not apt to receive an enthusiastic hearing. I suspect we will take the easy way of resolving the crowding-out issue—by cutting down the public sector, with the military suffering least; not by raising public revenues on a substantial scale, or by scrutinizing the needs and uses for credit in the private as well as the public realms. We will then see whether getting the government off our backs also pulls it out from under our feet. At least, when considered in this light, the deficit loses its paralyzing numerical spell and sheds its misleading familial analogies. It simply poses the issue of what will crowd out what in the social landscape of the future.

THE WEALTH OF THE NATION CAN HANDLE THE DEFICIT WITH EASE[5]

Numerous observers are worrying about how the country can finance Uncle Sam's red ink without deleterious consequences. We'll get a $200 billion shortfall this year and, the experts warn us, a number of that magnitude in future years as far as computers can project.

Individual savings are under $200 billion, and so we are told that the shortfall means higher interest rates. It means "crowding out" private borrowers, thereby aborting the recovery. High interest rates cause a strong dollar, which hurts exports and encourages imports, thereby fanning protectionist pressures at home, they maintain.

Investors shouldn't head for the storm cellars.

One needn't downplay the mischief of Uncle Sam's tangled finances to make a few reassuring, as well as realistic, observations about financing the deficit.

[5]Reprint of an article by M. S. Forbes Jr., deputy editor-in-chief, *Forbes Magazine. Forbes.* 132:23. Special issue. Fall '83. © 1983, *Forbes Magazine.* Reprinted by permission.

The Money Is There

First, there is more than enough liquid wealth in the nation—cash, savings, stocks, etc.—to finance Washington's red ink and a vigorous recovery as well. The money to service the national debt does not come just from the dollars you might save after you've paid your bills.

Second, a nation that is creating wealth, i.e., enjoying economic growth, producing more productive jobs and higher incomes, is in a better position to finance a wastrel government than one whose economy is stagnant.

Uncle Sam is perpetually in the red, the state and local governments are usually in surplus. For the past decade, in fact, the U.S. *net* government deficit was one of the lowest, as a percentage of GNP, in the Western World. Moreover, about $90 billion of what Uncle Sam or one of his agencies borrows ends up being relent to the private sector, primarily housing.

As the economy gains ground, the net red ink created by government will be shrinking. This is a phenomenon computers haven't been programmed to anticipate.

Corporate cash flows are getting better because of better business and because depreciation schedules were liberalized in 1981. Companies as a whole are generating more cash than they are consuming. This picture will brighten even more as sales pick up.

There is a bonus. In the inflationary 1970s companies discovered they needed more and more working capital to finance a given amount of activity. Now corporate treasurers are beginning to savor the opposite—their anticipated cash needs are not nearly so great. In addition, considerable capital was sunk on projects whose viability was based on rapidly rising prices. Adjusting to a noninflationary environment, not to mention the recession, has caused a number of companies considerable pain, but capital is now being used much more productively.

Add it all up—local government surpluses, improved corporate cash flows, as well as individual savings—and we have more than enough to cover the deficit and perpetuate the recovery, too.

This leads to an important point: Deficits don't have to be financed solely out of new savings. Government bonds can also be bought from the new wealth created by a rising securities market. Stocks and bonds today are worth a trillion dollars more than they were a year ago.

Moreover, with inflation at bay, people will be investing more in securities, including those of the government, than in traditional inflation hedges, such as land, gold, silver and Mickey Mouse watches.

Interest Rate Fears Overblown

The impact of the federal shortfall on interest rates is much exaggerated, as a handful of astute economists (that's not always a contradiction), such as John Rutledge and Alan Reynolds, have demonstrated. The deficit is higher today than a year ago. So are projections of future shortfalls. Yet interest rates are lower.

It is not only The Forbes Four Hundred who are richer today; so is the nation. And a richer nation can better cope with Washington's red ink than a poorer one.

If the recovery is allowed to proceed, the deficit problem will be tackled in two directions. It will shrink because of increased tax revenues that a vibrant economy will generate. And the increased wealth of an expanded economy will make financing the remaining shortfall that much easier.

THE DEFICIT'S SIREN SONG[6]

Ever since Geroge Bush labeled Ronald Reagan's proposals for massive tax cuts "voodoo economics," Reaganomics has been widely classified as a branch of wishful thinking. The supply-side economists who provided its theoretical underpinnings have been dismissed by many as merely the one lunatic fringe in the nation with the highest proportion of Ph.D.'s. So far, though, President

[6]Reprint of an article by Eric Gelman, economics reporter, with Rich Thomas and Connie Leslie. *Newsweek.* 104:78–9. O. 15, '84. Copyright 1984 by Newsweek, Inc. All rights reserved. Reprinted by permission.

Reagan's economic dreams have to a remarkable degree come true. Now, economists of many stripes are factoring in a new variable: the key supply-side tenet that a steadily growing economy coupled with spending restraint may be able to erase much of the budget deficit without tax increases. In short, the supply siders may be right.

More is at stake than economic theory. The way in which the deficit is approached will help determine the quality of American life for years to come. "If we allow the deficits to really get out of hand," says economist Alan Greenspan, "then trying to squelch them three or five years from now is going to be extremely difficult and very costly to the social fabric of the country." Democrat Walter Mondale has already put forth his program to raise taxes and cut spending to bring the deficit under control. It is not so clear what a re-elected President Reagan would do. He is committed to attacking the deficit with spending cuts and might even accept the tax hikes Congress would demand in return. Yet there are signs that he just might embrace the notion that a growing economy will provide enough added tax revenues to close the budget gap by itself. "It's a siren song to a receptive ear," says one administration economic official. "The president more than half believes that the deficits will succumb to growth."

Projections: Some of Reagan's most influential advisers are trying to fan that sentiment into wholehearted commitment. White House counselor Edwin Meese III has been transmitting to the president the views of supply siders Jude Wanniski and Paul Craig Roberts. Treasury Secretary Donald Regan insists that the deficit can be slashed without raising taxes. The true believers even managed to force Office of Management and Budget Director David Stockman, who has repeatedly called for tax increases to attack the deficit, to allow for the possibility that Reaganomics will work as planned. In its mid-August report, the OMB forecast a deficit for 1989 of $139 billion. But at the same time, the OMB also issued a more optimistic alternate projection. Using a higher estimated growth rate, it predicted a deficit of only $21 billion in 1989.

A growing number of influential business people and economists also seem willing to embrace the power of positive thinking.

The Chamber of Commerce has long been convinced supply-side theory would prove accurate—and now another trade group, the American Business Conference, also endorses the approach. "The supply siders have a great shot at being right," says Jack Albertine of the ABC, which represents mainly midsize high-tech firms. "And a lot of people are slowly beginning to realize it." Those two groups, along with the National Federation of Independent Business and the Business Roundtable, refused to join former Commerce Secretary Peter Peterson's recently formed Bipartisan Budget Appeal, which advocates cutting middle-income entitlements and defense spending and raising taxes to narrow the budget gap.

Even the nonpartisan Congressional Budget Office has begun, grudgingly, to give the supply-side proposition an outside chance of succeeding. "If getting the budget deficit down to around 2 percent of GNP is getting out of the problem, you can't say with certainty that that could not happen," says CBO Director Rudolph Penner, with a defensive flourish of double negatives. A sustained period of very rapid growth with low inflation could lead to a deficit of about $125 billion in 1989. "And by then, with a six-trillion-plus economy," he says, "some might think the deficit might not matter." As it is, though, the CBO is officially predicting a budget gap of $263 billion by 1989.

The strongest argument supply siders have is the economy's performance. Defying conventional wisdom, it has achieved sustained expansion without increases in inflation. And estimated budget deficits *have* to come down. In the fiscal year that ended Sept. 30, the actual deficit was $173 billion, considerably lower than the $231 billion forecast by the OMB early last year. The supply siders are saying that this trend can continue. "People who are saying this can't happen are the same who said we couldn't have a recovery at all, then that it couldn't be rapid and then that we'd have a big burst of inflation," says Richard Rahn, chief economist of the U.S. Chamber of Commerce.

'Fear of Flying': Rahn, however, does not expect the growth cure to get a fair test. He believes that the Federal Reserve Board will not permit the money supply to expand rapidly enough to sustain the level of expansion needed to erase the deficits. "But we believe a high-growth scenario is thoroughly possible and even likely if it weren't for the Fed's fear of flying," he says. The Fed, of course, is afraid of a resurgence of inflation.

The pivotal question is "Can high growth be sustained?" The most immediate threat is that the deficits will devour the economy—by keeping interest rates high—before the economy devours them. So far, though, the economy has achieved spectacular growth in the face of some of the highest real interest rates on record. The supply siders say they aren't asking for any miracles. "There is nothing inherently impossible about strong economic growth, a stable currency and low unemployment," says Alan Reynolds of Polyconomics. Adds Rahn: "All we're saying is that output from 1980 to 1989 can increase by 47.8 percent—high, but that's almost exactly the actual rate of increase from 1960 to 1969." One skeptical Fed official believes that such a performance would require annual productivity gains of 3.5 percent or even more for the rest of the decade, something that has never occurred.

Doubters: Some economists, in fact, do not even agree that growth is the main reason that deficits have declined. "Growth does help," says Penner, "but there is not a magic wand in action. It is the change of policies that is doing most of the work." Penner says the tax hikes and spending cuts in this year's Deficit Reduction Act alone will reduce the deficit by $70 billion in 1989. "That's a whole lot of money," he notes.

And there remain many who dismiss supply-side theory out of hand. Expressing a popular view, Steven Malin, an economist at the Conference Board, believes the economy has performed strictly according to conventional theories—and that Fed chairman Paul Volcker is the hero. To prevent an outbreak of inflation after the Reagan tax cuts, Volcker kept the money supply tight, inducing a recession. The recession put downward pressure on oil and commodity prices as well as wages. It also forced many businesses to streamline. When the Fed began increasing the money supply again in 1982, the economy was in fighting trim. The strong dollar, meanwhile, led to a flood of cheap imports. The only credit Malin will give to the supply siders is that "it was their program that forced the Fed to take those draconian measures that drove the economy off the cliff."

Another person who has no trouble resisting the siren song is Walter Mondale. He has promised to make a "down payment" on the deficit with a package of $25 billion in defense cuts and $87 billion in tax increases. For him, a walk on the supply side is out of the question. Says a Mondale economic aide, "You can't plan governmental policies on a one-in-a-hundred chance of lucking out."

Luck, though, has been the hallmark of the Reagan economic era. And the president has taken special delight in defying the "doomsayers"—those who have claimed his record budget deficits would inevitably crumple the economy. If Reagan receives the electoral mandate that many polls now promise, he may be inclined to let his luck ride and give growth a chance to balance the budget. It's still a risky long shot, but if he is proven right, he just might establish supply-side theory as a new economic model of how the world works.

IN PRAISE OF DEFICIT SPENDING[7]

The U.S. economy is paralyzed. Our real gross national product fell last year by 1.8 percent, and unemployment stands at 10.8 percent—postwar records for both of these gloomy indicators.

As the Reagan Administration and business leaders flounder around for a way out of this mess, their natural inclination is to follow the path marked by Martin Feldstein, chairman of the President's Council of Economic Advisers, and Peter Peterson, Richard Nixon's former Secretary of Commerce: sustantial budget cuts and tax increases.

It is precisely the wrong medicine.

The economy is suffering from a shortage of consumer demand. Many Americans—especially those standing in the unemployment lines—have no cash to spend. Others are reluctant to spend because they fear they may soon lose their jobs. As consum-

[7]Reprint of an article from *The Progressive*. 47:10. Mr. '83. Copyright © 1983 *The Progressive Magazine*. Reprinted by permission.

er demand declines, businesses lay off workers and defer spending on new plants or equipment.

To get out of this economic bind, the government must boost consumer demand, it must give consumers more money to spend on goods.

But raising taxes and reducing Government spending will deprive consumers of the money they need to help bring us out of this near-depression. When taxes go up, consumers have less disposable income. When Government spending is cut, people lose jobs.

No one wants to say it aloud these days, but what is needed is a large deficit in the Federal budget. Significant Government spending would create jobs and stimulate growth. Given the current decline of consumer spending, it is the only way out.

Critics insist, of course, that Government spending must be inflationary, and in the short term, they are right. In our economy, it is impossible to have growth without inflation. For the time being, however, we should be willing to trade some inflation for jobs and economic recovery.

In the long term, noninflationary growth is possible—if the structure of the economy is transformed. Today's economy revolves around such products and services as the automobile, oil, and private medicine—precisely those sectors that have generated the strongest inflationary pressures in the last decade. Government spending should be allocated, therefore, not to piecemeal public works programs but to mass transit, alternative energy sources, and health care systems—all avenues in which we can achieve growth without inflation.]

Take solar energy, for instance. Unlike oil or nuclear power, it is not a capital-intensive industry facing ever-increasing machinery costs. Nor is it vulnerable to manipulation by multinational giants or an OPEC-style cartel, one of the main inflationary engines of the 1970s.

Critics of increasing Government spending raise another objection: the "crowding out" phenomenon, a favorite catchphrase among economists. A big deficit, they say, will force the Government to borrow large sums in the private capital markets. Since the amount of lendable money is limited, such public borrowing will deprive industry of loans for the improvement of plants and machinery, and will raise interest rates across the board.

This fear is, at best, premature. Businesses will hardly search for new capital when their plants are currently operating at less than 70 per cent capacity. And once a recovery does begin, there is no guarantee that industry will invest scarce capital in areas of need rather than in real estate and mergers, speculative ventures that have fueled inflation in recent years.

The call for a reduced or balanced Federal budget is not only counterproductive but dangerous. It is not a prescription for lifting us out of the current recession but for sending us headlong into a depression.

The current budget deficit is more a symptom than a cause of economic paralysis. Workers who collect unemployment compensation don't pay taxes, and only noninflationary growth can begin to bridge the gap between Government expenses and revenues.

We need a well-designed jobs program that gets at the basic problems of our economy. Nothing less will suffice.

IV. POLITICAL CHOICES,
ECONOMIC IMPERATIVES

EDITOR'S INTRODUCTION

⌐Massive deficits are a reality, not to be wished or talked away.⌐ The executive and legislative branches of the federal government are faced in the mid-1980s with some very hard decisions, and their choices have not been made easier by President Reagan's adamant refusal to lower the military allocation in any substantial way or to consider new taxes. The first article, from *Great Decisions '85*, outlines the limited policy choices available to reduce the interconnected deficits in the federal budget and foreign trade.

⌐Passing a Constitutional amendment to require a balanced budget is not a new idea, and it has traditionally received only lukewarm encouragement from the White House. It is considered a less radical approach to an enforced balanced budget than calling a Constitutional convention for the same purpose, yet the convention needs approval by only a few more state legislatures before it must be called, while the amendment is unlikely to gain the required two-thirds majority approval of both houses of Congress any time soon.⌐ In the second and third articles, Alvin Rabushka states the case for a balanced-budget amendment and Roger G. Noll considers the case against it.

In the fourth article, Murray L. Weidenbaum argues that reducing federal expenditure is the only way to control the deficit, and that this may be accomplished in three areas: cut the cost-of-living adjustments (COLAs) to entitlement programs; lower projected military outlays; and drastically slash the generous subsidies paid to such groups as dairy and tobacco farmers and sugar producers. Felix Rohatyn, in the fifth article, suggests several novel ways of increasing federal revenue and reducing federal expenditure, including a tax on consumption and a spending freeze. In the sixth article, Robert D. Kilpatrick raises a businessman's alarm about the deficit, and recommends a close reexamination of

all federal programs and a removal of the deficit from the arena
of partisan politics.

ECONOMIC POLICY CHOICES[1]

The state of the economy is as much a measure of U.S.
strength as its military forces. Americans found that out in the late
1970s, when, with an economy dependent on oil imports and
weakened by inflation, America's leadership was seriously ques-
tioned.

The "American renaissance" Reagan speaks of is above all an
economic renaissance, brought about by the 1983–84 recovery.
How can the U.S. retain its economic leadership? How can the
U.S. stay competitive?

The Budget Deficit

The budget deficit is considered the worst economic problem
of the U.S., according to a *Washington Post*–ABC News poll. The
painless way to get rid of it would be through economic growth.
But the economy would have to grow at a real rate of 6% for the
next five years, instead of the 4% the Administration is projecting,
to eliminate the deficit without any changes in spending or tax
rules.

Barring such a happy, but unlikely outcome, Americans are
faced with the prospect of cutting spending, raising taxes, or learn-
ing to love the deficit. Following are the principal arguments advanced for each of the three choices.

• **Option 1.** *Cut spending*. Government spending is out of control.
Spending has been growing about 12% for each of the past three
years while nominal GNP has risen by about 8% a year. Said Wil-
lard Butcher, "We can't continue to spend the nation's wherewith-
al 50% faster than we produce it."

[1]Excerpted from *Great Decisions '85* by the Editors of the Foreign Policy Association. pp. 42–3. © 1985,
Foreign Policy Association. Reprinted by permission.

In addition to excess spending, there is wasteful spending. According to the President's Private Sector Survey on Cost Control, known as the Grace Commission, there are 2,478 ways that government can cut waste. These cuts could save the government $424.4 billion over three years.

Spending cuts, unlike a tax increase, will reduce the deficit without slowing the recovery, it is argued. A tax increase would burden Americans while putting more money into the hands of government, according to Reagan.

• **Option 2.** *Raise taxes.* Spending cuts are not possible unless the President wants to start cutting back on entitlement programs or defense, according to 1984 Democratic presidential candidate Walter F. Mondale. Discretionary domestic programs, where President Reagan has already cut the most, make up only 15% of the budget, and most of the cuts that can be made there have already been taken. The Grace Commission's recommendations are not politically practical: they include cuts in food stamps and Medicare. But the deficit must be reduced, or else high interest rates will hurt the recovery. Therefore, the argument goes, taxes must be increased.

The debate over spending is a debate over the role of government as well. Those who favor increasing taxes are concerned that important functions of government would be cut if spending is sharply reduced. Said economist Robert Heilbroner, "We will then see whether getting the government off our backs also pulls it out from under our feet."

• **Option 3.** *Stop worrying about the deficit.* It is the deficit that has brought about the recovery, for the reasons that Keynes described. According to Paul Davidson, professor of economics at Rutgers University, "The unprecedented deficit is not a symptom of illness in the economy. Quite the contrary, it is the medicine that promoted the robust recovery of 1982–84. . . . "

Spending cuts or taxes would likely cause a recession by taking away the stimulative effect of the deficit before the economy had reached a full employment level.

The Trade Deficit

Trade is a measure of U.S. competitiveness on the global market. Record deficits have forced policymakers to reexamine the various trade options available to the U.S.

• **Option 1.** *Free trade.* This has been the U.S. objective since the 1930s. If it has not worked as well as it might have recently, it is because we need freer trade, not restrictions, according to Brock. He has called for a new round of GATT negotiations that would cover areas not yet discussed, such as services trade.

The nature of capitalism is such that some industries will always be expanding while others are declining, free-traders note. To try to preserve a declining industry with trade restrictions is only likely to hurt a more competitive one as trading partners retaliate.

Three other trading strategies commonly discussed are basically ways of dealing with perceived shortcomings in free trade.

• **Option 2.** *Protectionism.* The U.S. is trading with countries that are playing by different rules. That, plus the strength of the dollar, puts Americans at a disadvantage, protectionists claim. Floods of low-cost imports have cost Americans jobs. The U.S. must protect its industries aggressively or it will risk losing its industrial base, they argue.

Furthermore, protectionism can work, its proponents say. The automobile industry needed time to retool after the onslaught of inexpensive imports in the 1970s. "Voluntary" quotas gave it breathing space, and in 1983 it had record profits, enabling it to employ more workers.

Critics say protectionism doesn't work. The automobile industry has made money because the lack of competition enables it to charge more for a car. The industry, critics say, has spent money on bonuses for executives, not new factories. Although auto workers have benefited, consumers have not. This, critics argue, is the problem with protectionism.

• **Option 3.** *Industrial policy.* The governments of the countries the U.S. trades with, such as Japan, play an active role in promoting their countries' exports. Proponents of an industrial policy argue that the U.S. is at a disadvantage when it trades because its exporters are on their own, competing against companies which have been subsidized by their governments.

The U.S. government needs to play a more aggressive role in promoting U.S. trade by giving aid to up-and-coming industries as well as encouraging other industries to export, industrial policy proponents argue. This is not the same as industry-by-industry protectionism, they say. In fact, a more coordinated U.S. trading policy would make the U.S. more competitive and would therefore offset calls for protectionism.

Critics say industrial policy looks after everybody but the consumer. " . . . If business, labor and government representatives were about to sit down and cut a deal, I suspect most consumers would start counting their silverware," said James C. Miller III, chairman of the Federal Trade Commission.

• **Option 4.** *Fair trade.* The U.S. should trade fairly with those who trade fairly with it and put restraints upon those who do not trade fairly. This is the basis for a "reciprocity bill" proposed by Senator John C. Danforth (R-Mo.) in 1982 that would put trade restrictions on countries that limit U.S. imports. This more flexible approach would give countries an incentive to play on an even field.

Critics say that fair trade is just a sugar-coated form of protectionism. Instead of encouraging freer trade, it would just make protectionism more reasonable. When dealing with a country such as Japan, which restricts trade in some way, the U.S. should look for ways to reduce restrictions, not for ways to retaliate.

U.S. citizens have a voice in determining the economic policies that have a significant effect on the world economy. What policies will help the U.S. achieve its foreign as well as its domestic goals? What impact will those policies have on the rest of the world?

A COMPELLING CASE
FOR A CONSTITUTIONAL AMENDMENT
TO BALANCE THE BUDGET AND LIMIT TAXES[2]

Introduction

On November 26, 1798, a decade after the U.S. Constitution was written, Thomas Jefferson wrote, "I wish it were possible to obtain a single amendment to our Constitution. I would be willing to depend on that alone for the reduction of the administration of our government to the genuine principles of its Constitution; I mean an additional article, taking from the federal government the power of borrowing."

Today, the need for such an amendment to the Constitution is greater than ever. Large and protracted federal deficits have brought havoc to today's economy. The nation's trillion dollar debt represents a true and onerous burden to the average American citizen. The carrying cost on the debt has skyrocketed. The bill we pay arrives in several forms: higher taxes, declining real income, higher interest rates and, at present, a recession.

Are deficits the only cause of our economic troubles? Of course not. Many of the undesirable consequences popularly attributed to deficits would have occurred if government spending and money creation had followed their historic path of the past twenty years even with the budget balanced. However, the burden of taxation on current and future generations would have been quantitatively different. Government debt would be lower, tax rates higher and inflation about the same. The disincentive effect of taxes on investment and employment would not have been avoided. Therefore, in order to preserve our economic and political freedom, it's necessary both to outlaw deficits and to place a cap on taxes such that the size of government, relative to the entire economy, does not increase.

[2]Excerpted from the chapter by Alvin Rabushka, tax specialist, in Richard E. Wagner, Robert D. Tollison, Alvin Rabushka, and John T. Noonan Jr., *Balanced Budgets, Fiscal Responsibility, and the Constitution*, Studies in Law and Economics, Cato Institute, 1982, pp. 57-8. © 1982 Taxpayers Foundation. Reprinted by permission.

Statutory Reform:
Historically and Inherently Flawed

Reforming the federal budget process has been and remains a popular topic with politicians, scholars and taxpayers. Many of the reformers believe that statutory changes in the way Congress conducts its business can bring about a responsible federal budget without resort to a constitutional amendment. Proponents of this view claim that statutory reform would avoid the time-consuming and cumbersome process of amending the Constitution to achieve fiscal restraint. They believe that Congress is capable of drafting legislation that will put its fiscal house back in order. This view has repeatedly been proven false, however.

Concern over reforming the congressional budget process has been debated extensively since 1921. For example, the Revenue Act of 1964 stated:

To further the objective of balanced budgets in the near future, Congress by this action recognizes the importance of taking all reasonable means to restrain government spending.

The Budget and Impoundment Control Act of 1974 enacted major reforms—the establishment of budget committees within each house, the creation of the Congressional Budget Office to supply timely information and analysis, and the development of a budgetary timetable—to enable Congress to consider individual spending measures in light of overall budget objectives. In the Humphrey-Hawkins Full Employment Act, a balanced budget was declared to be a national public policy priority. An amendment offered by Rep. (now Senator) Charles Grassley and Senator Harry Byrd, Jr. to an IMF loan program measure was enacted into law and requires that, beginning with FY 1981, total budget outlays of the federal government "shall not" exceed its receipts (P.L. 95–435). In 1979, a provision in a measure to increase the public debt limit stated that "Congress shall balance the federal budget" (P.L. 96–5), which required the congressional budget committees to propose balanced budgets for FY 1981 and subsequent years.

None of these measures have effectively constrained deficits. None has reduced the share of national income taxed or spent by the government. The most obvious reason for this is that no Congress can bind a succeeding Congress by a simple statute. A balanced budget or tax limitation statute can itself be repealed by the simple expedient of adopting a new statute or new budget which is in conflict with the earlier measure. The Byrd-Grassley amendment, which required a balanced budget for FY 1981, provided no deterrent whatsoever to the adoption of a budget with a $50 billion deficit for that year.

Indeed, legislation passed by Congress has exacerbated the problem of runaway federal spending. A convincing case can be made that control over the budget has steadily declined since the 1974 Act. Despite congressional adherence to the budget timetable, deficits have assumed record proportions: seven deficits exceeded $40 billion in the 1970s, and a regime of $100 billion deficits appears likely in the early 1980s. Control over off-budget outlays has eroded even more sharply: off-budget outlays have increased from less than $1 billion in FY 1973 to surpass $20 billion in FY 1982. Finally, those items in the budget which are known as "uncontrollable" have increased from 72 percent in FY 1973 to 77 percent in the FY 1983 budget. (Technically defined, an uncontrollable is budget authority or an outlay which would require substantive legislation to cancel. These consist chiefly of open-ended entitlements such as Social Security and Medicare, open-ended programs such as interest payments on the national debt and farm price supports, and contracts and obligations entered upon in the past and payable in the present.) Congress has thus been wholly unable to impose its own priorities on the budget.

The source of this failure lies in the fact that there is a structural bias within our political system that causes higher levels of spending, taxing, and deficits than are desired by the people, even though most members of Congress believe that large deficits and excessive government spending damage the economy. This spending bias has yet to be corrected by internal reform, because none of these reforms allow members to cope with spending pressures. As will be demonstrated, the removal of prior constraints calls for the imposition of a new constraint. A constitutional amendment would reimpose those constraints that the framers of the Constitution originally imposed or assumed. It would go a long way to correcting the serious defects in the institutional setting within which Congress now operates.

Amending the Constitution

Article V of the Constitution provides two methods of proposing amendments. The first method, by which all 26 amendments have thus far been adopted, requires the proposal of an amendment by two-thirds of each House of Congress, and ratification by three-fourths of the states. The second method allows for an amendment drawn by a constitutional convention, which must be called by Congress in response to the application of two-thirds of the states. Whichever method is invoked, the proposed amendment must be approved by three-fourths of the states (38) before it becomes part of the Constitution.

Since 1975, the National Taxpayers Union has worked with the state legislatures to pass resolutions—of which thirty-one have thus far been approved—calling upon the Congress to invoke Article V of the Constitution and convene a constitutional convention for the purpose of writing a balance budget amendment.

In early 1979, largely because of pressure being exerted by the states to convene a constitutional convention, the Senate Judiciary Subcommittee on the Constitution also began efforts to develop its own constitutional proposal to prohibit budget deficits. Senate Joint Resolution 58 (S.J. Res. 58), a combined balanced budget-tax limitation amendment, was reported out of the full Senate Committee on the Judiciary on May 19, 1981. Its companion in the House of Representatives is House Joint Resolution 350. The National Taxpayers Union is still actively working with several state legislatures—trying to bring the constitutional convention movement to a successful conclusion—in the belief that the continued pressure from the states will force the Congress to act.

A balanced budget amendment could overcome the inherent bias for increased federal spending by restoring the link between federal spending and taxing decisions. Under the terms of S.J. Res. 58, Congress could only adopt a planned budget deficit upon a three-fifths vote of the whole membership of both Houses. Moreover, unless Congress approved a bill by a majority vote of both Houses to increase taxes, federal revenues could not grow faster than the private economy; the amendment thus prohibits the federal government from consuming an ever-increasing share of our income.

Americans have come to the realization that the problem of deficits in this country is not one that can be resolved by any one individual or group of individuals. It is an institutional problem requiring a constitutional solution.

Many years ago, Many Americans believed that the election of fiscal conservatives would restore integrity to the conduct of the nation's fiscal business. They believed that a conservative President, Ronald Reagan, working with a conservative Congress would get control over the federal budget process. To their dismay, President Reagan has already abandoned his goal of a balanced budget by 1984. He has proposed future budgets with all-time record deficits, and he has even presided over an overall increase in government spending as a share of Gross National Product. The national debt, which surpassed $1 trillion in October 1981, is now forecast to grow by half-a-trillion dollars by 1985.

As a result of this abysmal failure to bring deficits under control, support for a balanced budget amendment now transcends both members of Congress and the state legislatures. Despairing of the federal government's ability to restrain spending and eliminate deficits, the American public has expressed its support for a constitutional amendment to require a balanced federal budget. According to Gallup, 80 percent of all Americans favor such an amendment.

Had the founding fathers not taken for granted the concepts of limited government, they might have incorporated a balanced budget amendment into the original constitution. Indeed, it was the Sixteenth Amendment, which authorized Congress to "lay and collect taxes on incomes," that is at the root of our present discontent with the budget process. Without a progressive income tax code, government spending might be substantially lower and the need for a restraining amendment correspondingly less.

175 Years of Fiscal Prudence

The founding fathers adopted two explicit constitutional provisions and assumed a third which served to restrain spending. One reserved powers not expressly delegated to the federal government to the states and to the people. The second provided for per capita distribution among the states of taxes on income. The third, implicit, assumed that federal spending would not exceed federal revenues except in times of war or recession. All three have been abrogated or eroded by time and events, especially by the adoption of the Sixteenth Amendment (income tax) in 1913. Indeed, it is the income tax amendment that lies at the roots of the current balanced budget amendment movement.

Someone born in the post-depression era would regard deficit financing as normal budget practice. Yet until the great depression, the balanced budget, save in wartime or recession, was considered part of our "unwritten constitution." Thomas Jefferson warned that "the public debt is the greatest of dangers to be feared by a republican government" and proposed the idea of a balanced budget amendment as early as September 6, 1789. Alexander Hamilton strongly urged the repayment of national debt. Presidents John Adams, James Madison, James Monroe, John Quincy Adams and Andrew Jackson all urged avoiding public debt. A balanced budget was synonymous with sound political economy.

Until the Great Depression of the 1930s, budget deficits occurred only in times of war and recession. The budget surpluses generated in good times were invariably used to reduce the national debt these deficits produced. Historical deficits of large proportions arose during the Revolutionary War, the War of 1812, the Mexican War of 1846, and during brief recessions in the late 1830s and 1850s. In each instance, the debts were immediately reduced at the onset of peace or prosperity. Between 1795 and 1811, Congress cut the national debt nearly in half from $84 million to just over $45 million. After the War of 1812, eighteen surpluses (of 21 budgets) between 1815 and 1836 virtually eliminated the national debt. A run of 28 consecutive surpluses following the Civil War lowered the national debt from $2.7 billion to $960 million. Finally, throughout the 1920s, consecutive surpluses reduced the national debt from $24 billion to $16 billion, at the very time that major tax rate reductions were approved.

Sustained deficits first arose during the depression years of the 1930s and the war years of the early 1940s, leaving in their wake a national debt of about $170 billion. These deficits were consistent with the national experience of wartime and recession. When peace returned, deficits again disappeared. Between 1947 and 1960, seven surpluses of $31 billion roughly offset seven deficits of $32 billion. However, for the first time in American history, no effort was made to reduce the national debt.

Why the Congress Can't and Won't Control Federal Spending and Deficits

Due to the operation of the unwritten norm of budget balance, the federal government was rarely troubled by budget deficits through almost 200 years of our history. Indeed, revenues and expenditures were not incorporated into an overall official budget until 1921.

But today federal budgets are wildly out of balance. Why?

The answer lies in the political reality that budget objectives and the budget process are in direct conflict. The Congress, as a whole, is concerned with stable prices, low interest rates, and full employment, which require some check on the scope of government spending. As individuals, however, congressmen confront pressures to increase spending. The reality of our system has shown convincingly that the collective need to control spending is no match for the pressures each individual member faces to increase it.

The tendency for federal spending to grow is clearly highlighted in historical debates on congressional reform:

The growth of the cost of government as expressed in the increase of Federal taxation has been astounding. . . . Our failure to reduce that cost has called attention to our need of the adoption of a system which will prevent waste and extravagance with inevitable inefficiency in the various departments.
Our present system cannot be conducive to economic administration, as it invited increased expenditures through the perfectly natural rivalry of numerous committees and the inevitable expansion of departments. . . .
Our present system is designed to increase expenditure rather than reduce it.
Each committee in the House quite naturally is jealous of both its jurisdiction and success in legislation. It will therefore push to the limit its jurisdiction over legislation and its demand for appropriation that enlarges the function falling under its jurisdiction. Appropriations from the several committees become a race between or among rivals to secure funds from

the Treasury rather than safeguard them. . . . The pressure is for out-lay.

These words stem from the various participants in the debate on the Budget and Accounting Act of 1921, not the 1974 Act! Yet they are the same misgivings articulated during the debate on the 1974 Act. And despite the 1974 Reform Act, the misgivings still remain.

The concerns they represent reflect the empirical fact that the American political process is biased toward higher levels of federal spending; levels which do not reflect the genuine will of the people on the overall size of the budget. Federal spending is skewed toward these artificially higher levels because members of Congress have powerful incentives to spend the taxpayers' money, yet they face few offsetting incentives to watch out for the taxpayers' interests.

Spending Biases

This bias toward more spending is due, first, to what analysts of government call the phenomenon of "concentrated benefits versus dispersed costs." This describes the fact that the benefits of any given spending program normally are concentrated among a small number of persons, while the costs of such a program are dispersed throughout a much larger class, the general taxpayer.

The competition between tax-spenders and tax-payers is highly unequal: it is simply not as worthwhile for an individual taxpayer to spend much time and effort to save a few dollars in taxes as it is for the spending interests to secure millions or billions of dollars for themselves. The latter intensely focuses on those few spending measures from which they derive benefit, while the individual taxpayer, who might normally be concerned about the broader impact, is less likely to organize for the purpose of defeating a particular spending measure. Spending interests are able to reward or punish legislators with their organized electoral support or opposition. Taxpayers find it more difficult to perceive their self-interest in the context of isolated pieces of legislation. Thus, whenever government programs are considered one by one, as they are in our budgetary system, there is a bias toward goverment growth. The result has been annual budget growth in the neighborhood of $100 billion, with even larger deficits forecast.

The explosion in federal spending is not due to the failure to elect the "right" people, it is an institutional defect. The federal budget process is inherently biased toward deficits, higher taxes, and greater government spending. The trends toward bigger government and economic instability reflect the decisions of reasonable men and women in Congress, who, as individuals, cannot successfully resist the pressures they face to increase spending.

A second source of bias toward greater spending is the separation of benefits, which are short-run, from costs which are typically more long-run. The benefits of spending programs are immediate, both to the recipients and the sitting congressmen who supported them. The cost of spending programs—in the form of potentially higher future taxes, higher future inflation, higher future unemployment or higher future interest rates—will be evident only at some future time, to be borne, perhaps, by future congressmen. Since the electoral time horizon of all House members and one-third of the senators is never more than a year or two away, short-term benefits invariably take precedence over potentially long-run adverse economic effects due to higher government spending.

A third bias arises within the structure of Congress itself. The committee system, whatever its original intentions, finds members of Congress gravitating to those specific committees that allow them to serve their geographic constituencies by bringing home their "fair share." Farm state members typically serve on the agriculture committes, Western legislators on interior policy committees, urban legislators on urban policy committees, and so on. Reelection rewards those congressmen who successfully serve their constituencies, at the same time the actions of Congress as a whole damage the growth rate of the economy. The driving elements in each congressmen's calculation is protecting his turf, getting his share of the pork barrel, not transgressing his colleague's committee jurisdiction; in short, concerns about self come first. It is not in the interest of an individual congressman to give up those dollars that benefit his constituents, since that reduction will have only a modest or even insignificant effect on overall spending. The same situation fits all 535 members of Congress. Unless the entire membership can agree to limit spending, no one member or group of members dare risk their constitutents' wrath by surrendering benefits that have no appreciable effect on the total size of government spending, while their colleagues, who do not forgo spending, continue to earn the support of their respective constituents. The only viable solution to this dilemma is to alter the incentives which confront members of Congress. That is, we must change the rules under which congressmen operate.

Currently, there are two major gaps in these rules which nourish Congress's spending bias and flout widely recognized customs of fiscal prudence. First, members of Congress enjoy virtually unlimited access to deficit spending. As the "unwritten" rule of budget balance has been discarded, members of Congress can vote to increase spending without a concomitant vote to increase taxes. Spending decisions have become increasingly divorced from the availability of revenues. As a result, members of Congress can satisfy the demands of particular spending interests without either reducing spending for another interest or taking political heat for raising taxes. Rather than choose among alternative spending proposals, members jointly act to increase the deficit. The availability of deficit spending reduces the need for members to make hard political decisions of choosing among spending proposals.

A second element in the spending bias is that under our present tax system, members of Congress have access to annual, automatic tax increases. Our progressive tax code works to transfer more and more of our personal income to the government, because as individuals' incomes increase, they are taxed at progressively steeper rates. The rising share of national income paid in taxes is due to increases in real income or to inflation, a phenomenon known as "bracket creep," which has had the especially pernicious effects of raising tax burdens. In the last decade, government income tax collections have risen by about 16 percent for each 10 percent increase in personal income, largely as a result of inflation. In the last three years government receipts have outpaced inflation while average weekly earnings in private industry have fallen in real terms. Resources are being increasingly shifted from private to public hands. By trying to break even with cost of living increases, the typical wage-earner actually falls behind.

A progressive tax system allows Congress to raise taxes without having to vote an explicit increase either in tax rates or the size of the tax base. Federal income tax yields have grown about 75 percent faster than the GNP, which has allowed Congress to simultaneously collect a growing stream of revenues and enact a sequence of nominal tax cuts. Although Congress passed "tax-reform" measures in 1954, 1964, 1969, 1971, 1976, 1977, 1978, and 1981, taxes have not declined. It is only their rate of increase that has slowed. The accelerating frequency of congressional action reflects the higher rates of inflation throughout the 1970s. In each instance of tax reform, a rising trend of taxation was interrupted, but the long-run trend has been upwards.

Here again, individual congressmen confront strong incentives to do what is far from in the best interests of society. The benefits that they must deliver to retain their office prompt congressmen to support inflationary policies which net them greater spending authority, hence the ability to meet the demands of special interest groups.

Congress has finally voted to correct inflation-generated "bracket-creep" by indexing taxes to inflation, to take effect in 1985. In that event, the progressive tax code would only transfer a greater share of personal income to government when real growth occurs. But many economists and politicians have begun to suggest repeal or postponement of the indexing provision before 1985 to prevent "a drain" on Treasury revenues, thus maintaining the automatic increase mechanism.

The Fiscal Experience since 1960

Since 1960, these biases have yielded the current spending habits of the Congress; that is, deficits have become the accepted practice of federal budgeting. Apart from one modest surplus of $3 billion in 1969, the Congress has imposed a regime of persistent deficits. A national debt of $330 billion in fiscal year 1962 rose to $437 billion in fiscal 1972, surpassing $1 trillion in October 1981. Eight deficits in the 1970s, were $400 billion or greater. Interest payments, which absorbed approximately six percent of the national budget twenty years ago, consumed about twelve percent in FY 1981. It is a figure half as large as spending for income security programs including Social Security. (Nor does this figure include the growing unfunded liability of social insurance programs and the implicit obligations of loan guarantees.)

The breakdown of the balanced budget norm fueled an explosive rise in federal spending. As recently as 1929, federal spending of $3 billion consumed only 3.1 percent of the gross national product (GNP). Since then, the federal sector has demonstrated a continuing propensity for growth, whatever the economic circumstances. In successive decades, federal spending grew to consume 10.0, 15.6, 18.5, 20.3, and 23.1 percent of GNP by 1980. In money terms, federal spending passed the $100 billion mark in 1962. A $200 billion budget was reached only 9 years later. In rapid-fire succession came $300 billion (1975), $400 billion (1977), $500 billion (1980), $600 billion (1981), with estimates of one trillion dollars by 1985.

A comprehensive picture of government spending must also include the spending totals of off-budget federal entities (e.g., Federal Financing Bank, Strategic Petroleum Reserve, Postal Service Fund, Rural Electrification and Telephone Revolving Fund, Rural Telephone Bank, U.S. Railways Association, and Synthetic Fuel Corporation). These have risen from $60 million in FY 1973 to $10 billion in FY 1978 to $21 billion in FY 1981. The Reagan administration, despite pledges to reduce off-budget outlays, even included the Strategic Petroleum Reserve as an off-budget item in its first year to lower the official budget deficit.

The growth of federal spending has carried with it an economic increase in federal tax burdens, which have risen from 15 percent of GNP in 1949 to 22 percent today. Taxpayers also face much higher marginal rates on income as inflation has pushed them into higher tax brackets. Households in the 70th percentile of taxpayers have seen their average top marginal rate rise from 20 percent in 1966 to 28 percent by 1981; for those in the 95th percentile, from 25 to 46 percent. Per capita tax receipts have nearly doubled in the past five years alone. The number of individual taxpayers paying more than 20 percent of their income to the federal government has nearly tripled in the past 15 years. Rising tax burdens, especially high marginal rates faced by many taxpayers, have eroded the incentives to work, save and invest.

Thus in sharp contrast with historical experience, the federal budget process has failed to show restraint in the post-WW II era. For the better part of 200 years, Americans held to a limited role for the federal government. Save for periods of war or recession, revenues from customs and excises were sufficient to fund those activities widely regarded as "proper" federal functions. This consensus has broken down in the last fifty years. The greater part of the current federal budget is devoted to activities not funded fifty years ago.

What It Means When Congress Orders a Deficit and the Effect It Has upon Our Lives

The federal government can finance its deficits in three ways. It can raise taxes. It can borrow in the capital markets. Or, it can print new money. By raising taxes, the government reduces the incentives of individuals and business to work, save and invest. By borrowing, the federal government competes with private borrowers, raises the rate of interest, and ultimately crowds out private borrowing. By printing money, the government fosters inflation which, in turn, reduces investment by increasing the risk-premium on long-term investment. In recent years tax burdens and high marginal rates have risen substantially. The 1981 tax rate cut attempts to correct this problem. Without new taxation, future deficits are likely to be financed largely by borrowing or new money creation. Let us examine the effects of these two methods.

Borrowing. When the government borrows to finance its budget deficit, it has an unfair advantage in its competition with private borrowers. Since governmental borrowing is backed up by the "full faith and credit" of the United States government, *viz.*, the power of tax, the government gets first call on the available supply of credit. Moreover, the government will pay whatever rate of interest is required to get the funds it needs to sustain government spending. Private borrowers are not so flexible.

The price of credit—the interest rate—is determined by the intersection of the supply of and demand for credit. In the past decade, the percentage of disposable personal income that was saved fell by about half, from nearly 8 percent in 1971 to about 4 percent in 1980. As a result, total real savings have fallen, reducing the supply of new credit. At the same time, the government has sharply increased its annual demand for new credit. Total federal and federally-related borrowings have risen from $33 billion in FY 1971 to $155 billion in FY 1981. The rate of increase in government demand for credit has outpaced new savings. As in any such situation of rising demand, the price of borrowing will rise because of the competition among borrowers for limited funds. But when interest rates rise, private citizens will borrow less. Thus private borrowing is crowded out.

Borrowing to finance large deficits need not crowd out private borrowers if the supply of new savings is large enough to satisfy both public and private demands for credit. In Germany and Japan, savings rates have been from three to five times as large as in the United States, which explains why the German and Japanese governments can run substantially larger deficits as a share of GNP than the United States government, without equally adverse economic effects. The conjunction of rising credit demands and lower savings rates in the United States has driven up real interest rates to levels higher than at any period in our nation's history. To the extent that deficit finance raises real rates of interest and reduces investment in plant and equipment, we have fewer tools or machines in our old age and leave fewer tools for our children. We consume relatively more today but we are poorer and have fewer goods available tomorrow.

It is important to note that private borrowing is used disproportionately more for investment than is government borrowing. Budget deficits that are financed by borrowing mean that funds which might be used for the creation of capital goods are instead used to subsidize consumption. Deficits thus crowd out some investment in favor of greater consumption. Although some capital investment will still take place, the amount is lower than it would have been in the absence of a budget deficit.

Money Supply Growth. The inflation which began in the late 1960s has been associated with large and continuing federal deficits. Apart from Treasury borrowing, the government can also finance deficits by printing new money. This result occurs when the Federal Reserve Board (the Fed) increases its ownership of Treasury debt, which, in turn, effectively increases the amount of money and credit in circulation. This process is referred to as monetizing debt, which is largely synonymous with printing money to finance deficits.

It is technically true that there is no necessary relationship between budget deficits and money creation. The Fed can keep its ownership of government debt unchanged despite deficits, or increase its ownership of outstanding government debt in the absence of a deficit. Assume it does the former. Persistently large deficits, coupled with inadequate savings, will place upward pressure on interest rates, thereby crowding out private investment. This, in turn, leads to recession and higher unemployment. To ease these effects, the Fed can increase its ownership of Treasury debt, thereby increasing the supply of money. As the supply of loanable funds expands, other things being equal, the rate of interest will fall and fewer private borrowers will be crowded out. However, money creation reduces the real value of the existing stock of money, thus contributing to inflation.

Persistently large deficits during a period of economic recovery foster long-run inflationary fears that the Fed might monetize some portion of this debt. In the past decade, purchase of government debt by the Fed has contributed to rising inflation. Inflation, in turn, disrupts savings, investment decisions, and the prospects for economic growth. Personal savings rates fell throughout the 1970s and the average service life of capital expenditures, so vital to future increases in production efficiency, began to shorten.

Inflation puts economic stability and growth at risk; it has undercut investment and employment by increasing uncertainty over the profitability of long-run investments. This uncertainly, which is embodied in investment calculations in the form of higher risk premiums, prevents a normal package of capital projects—especially those for which the profit expectations are skewed toward the later years of the investment, eight, ten, or fifteen years in the future—from meeting acceptable financial criteria.

Reflecting increased investment risk, price earnings ratios in the stock markets have fallen to their lowest levels in two decades, largely as a consequence of the increased discount rate imposed on expected earnings growth. An inflationary environment makes it more difficult and uncertain to calculate the rate of return on new investment. Inflation not only skews rate-of-return calculations, it also acts to shift the investment pattern toward shorter-lived projects in which the uncertainty is less.

High investment risk thus blunts capital formation and the level of economic activity. It replaces the creation of long-lived capital assets with undue focus on the short run. To restore long-term investments requires a high level of business confidence, which can only be obtained by a credible and sustained reduction in long-run expectations about inflation. This implies that budget deficits must be minimized, preferably eliminated, thereby removing the consequent pressures on the monetary system of large federal deficits.

Interest rates are high because the demand for credit is high, especially on the part of the federal government. Money supply growth in recent years has been excessive, in part, because the Fed feels compelled to suppress interest rates by at least partially accommodating the excess credit requirements. Thus the prospect of multi-hundred billion dollar deficits in the next few years implies (if savings do not increase dramatically) continued crowding out and high interest rates or purchase of additional debt and a renewed inflationary spiral, which was the cause of declining business investments in the first place.

In short, deficits matter!

In fact, deficits matter in ways other than those purely economic. Yet another effect of excessive government spending has been the erosion of public confidence in government. Surveys conducted by George Gallup, Louis Harris, the Institute of Social Research at the University of Michigan, and CBS/New York Times reveal major shifts in public opinion between 1957 and 1978. The percentage of respondents who said that government wastes money rose from 46 to 80. But the number of those who said they trust Washington to do what is right most of the time declined from 75 to 34 percent!

Americans have increasingly felt the effects of inflation. Between 1958 and 1973, for example, the number of Gallup's respondents naming inflation as the nation's most important problem was always less than 20 percent. Since 1974, the percentage has ranged from a low of 25 to a high of 79. Complaints about taxes and government waste have escalated as taxpayers endured rising rates of inflation and stagnant real income. Indeed, according to Gallup, 80 percent of the American people favor a constitutional amendment to require a balanced budget.

SENATE JOINT RESOLUTION 58. A BALANCED BUDGET–TAX LIMITATION CONSTITUTIONAL AMENDMENT

Since 1979, members of the Senate Judiciary Subcommittee on the Constitution have sought to develop a "consensus" measure that would attract the support of as many proponents of a constitutional initiative as possible. Senate Joint Resolution 58, a combined balanced budget and tax limitation amendment, was voted out of the Subcommittee by a 4-0 vote on May 6, 1981, and reported out of the full Senate Committee on the Judiciary by an 11-5 vote on May 19, 1981. The measure enjoys the support of both the National Taxpayers Union, progenitor of the balanced budget constitutional convention movement, and the National Tax Limitation Committee, formerly sponsor of the Heinz-Stone spending limitation amendment.

Let us examine each section of the proposed amendment to see how it would redress the present imbalance in our budgetary process.

BALANCED BUDGET

Section 1. Prior to each fiscal year, the Congress shall adopt a statement of receipts and outlays for that year in which total outlays are no greater than total receipts. The Congress may amend such statment provided revised outlays are no greater than revised receipts. Whenever three-fifths of the whole number of both House shall deem it necessary, Congress in such statement may provide for a specific excess of outlays over receipt by a vote directed solely to that subject. The Congress and the President shall ensure that actual outlays do not exceed the outlays set fourth in such statement.

The purpose of Section 1 is two-fold. First, Congress would be required to plan to balance its budget every year. It would do so by adopting a "statement" or budget prior to the start of each year, in which planned outlays (spending) do not exceed planned receipts (revenue). Congress could violate this rule and plan for a deficit only by a three-fifths vote of the whole number of each House of Congress, not just three-fifths of those present and voting. In contrast, a simple majority could approve a budget surplus. Section 1 also mandates that actual outlays do not exceed the spending levels set forth in the approved statement or budget.

It is important to point out that the amendment establishes the basis for a *planned* balanced budget. It does not require that the budget be in *actual* balance during the course of the fiscal year. In some circumstances, actual outlays may exceed actual receipts. For example, a recession might reduce actual receipts below the level of receipts set forth in the planned statement. This is permissible under the amendment, but actual outlays could not exceed statement outlays. Deficits caused by increased spending would also not be permitted.

If circumstances warrant, the Congress may adopt an amended statement of receipts and outlays for the fiscal year (provided again that outlays do not exceed receipts) at any time during the fiscal year. An amendment statement containing a deficit would require a three-fifths vote only if such deficit was greater than the deficit in the previous statement. Thus the budget would not be "locked in" and could be changed by an explicit vote of Congress in response to changing economic conditions.

An important feature of Section 1 is that it imposes upon the Congress and the president a mandate to prevent total actual outlays, which includes both on- and off-budget items, from exceeding statement outlays. For example, should the economy perform below expectations, leading to increased spending on "entitlements" or on debt service due to higher interest rates, the Congress would be called upon *either* to increase statement outlays and approve a deficit (by a three-fifths vote), or to postpone spending programs and/or to reduce eligibility for "entitlements." To guard against the possibility that actual outlays might exceed statement outlays through unintentional and presumably modest error, an obvious remedy would be for Congress to plan a surplus of equivalent size for the next fiscal year.

The Congress is expected to adopt the most accurate estimates of receipts and outlays that it can in drafting its budget, but in all cases a congressional majority will be the final arbiter among the choice of estimates. As the fiscal year unfolds, actual receipts may or may not meet expectations. An unexpectedly more robust economy may yield receipts above statement receipts; an unexpectedly weaker economy may yield receipts below statement receipts. Either result is permissible. The amendment imposes no obligation upon the Congress to react to the flow of actual receipts during the fiscal year, only to the flow of actual outlays.

Recent years have witnessed congressional failure to adopt a budget by the October 1 date on which a new fiscal year begins. Congress has funded government operations in such instances by adopting continuing resolutions. Under the amendment, this practice would be banned. Failure to adopt a statement of receipts and outlays by the October 1 deadline would be construed as an implied adoption of a statement in which both receipts and outlays are zero. In that event, the Congress and the President would be mandated constitutionally to ensure that fiscal year outlays also would be zero. In short, the government would shut down on October 1 without prior passage of a budget by September 30.

Loans for which the federal government guarantees in whole or in part the repayment of principal and/or interest impose no funding obligation on the treasury unless and until such loans come into default and the treasury must discharge the guarantee obligation. Such a discharge is intended to be construed as an outlay in the fiscal year of discharge.

A large portion of federal spending is currently on automatic pilot. That is, spending for "entitlements" grows every year as a share of federal spending. An amendment prohibiting deficits would create a strong incentive to bring these "uncontrollables" under control, since they would compete directly with discretionary programs. At present, the automatic growth of spending on "uncontrollables" erodes the ability of Congress to impose its own priorities on the budget, which is tantamount to passing the congressional buck.

Section 1 proposes to overcome the spending bias of Congress by restoring the linkage between federal spending and taxing decisions. It does not propose to read any specific level of spending or taxing forever into the Constitution, nor does it intrude into the day-to-day decisions of the government as to how the federal dollar is allocated. It merely restores the balance between tax-spenders by constraining spending totals to available revenues.

The amendment would compel public officials to determine first what resources are available to government (see Section 2 below) and, against that constraint, choose among the many competing claims on public spending.

Under the amendment, if politicians voted new spending programs, they would have to eliminate old programs or vote to raise additional taxes. Resistance to the elimination of existing programs or to tax increases would discourage many new spending proposals, thereby eliminating the current bias toward overspending. It would end future deficits and reduce the inflationary effect of new money creation, which has in past years both financed a portion of these deficits and raised taxes via bracket creep.

Political values and perceptions are important determinants of government action. For this reason, a balanced budget amendment is especially attractive. It is easy to understand—every household understands the need for living within its means. It is also widely supported.

TAX LIMITATION

Section 2. Total receipts for any fiscal year set forth in the statement adopted pursuant to this article shall not increase by a rate greater than the rate of increase in national income in the last calendar year ending before such fiscal year, unless a majority of the whole number of both Houses of Congress shall have passed a bill directed solely to approving specific additional receipts and such bill has become law.

The purpose of Section 2 is to prevent tax receipts from growing more rapidly than the general economy, as occurs with our progressive tax code. Under the amendment, a "whole" majority of the membership of both Houses would have to vote to permit receipts to outpace general economic growth. In particular, Congress would be required to enact a bill expanding a specified tax base and/or increasing specified tax rates.

Put another way, Section 2 states that the balanced budget requirement in Section 1 should not occur at levels of receipts and outlays that consume an increasing proportion of the national economy. It attempts to achieve this result by limiting the increase in receipts for a new fiscal year to the percentage increase in the national income during the prior calendar year. If present tax laws are likely to yield revenues in exess of this limit, the Congress must modify the revenue laws to reduce anticipated receipts.

The relationship between the growth of national income during the prior calendar year and the growth of receipts during the following fiscal year provides the Congress with reasonably precise guideposts in its budgeting process. Quite accurate estimates of the growth in national income are available by mid-July prior to the beginning of the fiscal year.

Take fiscal year 1981, for example, which began October 1, 1980. The rate of increase in statement receipts for fiscal year 1981 would have been limited to the rate of increase of national income for calendar year 1979. Since national income rose 11.4 percent in 1979, statement receipts for fiscal 1981 could not have exceeded fiscal 1980 statement receipts by more than 11.4 percent. The planned increase for FY 1981 with no changes in the current tax law was set at 14.5 percent. Had the amendment been in effect, the tax law would not have produced this automatic tax increase. Taxes would have been about $16 billion or lower. To increase taxes, Congress would have had to explicitly vote for a tax increase for FY 1981.

Statement receipts may also rise by less than the proportionate increase in national income. In that event, the new lower level of receipts would then become the base for statement receipts in subsequent fiscal years, until the Congress voted a rise in allowable receipts.

Let's recapitulate how the budget process would work under the amendment. First, the Congress would determine the increase in national income during the prior calendar year. That percentage rise, in turn, would determine the maximum increase in receipts the government could collect for the coming fiscal year. If, say, national income rose 10 percent during the last calendar year, then receipts could rise by *no more than* 10 percent for the new fiscal year. Since outlays cannot exceed receipts (the budget must be balanced or in surplus), government spending could not rise by more than 10 percent. Sections 1 and 2, in conjunction, establish a *de facto* spending limit. Thus neither taxes nor spending can grow more rapidly than the economy.

The amendment permits federal spending to grow more rapidly than the economy *only* if Congress explicitly votes to allow receipts to rise more rapidly than the growth of the economy. It takes a direct vote of a constitutional majority of both Houses of Congress to permit growth of federal spending to outpace growth of the economy. Or, federal spending may outpace economic growth if Congress approves, by a three-fifths majority vote, a deficit in which outlays from year to year exceed economic growth rates. Thus the federal government is not hamstrung; it can meet what may be regarded as increased genuine needs of the people, if it also were prepared to vote on the record for higher taxes or deficits to finance higher spending.

WARTIME WAIVER

Section 3. The Congress may waive the provisions of this article for any fiscal year in which a declaration of war is in effect.

In the event of a declaration of war, Congress has the discretionary authority to operate outside of the provisions of the amendment. Such a waiver would be on a year-to-year basis by concurrent resolution of Congress, as defined under Article 1, Section 8, of the Constitution. Congress would have to adopt annually a separate waiver for each fiscal year at issue.

BORROWING AND REPAYMENT OF DEBT

Section 4. Total receipts shall include all receipts of the United States except those derived from borrowing and total outlays shall include all outlays of the United States except those for repayment of debt principal.

The purpose of Section 4 is to exclude the proceeds of debt issuance from receipts. Thus, treasury notes and bonds would not count as receipts, but as the proceeds of selling debt. Similarly, the term "outlays" is intended to include all disbursements from the Treasury of the United States, both "on-budget" and "off-budget," either directly or indirectly through federal or quasi-federal agencies created under the authority of acts of Congress. Section 4 states that funds used to repurchase or retire Federal debt would not count as outlays. Interest accrued or paid in conjunction with the debt obligation would, however, be included in outlays.

The amendment permits Congress to plan for a budgetary surplus. Those surplus receipts, subject to the increase limit of Section 2, used to repay principal—that is, retire national debt—would not be counted as outlays. Should the government fully retire the national debt, the amendment would still allow the government to plan for an annual surplus, and even accumulate reserves. Interest earned on these reserves, however, would be subject to the revenue limit. (Admittedly, it would take generations for this scenario to develop.)

DATE OF IMPLEMENTATION

Section 5. This article shall take effect for the second fiscal year beginning after its ratification.

Section 5 stipulates when the amendment would take effect. If ratification were completed before September 30, 1982, the amendment would require Congress to adopt its first balanced budget statement before September 30, 1983; if ratification was completed before October 1, 1982, and before September 30, 1983, the first balance budget adoption would be required by September 30, 1984, so on.

THE CASE AGAINST THE BALANCED BUDGET AMENDMENT[3]

Since the publication of Arrow's classic work, *Social Choice and Individual Values*, a hardy, growing band of scholars has at-

[3]Excerpted from the chapter by Roger G. Noll, economist, in Laurence H. Meyer, ed., *The Economic Consequences of Government Deficits*, Economic Policy Conference Series, Kluwer-Nijhoff Publishing, Dordrecht, The Netherlands, 1983, pp. 201–209. © 1983 Kluwer-Nijhoff Publishing. Reprinted by permission.

tempted to use social choice theory to build a positive theory of government. Alternatively called social choice theory, public choice and formal positive political theory, this work investigates methods of collective decisionmaking in terms of their efficiency, their distributional effects and the existence and uniqueness of equilibrium. Applications have been made to small group decisionmaking, the structure of legislatures, and procedures for electing political leaders as well as undertaking referenda on policy issues.

The most fundamental level at which this theory can be applied is to the question of designing a constitution. A constitution establishes the rules of the political game. It defines the rights and obligations of citizens acting in various capacities as voters, owners of private property, candidates for public office and government officials. It describes the process for organizing the government, establishes the range of actions that government can take, defines the powers and responsibilities of various parts of government in the policymaking process, and even sets forth rules for changing the rules themselves. Moreover, the constitution is preeminent in the hierarchy of rules and procedures established by all organizations in society, private and public: constitutional principles always take precedence, by definition.

The papers by Aranson and Rabushka [previous articles defending the balanced-budget amendment] attempt to undertake a theoretical analysis of an issue of constitutional design: namely, what is the effect, normatively and positively, of adopting a constitutional rule requiring a balanced federal budget? I have phrased the question in a somewhat altered form than can be found in either paper, but the change is intentional—to emphasize that the problem is one in comparative equilibrium analysis, and that it has both positive and normative aspects. These distinctions are not always clearly made in the two papers. I have also been rather more comprehensive in defining the point of a constitution. To state, as does Rabushka, that the purpose of a constitution is to limit government is, in my opinion, narrow, confused and loaded. A view that I find more useful is that a constitution is a contract among citizens defining their rights, their mutual obligations, and the procedures they will follow to make collective decisions.

Both papers attack the issue of the balanced budget limitation in the following way. Both examine the formal theory of the political process to determine whether (a) it has a systematic tendency to produce a public sector that is too large; (b) it has a systematic tendency to produce lower tax revenues than expenditures; and (c) if the first two are true, an amendment to balance the budget will cure these problems. The two papers reach different conclusions: Aranson believes that one should answer the questions, respectively, as "probably," "probably," and "maybe," whereas Rabushka gives a confident "YES" on all parts.

In these brief remarks I simply want to dissent on all three points. I do so as a matter of political theory; my answers to the three questions would be: "Who knows," "probably not," and "probably not." But I wish to emphasize one central point: the economic theory of politics applied to the American system of government yields no firm results on any of these issues. Indeed, like most of rational choice theory, including microeconomics, it is far too general to produce definitive qualitative results. It is not even intended to do so. Instead, its purposes are to help one organize one's thoughts about how political processes work and, especially, to guide empirical research to explain and predict changes in political outcomes. It is not designed to tell us whether we need or want a constitutional amendment to balance the budget any more than it is designed to tell us whether women should have the franchise or citizens should be guaranteed freedom of speech.

First, rational choice models of the political system do not tell us that government is too big. At best, some parts of formal political theory tell us that some aspects of the political process work in this direction, under some conditions. The most famous body of theory in this field is the Arrow paradox and its ramifications. It says that in general majority-rule elections do not have a unique equilibrium and, moreover, that with appropriate selection of the agenda for voting on alternatives one generally can produce a final outcome that is strictly Pareto dominated by others. Interpreted in the context of the size of government, this theory implies that to err on one side is as likely as to err on the other. Government, *a priori,* cannot be said to have a systematic tendency to be either too big or too small.

Other theories that are richer in institutional details, while costly in making more assumptions, pay off in clearer results. But the effect of the American system of representative democracy on the size of government is still ambiguous. The primary results of these models deal with the mix and efficiency of government provision of goods and services. They state that certain kinds of policies will tend to be favored over others, and that certain methods of producing government services will be preferred over others. The foundation of these results is in the fact that the act of participation in the political process is itself a public good. Effective political participation has spillover effects because the resulting policy will affect everyone. Consequently, people will be moved to participate only when they have large enough stakes in an issue to make it worth their while to pay the costs of participation and when for some reason they do not elect to free ride. The conclusion derived from this is that narrow issues pertaining to well organized groups will receive relatively more attention than more diffuse issues spread over unorganized citizens, even if the aggregate stake of the latter exceeds that of the former. Using this conceptual model, it is not hard to think of situations in which public goods are undersupplied rather than oversupplied. For example, nuclear waste facilities provide diffuse public benefits of great value, but concentrate the risks on people who would live near them. Hence, attempts to build them tend to meet with such organized, vehement opposition that government is afraid to undertake them. The result is a hazardous condition of improperly managed nuclear wastes and an undersupply of waste management facilities. The general point is this: there is a tendency in a democratic form of government for the concentrated effects of a political action to be given greater weight than the diffuse effects. Consequently, some types of public goods will be in relatively too large a supply compared to others.

It is natural for journalists to observe that part of government tends to be a gigantic pork barrel machine, and therefore to conclude that government is too big. The problem with this conclusion is that it is based upon a fallacy that ought to be well known to social scientists: sampling on the dependent variable. Obviously, relatively little government activity will take the form of programs that are too small or even nonexistent, whereas much of it will be programs that are too big. It is correct to say that we probably spend relatively too much on public works; it is not at all correct to conclude, therefore, that government is too large because some programs are too large.

Another line of political theory investigates how the political process affects the design of government programs. The single member congressional district is the focus of this analysis, and the point is to explain and predict the consequences of the observation that representatives from such districts spend a great deal of time working as ombudsmen for constituents, as contrasted to making public policy. The result of this theory is that in order to preserve the possibility of responding effectively to citizen requests for help, a representative has an incentive to use bureaucratic means of providing public policies: regulations rather than emissions taxes or marketable emissions permits, project grants and contracts rather than block grants, etc. The result is inefficiency in the cost of providing public services. Costs of public goods are not minimized because it is worth it to legislators to use higher cost means of supply that enable them to intervene on behalf of constituents and thereby score points that will redound to their benefit on election day.

This theory says that government programs will cost too much per unit of output. Whether this means that total expenditures in the public sector are too high depends on the elasticity of demand for public goods. If demand is inelastic, expenditures are higher than they otherwise would be; but if demand is elastic, expenditures are too low. Whatever the expenditure effect, of course, the quantity effect is unambiguous if demand curves have negative slopes—higher price means less quantity. Hence, the effect of facilitation activities is almost certain to be to reduce the real output of the public sector.

So much for government being clearly too large. But what if, as an empirical matter, it is? This brings the second issue: is there a persistent tendency for deficits to be too large? Worth noting is the obvious: this is the only argument that supporters of the balanced budget need. The discussion of the actual versus optimal size of government is necessary only for an argument to limit expenditures.

The basic argument advanced in support of the notion that government is too prone to run deficits is that expenditures and taxes are more visible to individual citizens than are debts and money creation. A secondary argument is that deficits represent an intergenerational transfer from the future to the present. I will ignore the latter; it confuses the means of finance with the political selection of a division between consumption (private and public) versus investment (private and public). The less said about this argument the politer.

Certainly the question of the politics of tax policy is one of the most interesting—and least developed—components of formal political theory. Thus, we can speak less confidently about it than we can about the question of the size of government. Nevertheless, theory in this domain is developing quite similarly to theory about expenditures. Specifically, the most important results are about the form of taxation, rather than its level relative to expenditures.

Recall that the theory of expenditures relied upon two phenomena: the relative responsiveness of the public sector to well organized, narrow interests in relation to more diffuse, broader interests, and the activities of legislators as ombudsmen. Suppose in this milieu that citizens wish tax relief. Each citizen will have two types of avenues available: as a member of a diffuse group of voters who, *ceteris paribus*, can vote for politicians who favor lower taxes, and as a member of various particularistic interests, who will, among other things, favor particularistic tax preferences for themselves. The part of political theory that deals with the greater relative influence of narrow interests says that the latter avenue will tend to be more successful than the former. It also says that when a legislature raises taxes, it will tend to increase taxes that have an effect on more diffuse groups. The ombudsmen feature of representatives reinforces this tendency. Each legislator will try to provide specialized tax breaks for complaining constituents. Senator Russell Long, commenting on one of Congress' annual "Christmas Tree" tax bills, put the matter rather pointedly: "Don't tax you, don't tax me; tax that guy behind the tree."

The key point about formal political theory is that it imagines voters to be in a prisoner's dilemma on election day. They know that their representatives in the House and Senate have little

chance of affecting the winning position in Congress on major issues of public policy, such as the level of taxation or, indeed, the
overall size of any program or of the government itself. They do
know, however, that as government grows, it is increasingly important to have a legislative facilitator, someone who can provide
favors to constituents. And Congress, by fractioning itself into
myriad specialized subcommittees for programmatic oversight activities, has created an ideal device for providing small favors
through a timely phone call to an agency or a personalized break
in the annual tax "reform" bill. The structure of Congress not only
gives stability to the otherwise unstable majority rule process in
Congress, but by encouraging specialization, it creates an environment for mutually beneficial trades among members who have different committee assignments. Hence, it makes sense for voters to
give weight to facilitation as well as to public policy in voting for
legislators. Applied to the taxation case, this means relatively less
attention will be given to the overall level of taxation.

Of course, the prisoner's dilemma can be overcome if the general state of policy becomes so bad that even after accounting for
diffuseness, it becomes important in an election. This places a
check on legislators. There is no reason for them to run the risk
of widespread voter revolt when, by being good ombudsmen, legislators can remain incumbents almost as long as they wish. And,
historically, one of the two diffuse issues that more or less regularly raises the specter of defeat for an incumbent (the other is international affairs) is the state of the economy. Hence, to the extent
that running big deficits undermines the economy, there is a good
reason for a legislator not to vote for them, especially in light of
the ongoing opportunity to defuse the outrage of some unhappy
constituents in the annual tax bill.

Thus, formal political theory probably does have something
to say about the structure of the tax system and about why tax reform and simplification are so difficult to accomplish. But it probably has little or nothing to say about the question of deficits, for
much the same reasons it has nothing definitive to say about the
direction of distortion, if any, in the size of government.

As a practical matter, the argument that government is biased
in favor of deficits has more severe problems than are encountered

by the argument about size. The first question is why are deficits so small? What checks them at all? The empirical observation in support of the position that there is a bias in favor of deficits is that, since fiscal 1961, the federal budget has been in deficit every year except 1969. But in most years the economic significance of the deficit has been small. During the first ten years of this period (1961–1970), in only two years did the deficit exceed five percent of federal expenditures, and in only one did it reach two percent of GNP. In the next ten years, the deficits averaged ten percent of expenditures and two percent of GNP; however, the economy was weaker in the 1970s than in the 1960s, and one would expect that automatic stabilization would have caused higher deficits during this period in the absence of any political action to encourage them.

The second question about the bias toward deficits is why it is so recent a phenomenon? No explicit constitutional change altered the incentive structure of legislators. Rabushka argues that there was an implicit balanced budget amendment before the New Deal; however, the question remains why legislators, facing no explicit requirement, failed to respond to the incentives inherent in the political system for the first 150 years of the republic.

Indeed, to look at only the sign and not the magnitude of the bottom line of the budget is to overlook two very important facts. The first is that by far the most important predictors of the degree of imbalance in the budget are (a) the state of the economy; and (b) whether the country is at war. If neither of the above is straining the system, budgets are normally very close to balancing. The most important factor explaining the fact that the budget has been in the red for twenty two of the past twenty three years is that we have spent most of that period in either recession or the war in Vietnam. Second, the budgets of the past two years set new indoor records. Fiscal 1983 will be the highest deficit in relation to federal expenditures and GNP since World War II. The contest is not even close: in 1983, the deficit will be five or six percent of GNP, whereas the previous postwar record was around three percent. There is something incongruous about a President who speaks of the need to have a constitutional amendment to restrain him from responding to political incentives that other presidents have been substantially more successful in resisting. Perhaps he simply wants to assure the permanence of his entry in the Guinness Book of World Records.

Unlike the argument about the size of government, the argument about deficits can be subjected to empirical scrutiny. When it is, the validity of the argument is cast in even greater doubt. There simply is no reason to believe that the political system is biased in favor of deficits for the reason given.

Nevertheless, a third question still must be addressed: will the balanced budget amendment as proposed be a binding constraint? The answer here is quite simple: it is substantially less binding a constraint than the veto power of the President. Presidential vetos require a two thirds vote to be overridden, whereas the proposed balanced budget amendment requires sixty percent. A President who wanted to balance the budget would have an easier time of it than erstwhile balancers in Congress would have under the amendment.

Even above this detail, there is a more important element of political reality to contend with. The problem is the enforceability of such an amendment. A deficit can be proven to be a reality after a fiscal year draws to a close. Prior to that, revenues and expenditures are based on estimates and forecasts. To enforce a balanced budget requirement necessitates estimating a deficit in a politically meaningful way—within the executive and/or congressional branches of the government. If the political incentives were present for a majority in Congress to enact a deficit and the President to sign it, they will also be present to employ the services of that mythological forecaster of recent years, Rosy Scenario.

Even if Rosy fails, the form of enforcement is a shut down of government. Grandma's social security check will not be in the mail, etc. This is an extraordinarily high political price for a legislator to pay. Moreover, if the deficit is too large for even Rosy to paper over, most likely the country will be in a recession, so that legislators will be equally dissatisfied with the alternative of raising taxes or cutting expenditures—assuming either could be enacted and implemented quickly enough to affect the overall budget balance. The easy path will surely always be to override the balanced budget amendment.

The preceding conclusion seems to be verified by the experience of states that have balanced budget requirements. A recent study by the Congressional Budget Office found that "states faced with statutory and constitutional limitations on debt appear to have avoided the limitations successfully by creating various authorities that are allowed to issue 'moral obligation' bonds." Moral obligation bonds pledge the coercive taxation powers of the state as collateral for the bond, thereby permitting a quasi-governmental entity outside the budget to finance itself by floating loans at the state bond rate. What this phenomenon illustrates is the ingeniousness of political entrepreneurs at "inventing around" institutional constraints. If there were a political bias in favor of a government that is too large and too much in deficit, a constitutional amendment to deal with these problems would face the difficulty of preventing ways to get around it by engaging in off budget activities that have the same overall effect on the economy. An obvious example is greater use of tax incentives and loan guarantees to channel private expenditures into areas the government would abandon if the budget had to be smaller. Another example is the use of regulation to require certain kinds of private expenditures as a condition for doing business, or Richard Posner's idea of "taxation by regulation."

On all three counts, then, the case for the balanced budget amendment is insubstantial. But suppose each of the three subissues had gone the other way: suppose we could prove that the government is too large, too prone to deficit, and susceptible to effective control in both regards. Would it naturally follow that the constitutional approach is the appropriate one?

Here the answer must be more speculative. It depends upon philosophical questions about the nature of the social contract, which inevitably turn on questions of individual values. Nevertheless, there is a compelling argument for thinking twice about limiting expenditures and deficits.

The guts of the question about the performance of government have to do with the way it allocates resources among groups, between public and private goods, and between consumption and investment. To limit the size of the federal government, subject to a requirement that a substantial majority (not a bare majority) approve a proposal to do otherwise, is to constrain future citizens in their attempts to find an optimal allocation of resources. It is also to give more voting power to those who favor private goods in comparison to those who favor public ones. Additionally, it is to build an institution that works against a precept that is generally regarded as desirable in government, namely positive responsiveness: i.e., the direction of a change in government policy should be the same as the direction of shift in the tastes of citizens. Finally, it is to set in concrete a current macrotheoretic wisdom, shared only by some, about how deficits and the size of government affect the overall economy. Rabushka, quoting Jefferson, elevates a particular macroeconomic theory to the status of universal truth. But it is a good thing lots of other universal truths of Jefferson's time—bleeding as a treatment of fever, for example—were kept out of the Constitution.

The American Constitution has proved to be remarkably resilient, and has served as the foundation for a remarkably durable system of government. One plausible reason this is so is that it stands for the most part above matters of day to day politics. It deals with how we should govern ourselves and what individual rights the government should protect, but leaves to the political process the problem of deciding the amount of public goods to be provided and the method of paying for them. The proposed budget amendment upsets this feature of the political system. It elevates to the status of enduring, universal value the concept of a fixed size of the federal budget as well as whether the bottom line is written in red or black. And by so doing, it inhibits the responsiveness of government in ways that cannot be justified to losers on the ground that to do so protects some democratic principle related to fairness, justice and the rights of individuals. Unlike most of the Constitution, the proposed amendment appears to losers as the work of one faction to enhance their control of the policy outcomes of the government. It strikes me that this is the stuff of which political instability is made.

DEALING WITH DEFICITS
AND THE RISE IN FEDERAL SPENDING[4]

At a time when, alas, economist jokes are in vogue, I would like to add my favorite wisecrack about our profession: If all the economists in the world were laid end to end, it might be a good thing. This sour remark is instigated by my having to listen to, and occasionally participate in, what seems to be endless debates on whether budget deficits really matter, and, if so, on what arcane basis of measurement. I finally have found a short cut that reconciles the great intellectual wisdom of our profession with the practical concerns of participants in and observers of financial markets. Thus, I conclude that deficits do not matter—but that Treasury borrowing and money creation surely do!

Having disposed of this weighty subject so quickly, let me go on to examine several current policy questions relating to federal finance. First, let us consider the nature of the changes made in federal outlays by the Reagan Administration and second, let us analyze some of the economic implications, covering both military and civilian programs. This task, it turns out, is a bit more complicated than one might expect.

How Much Has the Budget Been Cut?

To begin, it is difficult to directly compare the current estimates of outlays under the Reagan program with those contained in President Carter's last budget message, presented in January, 1981. Since then, the publications of the Office of Management and Budget have generally "adjusted" the Carter numbers for a change that it believes President Carter should have made— providing for what is now considered to be an adequate national defense. That procedure does have its advantages. That is, by as-

[4]Excerpted from the chapter by Murray L. Weidenbaum, economist and former chairman of the President's Council of Economic Advisers, in Laurence H. Meyer, ed., *The Economic Consequences of Government Deficits*, Economic Policy Conference Series, Kluwer-Nijhoff Publishing, Dordrecht, The Netherlands, 1983, pp. 223-234. © 1983 Kluwer-Nijhoff Publishing. Reprinted by permission.

signing the present Administration's increases in national defense
to the numbers associated with the previous Administration,
OMB can take credit for its cuts in civilian outlays while ignoring
the increases in military outlays. It should be noted that this unusual procedure is an OMB practice. The White House Office of
Policy Information, in at least two of its recent publications, uses
the more straightforward approach of comparing Carter's numbers with Reagan's numbers, assigning to the present Administration all of the changes it made in the budget, both up and down.
However, these latter publications lack the detail contained in the
budget statements.

What all this means in practice is that, if we want to compare
Reagan with Carter, we must dig the Carter reports out of our
archives and compare the data in them with the figures in the most
current Reagan budget publications. I will note in passing that
this is a chore that the average journalist working under a tight
deadline may forgo. In any event, I find such statistical explora-
tions useful for those engaged in more leisurely scholarly pursuits.

Table 1 contains a first effort to make such a comparison. It
compares total outlays for fiscal years 1982–1984 as estimated in
the last Carter Budget report with those shown in the most recent
Reagan Administration budget report. Clearly, the Reagan

Table 1. Reagan and Carter Budget Estimates
(In billions of current dollars)

Fiscal Year	Defense		All Other		Total		Differ- ence
	Carter	Reagan	Carter	Reagan	Carter	Reagan	
1982	$184.4	$187.7	$554.9	$543.3	$739.3	$731.0	$ −8.3
1983	210.4	221.5	606.9	540.0	817.3	761.5	−55.8
1984	237.8	253.4	652.5	559.1	890.3	812.5	−77.8
1985	267.8	292.5	700.1	582.2	967.9	874.7	−93.2
1986	299.5	332.0	750.8	600.7	1050.3	932.7	−117.6

Source: Federal Budget for Fiscal Year 1982; Mid-Session Review of the 1983
Budget

spending totals in current dollars (unadjusted for inflation) are lower in each year than the Carter figures. The current Administration's much slower growth in civilian spending more than offsets its increases in defense outlays, but by about one half of the 1981 tax cuts—about $350 billion versus over $700 billion for the five year period 1982–86.

More sophisticated comparisons can be made. For example, the comparison can be restated in terms of constant dollars using in each case the inflation assumptions that accompanied the respective current dollar estimates. The results based on the GNP deflators are contained in table 2. The differences between the two sets of projected outlays are very much smaller than in table 1, about $23 billion when viewed in real (deflated) terms over the period 1982–86.

A variation of this theme is contained in table 3, where the CPI assumptions are used to adjust both sets of outlay projections. In this case, the results are more ambiguous. That is, using the CPI as a deflator, the aggregate estimates for fiscal years 1982–1986 under the Reagan programs are shown on balance to be a bit higher than the Carter estimates—by about $7 billion.

Table 2.   Reagan and Carter Budget Estimates
(In billions of constant 1972 dollars, using GNP deflators in respective documents)

Fiscal Year	Amount		Differ- ence
	Carter	Reagan	
1982	$345.0	$354.9	$ +9.9
1983	351.7	347.1	−4.6
1984	355.4	347.7	−7.7
1985	361.2	353.0	−8.2
1986	368.8	356.1	−12.7

Source: Federal Budget for Fiscal Year 1982; Mid-Session Review of the 1983 Budget

Table 3.   Reagan and Carter Budget Estimates
(In billions of constant dollars, using CPI deflators
in respective documents)

Fiscal	*Amount*		Differ-
Year	*Carter*	*Reagan*	ence
1982	$241.0	$253.5	$ +12.5
1983	245.0	247.4	+2.4
1984	247.6	247.0	−.6
1985	251.7	250.0	−1.7
1986	257.0	251.5	−5.5

Source: Federal Budget for Fiscal Year 1982; Mid-Session Review of the 1983 Budget

It does seem clear that, especially in relation to the 1981 tax cuts, the net spending reductions in the past twenty months seem to be quite modest. It is not surprising, therefore, that current estimates of the budget deficit for the next several years are unusually high (see table 4).

Table 4.   Projections of the Federal Budget
(Fiscal Years, In billions of dollars)

	1982		1983		1984		1985	
	OMB	CBO	OMB	CBO	OMB	CBO	OMB	CBO
Outlays	$731	$733	$762	$788	$812	$844	$875	$910
Revenues	622	621	647	633	720	692	801	757
Deficit	109	112	115	155	92	152	74	153

Source: Office of Management and Budget, Mid-Session Review of the 1983 Budget, July 15, 1982; Congressional Budget Office, The Economic Outlook: An Update, September 1982.

The Problem of Entitlements

When we probe beneath the aggregate spending levels, we find that entitlements or payments to individuals constitute the largest category of the budget. In recent years, entitlement payments also have been the most rapidly growing budget category. It therefore is quite appropriate that increasing attention is being given to this area. I have little to add to the extensive public debate. I am, however, struck by the vast amount of ignorance attached to the largest entitlement, social security benefit payments.

Given the current focus on the desire to reduce those outsized budget deficits, any discussion of possible change in social security outlays is immediately attacked as an effort to balance the budget on the backs of social security pensioners. It is true that facing the problem of social security financing would likely result in smaller budget deficits. But—and this is the fundamental point that is usually ignored—even if the federal budget were in such great shape that we could declare dividends out of the surplus, we would still have to face the basic problem that the social security system is not adequately financed.

Over the years, Congress has been more aggressive in voting benefit increases than in enacting the social security tax increases to pay for them. Also, demographic and economic trends have turned out in recent years to be more adverse than assumed in the system's actuarial calculations. Thus the public debate on social security seems to have the issue backwards: our attention is needed on the question of social security finance, not because of the budget deficits but to ensure that the program fully meets the disbursements to which it is committed. But we must recognize that, although it is the largest single item, social security is only one of the many entitlement programs. A comprehensive budget restraint effort must take a hard look at the other components in this category, including veterans' pensions and government employees' retirement benefits.

The Question of National Defense Spending

Let us turn to the second largest category of budget outlays, national defense. Here we should acknowledge at the outset that there is a broad based agreement on the need to expand US national defense spending. Both the Carter and Reagan budgets projected significant growth in defense spending in real terms for each of the five fiscal years 1982–1986. As would be expected, there has been considerable discussion and disagreement over the specifics of the buildup, including the question of how rapid an expansion in military spending is desirable. But it should be recognized that none of this is a debate between hawks and doves.

Among the specific questions raised is the economic feasibility of the currently contemplated schedule of military outlays. As the Council of Economic Advisers (CEA) stated in its annual report accompanying the President's Economic Report of February 10, 1982, "any economic effects . . . must be assessed in the context of the overriding need for maintaining the level of defense spending necessary for national security." Moreover, the 1981–82 recession has resulted in such substantial amounts of excess capacity in American industry that, at least for the next year or two, there is likely to be adequate industrial capacity to meet military and civilian needs. But it is useful to look beyond, to the middle of the decade when significant economic growth may coincide with the peak of the military buildup. In such circumstances, capacity questions would arise. The CEA annual report deals with that eventuality, pointing out three results of the defense buildup that can be anticipated:

1. The substantial transfer of resources in the durables sector to defense production may increase relative prices in at least some of the affected industries. Both the Department of Defense and private purchasers may have to pay more for goods from these industries. This premium is likely to increase with the size of the defense budget.

2. Increased demand may produce delays in the delivery of military goods. Delivery timetables that seem realistic today may, in some cases, become obsolete as producers try to accommodate both the defense buildup and rigorous expansion in civilian investment at the same time.

3. Some temporary crowding out of private investment may occur. Defense procurement uses many of the same physical resources needed for private investment in civilian producer durables and the Defense Production Act gives defense priority in the market place. Some private firms may turn to foreign sources for materials while others may cancel or postpone plans for expansion.

Along similar lines, a private economic consulting organization—Data Resources, Inc. (DRI) of Cambridge, Massachusetts—has stated that the concentration of the planned military increases within the procurement and research and development accounts implies weapon production growth rates more rapid than those which occurred at the peak of the Vietnam buildup. Moreover, the present expansion occurs after a decade of steady reductions in the defense industrial base.

DRI also pointed out:

. . . the combination of the increasing defense shares and the acceleration in growth rates raises concerns about industrial capabilities and spillover impacts on the economy.

DRI goes on to note that, with the implementation of significant investment programs in both plant and equipment and skilled labor forces, the problems of price pressures, bottlenecks and crowding out of civilian demand "could be constrained to isolated instances." See table 5 for some examples of extremely rapid growth rates in future defense industry requirements. Over the six year period 1982–87, double digit increases in annual output are shown for many industries, ranging from semiconductors to computers. The DRI conclusion is that the uncertainties about the capabilities of the defense industrial base and its linkages to other critical economic variables "will continue to cloud decisions regarding the defense budget." This point is enhanced when we consider that the author of the paper just cited heads up the ongoing analysis, commissioned by the Pentagon, of the economic impacts of the defense program.

A more recent Data Resources report is even less sanguine, pointing out that, since 1948, there has never before been a period of sustained growth in real defense spending such as that now planned. This more recent study concludes that the projected requirements for such large increases in defense output raise obvious questions about the ability of industry to meet them without ad-

Table 5.   Projected Increases in Output
in Major Defense Supplying Industries, 1982–1987
Average annual real percentage growth in projected output

Industry	Annual Increase in Total Output, 1982–87	Annual Increase in Defense Output 1982–87
Radio & TV communication equipment	11.2%	15.7%
Aircraft	12.8	18.6
Aircraft engines and engine parts	13.0	16.3
Aircraft parts & equipment, n.e.c.	11.2	14.7
Complete guided missiles	11.5	15.2
Electronic components, n.e.c.	11.2	17.2
Tanks and tank components	22.6	27.1
Ammunition, excluding small arms, n.e.c.	15.0	15.2
Motor vehicles parts and accessories	6.3	20.5
Motor vehicles	6.7	27.8
Other ordnance and accessories	13.5	14.4
Communications, excluding radio and TV	6.9	10.3
Semiconductors	13.7	20.2
Miscellaneous machinery	6.9	15.3
Electronic computing equipment	12.6	16.8
Aluminum rolling and drawing	7.9	17.9
Miscellaneous plastic products	8.5	17.3
Primary aluminum	7.3	17.1
Plastic materials and resins	8.8	17.8
Special dies, tools and accessories	8.2	15.8
Telephone and telegraph equipment	11.5	16.4
Metal stampings	7.0	18.6
Industrial trucks and tractors	9.9	14.1
Machine tools, metal cutting	9.2	15.7
Iron and steel foundries	4.3	13.2

Sources: Compiled from Data Resources, Inc., Defense Economics Research Report, August 1982.

verse implications in terms of costs and leadtimes. A variation of that theme appears in a recently released study by the US Department of Commerce which reminds us that defense expenditures do not affect all industries equally, but have "highly concentrated industrial impacts."

Table 6.　　　Demand and Supply Balance
of Selected Defense-Intensive Industries, 1979–1988

Industry	Growth in Output Requirements 1979–1985	Potential Increase in Supply Economically Efficient[a]	Maximum Attainable[b]
Guided missiles and space vehicles	86%	86%	98%
Ammunition, except for small arms, n.e.c.	50	119	133
Tanks and tank components	83	83	107
Small arms	7	40	50
Small arms ammunition	82	72	89
Ordinance & accessories, n.e.c.	33	112	128
Iron and steel forgings	19	33	39
Lead smelting and refining	12	−4	11
Aluminum production and refining	15	16	16
Nonferrous rolling and drawing, n.e.c.	33	33	37
Brass, bronze and copper foundries	32	25	37
Electronic computing equipment	83	106	122
Semiconductors and related devices	76	106	116

[a]Based on concept of preferred capacity, defined as the level of operations plant managers prefer not to exceed because of considerations of cost and economic efficiency.
[b]Based on concept of practical capacity. Assumes no material, utility, or labor shortage and no consideration of increased pay or other input costs as limiting factors.
Source: US Department of Commerce, Bureau of Industrial Economics.

The Commerce Department examined a somewhat different time period than did DRI, but the conclusions are fairly similar. For most of the 58 major defense supplying industries which it studied, the Department of Commerce reported that existing capacity is sufficient to supply the projected military and civilian demands through 1985. However, the Department said that, should further capacity expansion not take place in some of these industries, meeting projected 1985 requirements would mean using outmoded, economically inefficient capacity, which would increase costs and prices. For example, requirements for lead smelting and refining are projected to rise by 12 percent from 1979 to 1985, but economically efficient capacity is estimated to decline by 4 percent. Likewise, requirements for brass, bronze, and copper foundries are shown to increase by 32 percent, but economically efficient capacity is expected to rise by 25 percent (see table 6).

The Commerce study reported that some of our basic metal-processing industries will likely need to increase their dependence on foreign sources of supply in order to meet the stepped-up military demands. For example, the electrometallurgical products industry (which was specifically noted because of its "qualitative importance to defense") met 27.6 percent of its needs with imports in 1979, and is expected to increase that dependency to 45 percent in 1985. Likewise, zinc smelting and refining is anticipated to increase its import dependency from 33.4 percent in 1979 to 45 percent in 1985. Imports of miscellaneous refined nonferrous metals are estimated to comprise 66 percent of the industry in 1985, compared to 55.7 percent in 1979 (see table 7). It is ironic to note the matter-of-fact way in which the Commerce Department reports such increased foreign dependence for some of the key defense producing industries when on many other occasions, the hoary national security argument is trotted out to justify a host of subsidies to sectors of the economy far less closely related to defense output.

The point of these data should not be misunderstood. Drawing attention to the economic impacts of the contemplated expansion of military outlays does not call in question the desirablity of the expansion but, rather, its feasibility and cost in the period contemplated. An implicit assumption arises from these concerns: any adjustment of scheduled defense outlays to conform more closely with expected domestic production capabilities would result in slowing down the rate of increase in defense spending in the next few years and thus lower the projected deficits.

Table 7.   Changing Import Dependence of Selected
Defense Industries

Industry	Imports as Percent of Total Supply	
	1979	1985[a]
Iron and ferroalloy ores mining	25.0	28.1
Small arms	9.4	10.6
Blast furnaces and steel mills	10.1	13.0
Electrometallurgical products	27.6	45.0
Lead smelting and refining	8.8	11.0
Zinc smelting and refining	33.4	45.0
Aluminum production and refining	8.9	10.0
Refining of nonferrous metals, n.e.c.	55.7	66.0
Machine tools, metal-cutting types	17.2	23.0
Machine tools, metal-forming types	9.2	13.6
Ball and roller bearings	10.5	14.0
Instruments to measure electricity	8.9	13.0
Semiconductors and related devices	20.6	30.0
Electronic components, n.e.c.	8.0	11.5
Optical instruments and lenses	14.1	19.5

[a]Estimated
Source: US Department of Commerce, Bureau of Industrial Economics

Conclusions

In responding to the concerns over the continuing large federal deficits projected for the next several years, I have emphasized the desirability of another hard look at the spending side of the budget. Unlike another round of tax increases, restraining government expenditures is entirely consistent with the efforts of President Reagan to strengthen the private sector by reducing the size of the federal government.

Three major areas of the budget appear to be promising candidates for further pruning of outlays—above and beyond the Reagan Administration's important existing efforts to ferret out low priority and postponable items and to curb waste, fraud, and abuse:

The So-called Entitlements. These open-ended commitments on the budget range from social security and medicare to medicaid, welfare, veterans' pensions, and the retirement systems for federal employees, military and civilian. In the short run, reductions could be made in the generous formulas for computing annual cost-of-living increases (the COLA clauses) contained in many of these programs. More fundamental changes could be made by recognizing the great extent to which many of these "social insurance" programs have taken on a subsidy or welfare aspect— e.g., providing benefit payments far more generous than those that would result from basing the benefits solely on employee/ employer contributions plus earnings on those contributions. Making benefits subject to income taxes—as is now done with private retirement benefits—would reduce the net subsidy payment, especially to those taxpayers with substantial amounts of other income.

The Defense Budget. Official projections of future military outlays, in real terms, have risen successively during the last two years from five percent to seven percent to nine percent or more per annum. There seems to be little justification offered of the economic feasibility of this sharply upward movement. Without prejudging the results, intensive analysis should be given to the military budget, comparable to the tough minded attitude quite properly taken toward many civilian spending activities of the federal government. Surely, reducing the extent of cost overruns and bottlenecks in defense production will help to maintain the necessary support for the strengthened national defense that is needed in the dangerous world in which we live.

Because of the potential capacity problems, a given cutback in nominal military spending would actually result in less than a proportional reduction in real procurement outlays. This would come about because of reduced price pressures on military purchasing generally.

Imbedded Subsidies. Advocates of smaller federal budgets typically focus on entitlements and/or defense spending because these are the two largest categories. However, it does not take a great deal of research to discover a third category of the budget, "all other." Contrary to widespread belief, not all of the items in this part of the budget are social programs, nor have they been cut to the bone. Generous and expanding programs such as subsidies to dairy and tobacco farmers and sugar producers quickly come to mind. There is no serious justification for these subsidies, and many others like them in other departments of the federal government. Such special benefits to specific segments of the society are in the budget simply because of the political muscle of the producer or other special interest groups supporting them. The Congressional Budget Office has presented several comprehensive listings of potential budget cuts that could be made. There is no shortage of information. All that is lacking is the will to cut more.

On reflection, we need to realize that at times—such as earlier this year—the failure to curtail federal spending leads to pressures for tax increases. Given the outlook for rising deficit financing, if we are to avoid further reversals of the Administration's most welcome tax cuts, more of the existing sacred cows in the federal budget should be taken out of pasture and led to slaughter.

THE DEBTOR ECONOMY: A PROPOSAL[5]

The economy this autumn is still growing, inflation is low, unemployment is down. Whether this proves the success of supply-side economics or is just another deficit-driven Keynesian recovery will be argued for years to come. It seems to me clear that the enormous federal budget deficit was largely responsible for the recovery and that it could become extremely dangerous if it is not controlled. The important question now is how the recovery can be sustained in view of all the urgent financial problems facing the economy. These include the record domestic budget deficit and

[5]Reprint of an article by Felix Rohatyn, investment banker and chairman of New York State's Municipal Assistance Corporation. *The New York Review of Books*. 31:16–21. N. 8, '84. Reprinted with permission from *The New York Review of Books*. Copyright © 1984 Nyrev, Inc.

the record deficit in the balance of trade; they also include a national debt that will soon amount to \$2 trillion and a third world debt that will soon amount to \$1 trillion. In effect, we are now borrowing heavily from our children to finance a great many expenditures we really cannot afford. This is neither moral nor prudent.

Will the current growth of the economy eliminate these deficits? Those who believe that it will might recall that the most important rule in business is never to bet the entire company. By betting so heavily on growth, we are running the risk of having our national debt overwhelm the federal budget. Financing that debt threatens to absorb far too much capital needed for investment in the domestic economy if it is to sustain growth, improve its comparatively low rate of productivity, and compete successfully abroad.

The Congressional Budget Office has estimated that by 1989—even assuming an average real growth rate of 4 percent between 1983 and 1989—the national debt will amount to almost 50 percent of GNP, up from 35 percent in 1983. Interest on the national debt will be 16 percent of the budget and it will be growing swiftly. To pay that interest, a government would have to make a grim choice: either to cut social programs and the military budget beyond anything now contemplated or to increase taxes constantly.

It has been argued that the level of the debt need not cause concern because, in 1960, the national debt stood at close to 50 percent of GNP. Important differences, however, exist between 1960 and today. First, more and more of our debt is now financed from abroad (last year about \$80 billion), a situation unlike that of 1960. We are therefore at the mercy of foreign investors who, should they lose confidence in the US economy, could create a dollar crisis and higher interest rates in short order. Without the additional capital available from abroad, our low rate of national savings would not be sufficient to accommodate the foreseeable needs of both government and private business.

Two other differences from the economic situation in 1960 are instructive now. The 1960 debt was the result of borrowing during World War II and the Korean War; and the budget deficits between 1960 and 1965 hovered between zero and 1.3 percent of GNP. A rapidly growing economy in the 1960s kept the deficit below 3 percent of GNP even at the height of the Vietnam War. The debt as a percentage of GNP dropped rapidly, and lower interest rates kept the impact on the budget within bounds.

Now we have a completely different situation. Despite a growing economy the continuing deficit requires the government to borrow between $180 and $240 billion each year. The debt is growing much more rapidly than GNP. Interest on a steadily growing debt feeds on itself, like a form of financial cancer. The situation of the US too closely resembles that of New York City between 1970 and 1975 and that of Argentina, Brazil, and Mexico between 1975 and 1982.

There is much talk of the need for greater fairness in any future economic policy, and much of it is justifiable. Between 1980 and 1984, the share of disposable family income of the poorest fifth of the population actually declined from 6.8 percent to 6.1 percent. The share of the most prosperous fifth of the population increased from 37 percent to 38.9 percent. Clearly that is not an acceptable trend in any society committed to the idea that all parts of the population should benefit from growth and prosperity.

In dealing with our budget problems, however, we cannot create the illusion that fairness means that the government will simply do more for the poor, the unemployed, the retired, the minorities. All these groups stand to suffer from a fiscal breakdown that could cripple economic growth, or cause a great surge of inflation, or both. If sacrifices have to be made to avoid those consequences, fairness means that the largest sacrifices must be made by those who can best afford them; but, unfortunately, some sacrifices will also have to be made by all groups above the poverty level.

This was the general principle we tried to follow in resolving New York City's fiscal crisis. It should be the basis for the new policies for taxes and entitlements that will be needed to deal with the problems of the budget and the national debt. In one way or another, the most urgent problems facing the US in the world economy—the rise of the dollar, the safety of our banking system, the dangers of protectionism—are all related to our federal budget deficit.

The Budget and the National Debt

The budget deficit is causing the national debt to grow at a rate almost twice the growth in GNP. That is a prescription for national bankruptcy. If that rate continues, interest on the national debt will grow more than $200 billion a year by the end of the decade, preventing more and more vital government programs from being carried out as government revenues are consumed in debt payments. In addition to the obvious costs being incurred domestically, the international effects are increasingly dangerous. As a result of escalating indebtedness, the level of the dollar is constantly pushed upward, putting many American industries in difficulty, unable to compete with cheaper foreign imports at home or to sell in markets abroad. The government's borrowing requirements, a major factor in maintaining interest rates at very high levels, increase the risk to our banking system of large-scale failure by third world countries to pay their debts. We are fostering speculation instead of investment. We are purchasing short-term prosperity by starving the rest of the world of badly needed capital and destablizing the international monetary system. Since we live in a world market whether we like it or not, we cannot continue much longer.

Some, including President Reagan, have argued that rising interest rates are largely a matter of psychology—that they move up in response to the premature and self-protective fears of bankers that deficits will lead to inflation. Although high interest rates are not solely caused by deficits, this is a superficial view. Several factors are at work in the rise of interest rates, among them the deregulation of financial institutions. But the most important factor of all, in my view, has been the vast increase in the use of debt by all the sectors of the economy. The US government debt grew from $290 billion in 1960 to $1.4 trillion in 1984. Corporate debt grew from $40 billion in 1960 to $400 billion in 1983. Mortgage debt grew from $470 billion in 1973 to $1.7 trillion in 1983. Third world debt grew from $80 billion in 1970 to $800 billion in 1984.

Neither the savings rate nor the capital of financial institutions or corporations has kept up with this explosive growth of debt, much of which has to be constantly rolled over and refinanced. Monetary policy is not the answer to this problem; we must reduce the demand for credit. While there is no magic number for the appropriate proportion of debt to GNP, it makes obvious sense to stabilize an apparently runaway situation and to limit the growth of the debt as closely as possible to the growth of GNP.

Eventually we will be forced to do something about the deficit. But what should we do and when? The answer to "when" is easy; as soon as possible and preferably before the next economic downturn. If we have to close the budget gap during a period of recession we would run risks that seem to me very dangerous indeed. We could then be faced with a growing deficit as a result of recession, increasing interest rates and a collapsing dollar as a result of capital outflows, and a banking crisis as a result of both. This is not a risk worth running. A deficit reduction program should begin as soon as possible after the election and no later than early 1985. The question of "how" and at what velocity is more difficult.

Vice-President Mondale has proposed to reduce the deficit by two-thirds—or about $160 billion—by 1989. He proposes about $85 billion in new taxes (about $25 billion in corporate taxes, and the rest from income taxes); about $24 billion in expenditure reductions and $51 billion as a result of interest cost reductions. President Reagan, for his part, has asserted that no new taxes are required and that continued growth and savings in government efficiency will eliminate the deficit—a position he restated in the first debate with Mondale. That hardly seems likely.

I have several reservations about the Mondale plan. It relies too heavily on tax increases—especially personal income taxes—and is vague on how expenditures would be controlled. As a result, the financial markets and the Federal Reserve will likely be skeptical about its effectiveness and the reduction in interest rates Mr. Mondale hopes for would not take place. But the plan is, at least, a serious one, worth serious discussion. It does not, as the administration has done so far, wave away the deficit and debt problems with assurances that growth and tighter control of executive spending will somehow make them go away.

With the economy as strong as it is now, I would suggest a program to close the gap more rapidly and more rigorously by about $150 billion over three years—half through taxes, half through budget cuts. The Congressional Budget Office projects a deficit of about $216 billion for fiscal 1987. Such a reduction would leave about $60 billion of deficits—about 2 percent of GNP. The lower interest rates that would result from a lower deficit should eliminate much of that balance as the cost of government borrowing falls.

Taxes

Higher taxes will not create economic growth. Simply taxing the rich will not abolish poverty, or create jobs, or lead to investment in improved technology. If taxes are increased, this should be done in the way least likely to slow down the economy. Any tax increase, moreover, should also be combined with a simplification of the tax system that would result in lower personal rates and fewer deductions and loopholes.

Taxes should be increased in two ways. First, by a tax on consumption—not an indiscriminate sales tax, but on a tax on energy consumption that would encourage energy conservation and the use of small, fuel-efficient cars instead of the present return to large ones. (Its other advantages could be considerable, as we shall see.) Second, a minimum tax should be imposed on corporations, which are, in many cases, paying little or no taxes at all. In 1975, corporate taxes made up 15.6 percent of federal revenues; in 1983 they made up only 6.2 percent of revenues.

The bill of Senator Bradley of New Jersey and Congressman Gephardt of Missouri suggests, in my view, the most useful pattern for personal taxes. It proposes a minimum rate of 14 percent—which would apply to four out of five taxpayers—and a maximum personal income tax rate of 28 to 30 percent, while eliminating many deductions and most tax shelters. If the maximum personal income tax rate is around 30 percent, moreover, there would be no need for the proposed "indexation" that would adjust tax rates to take account of inflation. Indexation is a necessary brake on spending when marginal tax rates are high; its benefits are reduced as marginal rates come down. Under this tax structure, moreover, capital gains could be taxed at the same rate as ordinary income. A minimum corporate income tax somewhere between 15 and 20 percent (depending on the definition of income) seems to the equally sound. The Bradley-Gephardt plan, if it were combined with the elimination of indexing and a minimum corporate income tax, could raise an additional $20 billion by the third year.

A consumption tax on energy could be applied through a combination of excise taxes on crude oil and oil import fees. These energy taxes should raise between $40 billion and $50 billion annually; phased in over three years, they would not hurt the economy. Part of these taxes would undoubtedly be translated into higher gasoline prices. However, gasoline prices in Europe are $2.50 to $3.00 per gallon; here such a tax would still leave gas prices at 50 percent of European prices.

The critical question concerning any new tax increase is whether the revenue raised will simply be translated into spending or whether it will genuinely be used to reduce the deficit. The only way to ensure that the energy tax revenues would be used to offset the deficit would be to set them apart from other revenues. One way to do so would be to create a trust fund into which all new energy taxes would be paid. The trust fund would be managed by the Federal Reserve Bank, which would use the proceeds solely for the purpose of retiring a part of the federal debt.

In order to make this arrangement an effective deterrent to spending, two additional features could be attached: first, it could be combined with a limitation on the growth of the federal debt to a fixed percentage of GNP. Second, it should provide for the energy tax (or another tax segregated for debt repayment) to increase automatically by the amount that the debt limit is raised, in any one year, beyond those limits.

These provisions would ensure that the government's unrestrained freedom to borrow would be both sharply curtailed and combined with an offsetting tax penalty. By reducing the need for government financing by some $40 to $50 billion per year, it would also make more money and credit available to the financial markets for investment. It would ease the pressures driving up interest rates and might allow the Federal Reserve to carry out an easier monetary policy without risk of inflation.

A variation of this arrangement was used when New York City sales taxes were segregated from the expense budget to guarantee the payments on MAC bonds. Segregating a new source of federal revenue for the sole purpose of reducing the size of the national debt deserves serious consideration now. It will not relieve either the president or Congress of the need to control the growth in expenditures; on the contrary, a comprehensive revision by Congress of our tax and budget structure remains our most urgent national need. However, if deficits are inevitable because of the demands of a great many political interests, a mechanism such as the energy trust fund not only would help to keep down interest rates, but would offset to some degree our low national savings rate. In effect, the trust would be a national savings plan. As for a constitutional amendment to balance the budget, that would be like a unilaterally declared nuclear freeze: it would give a quite unreal illusion of safety, without any guarantee of the real thing.

Military Budget Cuts

Annual defense outlays will grow from $300 billion to $400 billion from fiscal year 1986 to fiscal year 1989. Virtually every conceivable military system is being acquired: MX, B-1, Trident II, air-, sea-, and ground-launched cruise missiles, Stealth, to name just a few. Funds have already been appropriated for the "Star Wars" defense system. I am not a military expert, but I am familiar with large organizations. There is no question in my mind that the military budget, like that of practically any huge organization, can be cut significantly without affecting our military capacities. The Congressional Budget Office, among others, has made a convincing case for a multibillion-dollar annual savings in the procurement of weapons systems. The Committee on National Security has proposed a "prudent defense budget" slowing the growth of outlays from $282 billion in fiscal year 1986 to $365 billion in fiscal year 1989. Military pensions and other personnel costs also seem to me capable of being cut substantially. An annual rate of savings of $25 to $30 billion, by the third year of such a program, can and must be achieved.

Social Programs

No one can talk convincingly about reducing the budget deficit without also discussing entitlements—social security, Medicare, Medicaid, etc. Establishing fair limits to the growth of entitlements may be the most important issue facing this country. Medical advances are being made on every front—in pharmaceutical and DNA research, in diagnostic techniques, in operating-room procedures and equipment. The resulting increase in life expectancy could be dramatic. How this will affect not only social costs, but the agonizing choices to maintain life or accept death, is now only dimly perceived. Recent speculation that applying every available technology to every patient could eventually require more than 100 percent of GNP is not as wild as it may sound. Significant changes and savings are obviously necessary and a detailed program for ways of containing costs will have to be worked out. Lowering social security benefits for people in the higher income brackets will probably become necessary. So will taxing some benefits, putting a limit on cost-of-living allowances, changing benefits for new entrants into the social security system, etc.

I doubt that the problem of medical care, however, can be dealt with just as a matter of making a number of more or less painful adjustments. We have to reexamine the entire system, in which the various attempts to regulate the rising fees charged by doctors have not been notably successful, and in which a two-class system of medical care has, for the most part, prevailed.

We would do well to examine objectively other systems of medical care to see what we can learn from them. The following description of the Canadian system is suggestive:

Canada's provincial health-insurance systems, like ours, use third-party reimbursement. You go to the doctor, and the insurance system pays the bill. But in the United States, the insurer might be Blue Cross Blue Shield, or Prudential, or Medicare or one of hundreds of others. In Canada, there is only one insurer—the provincial health plan. Each patient simply pays the bill with a credit card, and the insurance system reimburses the provider. As a result, Canadian hospital administrative costs are about one sixth those of American hospitals. Moreover, with one unified system, the state has a much easier time regulating rates, procedures, and fees. In the early 1970s, when Canada first adopted its comprehensive plan, it was spending about the same total health outlay as the United States: roughly 7.3 percent of GNP. Since then, health-care costs in Canada have stabilized at about 7.5 percent of GNP, while in the United States, they have soared to the 9–10 percent range.

This does not mean that the US should or could simply adopt the Canadian system. But if the Canadians have managed to contain costs and provide reasonably good medical services through comprehensive health insurance, then Congress should ask why we have not been able to do so here.

Freeze on Spending

In view of the complexity of these budget cuts and their urgency, I believe a one-year freeze on all spending programs is worth considering while a new tax plan is worked out. This would save about $40 billion during the first year and may well be the most practical approach for the time being. In any case, Senator Dole was right to recommend that a bipartisan economic "summit" conference be held immediately after the election, to deal with the budget. If we wait until the next recession, it will be too late.

Any new approach to social programs will be irresponsible if it does not confront the deep question of poverty in the US. It is a melancholy, but undeniable, fact that there are more poor people in this country today than there were a few years ago. The income disparity between classes seems to be growing larger, and there is little on the horizon to suggest change for the better. The recent Urban Institute study stated:

From 1980 to 1984, the typical middle class family's income rose from $18,857 to $19,034 or up about 1 percent. The average income of the poorest one-fifth of all families declined from $6,913 to $6,391, or by nearly 8 percent, whereas the average income of the most affluent one-fifth increased from $37,618 to $40,888, or by nearly 9 percent.

Although the tax and budget policies of the Reagan administration no doubt aggravated this problem, it derives from deep trends in the economy that would face any administration.

Economic growth and new technology now have a tendency to leave behind larger and larger numbers of people who lack the skills, education, or social advantages that would enable them to compete for jobs. The technological changes now being made will put the same downward pressure on employment in service industries as it has in manufacturing industries. More and more people will have fewer and fewer chances to accumulate even a minute amount of savings or capital.

A one-year freeze on expenditures would permit a serious review of social welfare programs on the basis of need and means. The current low inflation makes this the most appropriate time both to forgo current cost-of-living adjustments and to reconsider the entire welfare system. Any new approach must explicitly recognize the quite different claims of those who need Medicaid and school lunches, for example, and those who benefit from Medicare and federal pensions.

Taxes have to be weighed on the scale of fairness. Not only should American business pay a minimum corporate tax but the effects of any new energy taxes on lower-income families should be mitigated. Those in low-income brackets who drive to work could, for example, receive low-interest loans enabling them to trade in their old cars for fuel-efficient, small, new, American-made automobiles. Moreover, we can collect more in taxes from well-to-do people if we have a system of lower tax rates with few deductions than we could if we had higher rates and more shelters. Under such circumstances, gains on capital should have no preference over ordinary income.

President Reagan's election in 1980, and the subsequent tax and budget programs of his administration, showed that there was, rightly or wrongly, a political consensus that income redistribution had gone too far. However, taking from the poor to give to the well off, in time of high prosperity, is not tolerable for long in a democracy. Income redistribution may not solve all the problems of poverty but the current trends have to be reversed at the very least.

Again I think we must examine a wider range of possible solutions. Recently, for example, Dr. David Owen, one of the leaders of the Social Democratic party in England, proposed a new plan for creating capital and savings for those at the low end of the British economic scale. He suggested that the British government distribute the shares of government-owned companies such as British Airways, British Telecommunications, etc., to those below a certain level of income. This would create some capital and savings for people who would probably have little access to both for many years. The London *Financial Times* supported this suggestion.

Although the US government does not own industrial concerns to the same extent that the British government does, nevertheless the US government is in many businesses. It not only owns TVA and Conrail but has large holdings of coal, timber, and gas and oil leases, among others. The recurrent proposals to "get the government out of business" in the US might be reconsidered with such a plan as Dr. Owen's in mind. Instead of selling Conrail, TVA, or others, the government might set them up as operating companies and devise ways to distribute their shares to those at the lower end of the income scale. Instead of transferring more income from one set of Americans to another, we could transfer capital assets from the government into the hands of its needy citizens.

A year's freeze of the budget would enable the administration and Congress to consider other fundamental changes needed by our society. Aside from slowing the growth of military spending, should there not be a shift from military to domestic public construction in view of the shameful conditions of our inner cities, many of our roads, much of our low-income housing? The Japanese and Germans are suggesting a gradual loweing of the work week to spread employment. The forty-hour work week has been in effect for forty years while technology has exploded and productivity in many industries has grown significantly. Bearing in mind the need to stay competitive, and the dangers of interference in labor-management relations, the government could still stimulate reconsideration of such longstanding industrial practices. These and many more questions concerning our basic social priorities should be assessed apart from the passions of an election year.

The Dollar and the International
Monetary System

By most standards, including purchasing power and relative levels of inflation, the dollar is overvalued by 25 to 30 percent in relation to the major European currencies and the yen. The result has been a projected $130 billion trade deficit for the US balance of trade and a disaster for many domestic industries, which have been making strong demands for protectionist measures. The level of the dollar is partly caused by high interest rates, partly by the fact that we are forced to borrow abroad to finance the deficit, and partly by the attractiveness of US markets as political and economic havens for capital. For Japanese and European exporters, the overvalued dollar has meant high profits; it has helped to keep US domestic inflation down by keeping commodity prices from rising. At the same time, the cost of the dollar has been extremely harmful in the third world and to the nonindustrialized countries generally.

An orderly, gradual reduction in the value of the dollar, as a result of responsible budget actions, is highly desirable; a precipitous decline, as a result of large capital outflows, would create serious problems. The Federal Reserve, for example, might well raise interest rates to stem capital outflows and to finance the deficit just at the time when the economy could least afford it. That would produce the worst possible outcome. The dollar will always command a premium simply because of the political and economic power of the United States throughout the world; there is no need to superimpose a surcharge because of our budget problems.

Convincing action to cut the budget, and the fall in interest rates that should result, will help in turn to reduce the overvaluation of the dollar. Equally important, however, is the need to rebuild and maintain an orderly international monetary system. The dramatic gyrations of foreign exchange rates, the explosion in world indebtedness, speculative flows of money during the last twelve years have had a major destabilizing effect on world trade, on the economies of many countries, and, as a result, on the political stability of a large part of the world. Although it is impossible to get back to a fixed-rate system, we should seriously consider negotiating a system where the main trading currencies would be allowed to fluctuate only within certain limits. This would mean coordination among the major central banks and finance ministries of the US, Western Europe, and Japan. Only the US can take the lead in proposing such arrangements, and the US can do so only if it first takes serious action to put its own financial situation in order.

The Banking System and International Debt

Many factors were responsible for the current dangerous overextension of the US banking system. Petrodollar recycling and the creation of a trillion-dollar unregulated Eurodollar market in the 1970s; deregulation of financial institutions coupled with overaggressive lending and lax oversight in the US; careless borrowing by overseas borrowers—all these had a part in creating a dangerous situation. About $800 billion in international debt is owed to Western banks. Some $350 billion is owed by Latin America alone, about $100 billion to US banks. Banking regulation permits our banks to make loans in an amount roughly equal to twenty times their capital. A number of our largest banks have lent more than 100 percent of their capital to Brazil, Argentina, and Mexico alone, which have a combined debt of $230 billion. It is worth noting that the total capital of all US banks is probably less than $100 billion. Notwithstanding current claims in the press that the crisis is largely over, the problem will not go away.

There is no neat solution to this problem. A long process of adjustment is clearly needed in which the US government should have an active part. Two goals should be paramount: to protect the US banking system, while maintaining our banks in a position to finance our economic growth; and to adjust the interest and the maturity dates of the debt to the social and economic capacity of the borrowers to pay, under continued but modified supervision by the IMF. Continued rollovers, as in the most recent agreement with Argentina, simply serve to buy time. In the case of Argentina, it may not even be very much time.

Lower interest rates throughout the world as a result of a reduced US budget will certainly help to achieve both objectives. To the argument that the government must not interfere with the market system, the answer is that we are doing so right now. In rescuing the Continental Illinois Bank from bankruptcy, we are now in fact nationalizing one of the ten largest banks in the country. The FDIC has already provided $5 billion to save the bank and the amount will probably go higher. The FDIC will ultimately own 80 percent or more of the bank.

Continental Illinois carried $40 billion in assets on its books. The FDIC and the Federal Reserve have unconditionally guaranteed all of its deposits, payments to all its general creditors, and complete liquidity in its operations. I have no doubt myself that the bank could not have been allowed to fail, but the sweeping nature of the US government commitments—far beyond anything we have seen since 1932—has yet to be analyzed and understood. If the government follows the precedent of the Continental Illinois rescue, and it seems safe to conclude that it will, it has unconditionally guaranteed all the depositors (not just those up to $100,000), all the general creditors, and the liquidity of all major US banks. That would be a trillion-dollar commitment.

After the election, the US should take the intiative in dealing with the international debt problem. It should not wait passively for demands to be made when politicians, treasury officials, and bankers here and abroad suddenly become fearful of collapse. A plan should be developed by the Federal Reserve and the US Treasury, together with the IMF and the banks, that will provide longer and easier repayment terms for Latin American borrowers. Some US government guarantees would have to be part of any such plan. The condition for revised terms should be continued fiscal restraint on the part of the borrowers, and open and safe markets for US capital. Such a plan should keep our banks strong and active while requiring them both to maintain higher levels of capital and to use more conservative accounting so as to protect depositors and investors. As in the Continential Illinois case, the costs would have to be allocated among bank shareholders, creditors, and US taxpayers.

Having already put the credit of the US behind our large banks, we should use the leverage conferred by this commitment to defuse a situation that could, if it is allowed to continue, cause havoc not only to the banks but to all of Latin America. The current formula for dealing with this problem is to impose austerity on Latin America in order to maintain the myth that our bank loans are worth 100 cents on the dollar. I believe this policy, if it continues, will create more communists during the next decade than Fidel Castro and the Sandinistas could during the next fifty years.

International Trade and Protectionism

As long as the international monetary system remains chaotic and the dollar overvalued, the strains in trade relations between the US and other countries will become acute. Both here and abroad, the demands for protection for domestic industries will rise, whether in the form of tariffs, export quotas, or government subsidies conferring advantages over foreign competitors.

Last May I recommended to the International Trade Commission an industrial policy that would give the steel industry *temporary* protection in exchange for explicit undertakings by the industry to modernize. These would include commitments by management to new investments in modern facilities and funds for displaced workers; by the unions to wage restraints; and commitments by both to profit sharing and improvements in productivity. The ITC, in announcing its decision to recommend steel import quotas to the president, specifically asked that they be made conditional on such undertakings. This is the central bargain of industrial policy. It should apply to the auto industry and the UAW when the issue of quotas on Japanese automobiles again arises during the coming months.

President Reagan's decision was to reject mandatory quotas but to require "voluntary" agreements from steel-exporting countries which are the equivalent of an 18 percent market share agreement. In order to maintain a façade of "free trade" and "market mechanism," the adminstration and the American consumers will get the worst aspects of protectionism (i.e., quotas and higher prices) without any of the benefits of an explicit industrial policy (i.e., industry commitments to invest and union commitments to wage restraint and productivity). An opportunity has been lost that we will all pay for.

If as a result of timely budget actions the value of the dollar is lowered, the need for quotas or tariffs would obviously be reduced; so would the period during which protection from foreign competition would be justifiable. Protectionism is destructive. Allowing our basic industries to be destroyed because of an overvalued currency is suicidal. Both can be avoided if interest rates and the value of the dollar are brought down as a result of new fiscal policies, and a rational use of industrial policy.

The current strength of our economy, coupled with the low rate of inflation, provides a spectacular opportunity to ensure long-term growth for our economy. If the problems I have discussed are dealt with soon, the American economy could respond strongly and steadily for the long term. However, if we wait for the next recession before we act, we could be faced with higher deficits, higher interest rates, a collapsing dollar, and a banking system under great pressure. The choices facing us then will make the current ones look easy.

DEFICIT REDUCTION: A NATIONAL IMPERATIVE[6]

My topic concerns this nation's most crucial economic issue: the federal deficit and the imperative to reduce it—not next year, not tomorrow . . . but now.

As the CEO of one of the largest financial services organizations in the country and in my capacity as Chairman of the Business Roundtable's Budget Task Force, I have spoken many times on this subject. In fact, I consider the debate so important, I'll speak to all who will listen and will help do something about it.

[6]Reprint of a speech by Robert D. Kilpatrick, chairman and chief executive officer of CIGNA Corporation, delivered at the Town Hall of California, Los Angeles, A. 2, '85. From *Vital Speeches of the Day*. 51:470-3. My. 15, '85. Reprinted with permission.

Today, I speak to you as a citizen who shares with you the same problems, the same hopes, the same desire to live in a country that will continue to grow and prosper. A country that will continue to provide the opportunities to create a secure and honorable life for our generation and for future generations.

These opportunities have been the source of America's unique greatness. But today—due to the federal deficit, a deficit we can control if our will is strong enough—our nation's ability to live up to its promise is being threatened. Not by an external enemy, mind you, but by our own hand and our inability to wrench ourselves away from the habit of profligate spending.

The issue is clear; it's as obvious, frankly, as a fist in the face. Continued and growing indebtedness can lead only to disaster. What is far less clear, of course, are the solutions. They are the source of the current debate—a debate that reflects the reluctance of many groups or interests to be the first to accept the pain that any major reduction in federal spending is bound to cause. We know that we must make hard choices. It's never easy, especially when most of us are enjoying a better life and a higher standard of living than ever before. But, ladies and gentlemen, I'm afraid the party is over.

In talking about the budget and the deficit, it's necessary to describe numbers that often seem indescribable. For the current fiscal year, for example, it's estimated that the budget deficit will reach more than $220 billion—four times the size of the deficit that existed 10 years ago. The amount is difficult to comprehend unless you can associate it with something familiar. I'm sure many of you have heard the analogies before: A billion seconds ago the U.S. entered the Second World War. A billion hours ago, the first primitive man reared up on two legs. And a billion dollars ago—in terms of this nation's spending—was this morning.

Yes, our government has already spent its first billion dollars of the day, with two more billions to go before nightfall. And we are spending $600 million a day more than we are taking in in revenues. Simply stated, that is the heart of the problem.

We in this generation are clearly responsible for the hole we are in. We have had the dance; now we must pay the piper. But what of our children and their children? We will saddle each child born this year with a federal debt of $50,000 and, if our spending ways continue unabated, we will add to that a liability of $1,000 for each year of their lives. If effect, you and I are asking our children to pay 22 cents for every dollar of services we are enjoying today.

This is the magnitude of the problem and the reason why it cannot continue unchecked. I do not ask or expect everyone listening to agree with the solutions I will describe today. But we must understand that if we do not solve this critical problem today, we will face a much deeper crisis tomorrow.

I do not mean to suggest that economic disaster is at our doorstep. Ours is a strong and vital economy. We have immense technological capacity and unmatched skills in the marketplace. In free markets, unfettered by artificial barriers, we can compete with anyone.

But the word "crisis" is not an exaggeration. Not when you realize the truly destructive effects an out-of-control deficit can have on our nation, our businesses and on each and every one of us. Excessive deficits:

—Devour our net savings.

—They are draining investment capital from other nations, and in the process, have made America a debtor nation for the first time since the First World War.

—They are a primary cause of high real interest rates.

—They add to the enormous burden of public debt;

—Threaten the health of the economy;

—Fuel the growing trade deficit; and

—Risk a new wave of inflation.

No, given all this, the word "crisis" is not an exaggeration. To brush aside the issue of the deficit is a dangerous deceit, and the only ones we deceive are ourselves.

Today, fewer and fewer Americans remain the victims of this self-deceit. A recent national poll tells us, for example, that more than half of all Americans expect the deficit to grow larger in the coming year, and they are becoming more worried about the economic impact of the shortfalls. The difficulty is that although Americans understand that higher deficits are a significant threat to the economy as a whole, only one in 20 single it out as a major threat to their own personal economic situation.

In this respect, the deficit is far more like a hidden cancer than a sudden heart attack. More like erosion than an earthquake. It eats away at our economic health without cataclysm, and so it is hard to muster either the support or the will to act until it is too late. But make no mistake. The deficit affects all of us personally.

Today, for example, it takes nearly 40 percent of all individual tax payments to pay the interest on the national debt, which now totals approximately $1.8 trillion. And that total debt will increase—to $2 trillion by 1986—as will the related interest expense, if the deficit is not brought under control.

A deficit-induced rise in mortgage interest rates also has a powerful effect on Americans. Just one percentage point—from 12 percent to 13 percent—translates into one million fewer families that could qualify for an eighty percent loan on a medium-priced home.

The deficit affects employment, too. High deficits have led to the over-valuation of the dollar, and this, over time, has badly hurt our ability to sell our goods and services overseas—as clearly evidenced by last year's record $123 billion trade deficit. The result? Diminished exports have already cost the American economy between one and two million jobs.

The flow of jobs out of the United States directly affects the hard-working citizens who comprise the real strength of America. The tragedy is that even if the deficit were reduced tomorrow, many companies already will have created international subsidiaries or will have begun purchasing their component parts from foreign sources. And so a job lost today may be lost forever.

Some people argue that there is no need to fix what isn't broken. The economy is prospering. We can grow our way out of the deficits, they say. But it should be clear to everyone that we cannot do this as long as our aggregate government spending grows faster than the economy. And that is exactly what it has been doing for the past five years. Without strong, immediate action it can only grow worse.

The Congressional Budget Office, for example, projects a $249 billion deficit in Fiscal Year 1988. At best, that is a staggering economic burden to carry. But if we should stumble a little along the way, if we should suffer a recession, the resulting deficits would make these projections look absolutely rosy. They would become an intolerable fiscal Sword of Damocles, hanging over our heads. So the question for us—for this nation—becomes not "Should we?" But "When?" Not "Can we?" But "How much?" Not "Who?" But "Everyone."

Clearly our first priority is to take a hard, objective look at federal spending and concentrate on its reduction. Our efforts must include sacred cows which have for years been considered untouchable. We must focus on the big ticket items in our spending plans, including defense, and all non-means tested entitlements: those programs in which benefits are paid automatically—like Medicare and Social Security—without respect to income or assets or ability to pay.

The Business Roundtable's Task Force has spent many months researching the deficit issue, working with some of the most respected economic minds in the country. It is clear to us— and I hope it is clear to you—that the Congress and the Administration must move forcefully in the next few months to cut the deficit and to move towards balancing the federal budget in the near term.

Last December, the Administration set goals to achieve that objective—to cut the deficit to no more than four percent of the gross national product next year, declining to no more than two percent in Fiscal Year 1988.

Unfortunately, the President's budget falls short of its own goals. Simply, the Administration has not gone far enough to reduce the deficit. And it has left virtually intact the two largest budgeted programs: defense and Social Security.

Certainly we of the Business Roundtable believe in a strong national defense. But we also believe that a strong defense presupposes and depends upon a strong economy. We believe defense must contribute more to deficit reduction than the Administration proposes. The Administration's proposed defense expenditures— described as a $9 billion cut—appear to us to be a $30 billion increase over the previous year.

We believe several possible approaches exist to cutting proposed defense expenditures. Three percent real growth for defense—rather than the eight percent figure in the proposed budget—for example, would cut outlays $64 billion below the levels in the budget and still meet our NATO commitments, as I understand them. And, I believe a one-year freeze on defense budget authority would save $94 billion through Fiscal Year 1988.

Some argue that a freeze on defense would cut too deeply. Others say to cut programs rather than freezing budget authority. But these are two examples of serious proposals to cut defense well below the proposed amounts. They are worthy of public discussion, examination and debate.

The Business Roundtable also is in favor of broadening the spending freeze to include cost of living adjustments for Social Security recipients. The Administration's budget proposes to freeze all other non-means tested cost of living adjustments. But this is not enough. It is necessary and appropriate that this concept be applied to the largest program in the budget as well. I believe our Social Security recipients, however, should only be asked to accept such a sacrifice if it is part of a broad-based effort to solve the most serious national problem that we have before us. The failure to find a solution will affect their future, as well as those yet to retire.

Of course, another approach to deficit reduction—offered by some—is to simply raise taxes. As a solution, this is an illusion.

If we do not first control our spending, the federal government will continue to buy out the store. It will have more money in its pockets, and the deficit will climb right back to where it was. No, ladies and gentlemen, just like at home, it is our spending habit that needs to be curbed before we talk about adding income.

As I mentioned cutting the deficit will be painful in the short term for almost everyone in America. But I am convinced that Americans are willing to share the pain if they believe that everyone else is carrying a fair share of the burden.

Unfortunately, whether the perception is right or not, many Americans do not believe that this is what the Administration intends. They see programs being threatened—like student loans or small business supports—that affect their pocketbooks, while defense, as an example, remains relatively untouched. Let me repeat—in achieving deficit reduction there can be no sacred cows. Defense and non-means tested entitlements must be considered as part of any reduction or freeze.

I would like to make two crucial points here.

First, I think we can all agree that the very poor should be spared as much pain as possible. Therefore, further benefit cuts in means-tested programs for the most needy should be avoided. We should continue to search for economy in these programs, of course—to root out waste and fraud—but that won't save the big dollars. A country as rich as ours can afford fairness and compassion. Those who are better off must bear the burden of putting our fiscal house in order. Thus, it is my hope that we as a nation can agree that further benefits cuts in means-tested programs for the most needy should be avoided.

Second, we should fully understand that most non–means tested entitlement dollars are directed to the elderly. In fact, at least 80 percent of all these entitlements go to this rapidly growing segment of our society.

Clearly, our budget problems cannot be solved without affecting the elderly in some fashion. Yet, it is clear that their advocates would support certain cuts—if only they could be sure that everyone else received a fair share of the medicine. The American Association of Retired Persons, for example, stated to the Senate Budget Committee that its members could support a package that included constraints on Social Security and Medicare if other budget items, such as tax breaks and defense, were similarly constrained.

I am sure that the AARP's willingness to share in the sacrifice provided the Senate Budget Committee with the encouragement it needed to recommend a one-year freeze on cost of living adjustments to Social Security, a recommendation the Committee made in its recently approved budget.

Such an example proves that we can make the right decision when faced with hard choices. To me, that is one of our greatest strengths as a nation. As proposed by the Senate Budget Committee, a freeze is a good beginning. It will lower the base from which we must cut and make further deficit reduction in subsequent years more manageable. But a freeze is not a permanent solution. It will not address the basic structural imbalance between federal spending and revenues. That will require additional cuts and, perhaps, the elimination of some programs.

All of these programs have a highly vocal constituency. And these are the voices that the Congress listens to each time it begins to act with courage and conviction. But let's make no mistake about it: We are the special interests. It is our children's college loans, our parents' Social Security, the SBA loan or crop subsidy someone in this audience wants—these are the programs we have to cut. We might as well fact facts: "We have met the enemy and he is us."

Ask yourself: Would we create today the programs the President proposes to eliminate? Would we spend as much on new education programs or on job training or to subsidize home mortgages, as we will even if Congress enacted all of the President's proposed cuts? We simply must hold existing programs to the same tough standards we would demand of new programs. We must measure them against the demands of today's fiscal crisis or we will not have the resources to meet new needs in the future.

This is where you can help. Nothing will be accomplished if the deficit remains a political football. Nothing will be gained by hoisting the flag to see who and how many salute each interest group's favorite program. Each of you needs to write your senators, your representatives and President Reagan. The country needs you to raise your collective voices today, when our economy is still strong, when our people still have jobs and the promise of a better future. Urge your own representatives to agree on a package of program cuts that will spread the immediate pain as broadly as possible to assure that the ultimate gain involves everyone as well.

Everything must be on the table. And the package—with the support of a consensus of Americans—must be voted on soon. If the delay is long and debate lingers, we will be into another election cycle. The gravity of the problem demands that we put partisanship and self-interest aside. If our political representatives hear from you and other community and business leaders, I believe they will act. I believe they will make the choices that are needed. Help convince your representatives that both the Administration and the Congress should make deficit reduction the number one priority and that nothing should sidetrack these efforts.

If we can agree on nothing else, I hope we can agree on this: from business, from labor, from the elderly, from the young, from educators, and financial markets, from the local and state governments, let us all recognize the critical importance of reducing the federal deficit, and let us make these concerns known. Let us act in unison.

Something must be done to remove the weight of an ever-increasing federal debt from our collective shoulders. Today, this debt comes to nearly $9,600 for every adult in the nation, and it affects every citizen who is worried about a mortgage, a college education for the kids, or just the monthly rent and food on the table. Without action, today's dreams will become tomorrow's real life nightmares. If we do not begin to reverse the tide of red ink now, interest payments alone in the year 2000 will equal the total annual deficit of Fiscal Year 1984.

Let government action on the deficit be fair and measured. Let us acknowledge the need for such action. And most important, let it happen now.

It would indeed be historic if, through this Town Hall forum, that kind of message could be sent to the Administration and the Congress. A message that says, "You have been given a mandate to re-examine the spending decisions you made in earlier years, to challenge the conventional wisdom that you can't do this or that or that the American people will not sacrifice if asked to do so with reason and fairness. Act with courage and with care to permit the economy to prosper by solving the deficit crisis and solve it quickly before it is truly out of control."

BIBLIOGRAPHY

An asterisk (*) preceding a reference indicates that the article or part of it has been reprinted in this book.

BOOKS AND PAMPHLETS

*Buchanan, J. M. Public debt. International encyclopedia of the social sciences, vol. 4, pp. 28–34. Crowell Collier and Macmillan, Inc. '68.

Buchanan, J. M., Burton, John, and Wagner, R. E. The consequences of Mr. Keynes. The Institute of Economic Affairs, London. Hobart paper no. 78. '78.

Buchanan, J. M. and Tollison, Robert D. Theory of public choice: political applications of economics. University of Michigan Press. '72.

*Buchanan, J. M. and Wagner, R. E. Democracy in deficit: the political legacy of Lord Keynes. Academic Press, New York. '77.

Federal Reserve Bank of Minneapolis Research Department Working Paper 210. '82. A monetarist approach to federal budget control. P. J. Miller.

*Foreign Policy Association. Great decisions '85. 205 Lexington Ave. N. Y., N. Y. 10016. '85.

Hardin, C. M. and Chilton, K. W. Budget control and indexed entitlements: are they compatible? Center for the Study of American Business, Washington University, St. Louis. '81.

Kuttner, Robert. The economic illusion: false choices between prosperity and social justice. Houghton Mifflin. '84.

*Lerner, Abba P. The burden of the national debt. In Income, employment and public policy: essays in honor of Alvin H. Hansen. Norton. '48.

McKenzie, R. B. Incentives for a balanced project. Washington, D. C.: Heritage Foundation backgrounder no: 207. '82.

Mills, Gregory B. and Palmer, John L. The deficit dilemma: budget policy in the Reagan era. The Urban Institute Press, Washington, D. C. '83.

*Noll, Roger G. The case against the balanced budget amendment. In Meyer, Laurence H., ed., The economic consequences of government deficits. Kluwer-Nijhoff. '83.

Organisation for Economic Co-operation and Development. Budget financing and monetary control. Monetary Studies Series. OECD, Paris, '82.

Palmer, John L. and Sawhill, Isabel V. The Reagan record. Ballinger. '84.

Pechman, Joseph A., ed. Setting national priorities: the 1984 budget. Washington, D. C.: Brookings Institution. '83.

*Rabushka, Alvin. A compelling case for a constitutional amendment to balance the budget and limit taxes. In Wagner, Richard E., et al., Balanced budgets, fiscal responsibility, and the Constitution. Cato Institute, Washington, D. C. '82.

Schick, A. Congress and money. Washington, D. C., Urban Institute. '80.

Shepsle, K. A. Constitutional regulation of the U. S. budget. Contemporary Issues Series 1, Center for the Study of American Business, Washington University, St. Louis. '82.

Stein, J. L. Monetarist, Keynesian and new classical economics. New York University Press. '82.

United States, Congress, Congressional Budget Office. Baseline budget projections: fiscal years 1982–1986. Washington, D. C.: Government Printing Office. '81.

United States Congress, Congressional Budget Office. Defense spending and the economy. Washington, D. C.: Government Printing Office. '83.

United States Congress, Congressional Budget Office. Reducing the deficit: spending and revenue options. Washington, D. C.: Government Printing Office. '83.

United States Congress, Joint Economic Committee. Subcommittee on Monetary and Fiscal Policy. Jl. '81. 97th Congress; 1st session. Deficits: their impact on inflation and growth. Staff study by R. E. Weintraub, Supt. of Docs. Washington, D. C. 20402. '81.

United States Congress, Senate. Balanced budget–tax limitation constitutional amendment; report to the Committee at the Judiciary, 97th Congress, 1st Session, report no. 97–151. Supt. of Docs., Washington, D. C. 20402. '81.

*Weidenbaum, Murray L. Dealing with deficits and the rise in federal spending. In Meyer, Laurence H., ed., The economic consequences of government deficits. Kluwer-Nijhoff. '83.

PERIODICALS

America. 143:71-2. Ag. 16-23, '80. Balanced budgets and the poor. R. Kazis.

America. 149:161-2. O. 1, '83. Fiscal and political deficits.

America. 150:229. Mr. 31, '84. Wishing away the deficit.

America. 150:310-11. Ap. 28, '84. Reducing the deficit.

Atlantic. 249:10+. My. '82. Endless deficits. James M. Fallows.

Atlantic. 251:18+. F. '83. Less red ink. M. Friedman.

Aviation Week and Space Technology. 120:24-5. F. 27, '84. High deficit called threat to defense fund support. W. Flora.

Black Enterprise. 14:27. Ap. '84. In the red again with Reagan: federal budget FY 85. D. C. Ruffin.

Business Week. p 54-5. My. 26, '80. Balanced budget that is bound to fail.

Business Week. p 81. Ag. 2, '82. A deficit time bomb is ticking. L. Walczak.

Business Week. p 84-7+. Ag. 16, '82. The built-in deficit.

Business Week. p 94. Ag. 30, '82. Dealing with the basics of closing the deficits.

Business Week. p 26-7. S. 6, '82. A deficit the markets can't forget.

Business Week. p 24-6. Je. 6, '83. Recovery shrugs off the deficit.

Business Week. p 45. O. 24, '83. Why Reagan can't jawbone the deficit away. S. H. Wildstron.

Business Week. p 15. N. 7, '83. How double deficits are distorting the economy.

Business Week. p 46. N. 7, '83. The perils of ignoring the off-budget deficit. S. Lee.

Business Week. p 42-3. N. 21, '83. Bob Dole's long-run strategy for shrinking the deficit.

Business Week. p 36-7. N. 28, '83. How the deficit could cripple long-term growth. S. H. Wildstrom.

Business Week. p 12+. D. 5, '83. Why the deficit hysteria is unjustified. P. C. Roberts.

Business Week. p 129. D. 19, '83. Dole will keep the deficit issue alive. L. Walczak.

Business Week. p 24. Mr. 12, '84. The market prods Congress into tackling the deficit.

Business Week. p 49-54+. Mr. 26, '84. How to cut the deficit.

Business Week. p 16. Je. 11, '84. Only a bold stroke can cure deficit hysteria: a flat-rate tax. P. C. Roberts.

Business Week. p 23–4. Jl. 2, '84. Finally, a deal shapes up on the deficit.

Business Week. p 157. Ag. 13, '84. Deficit infighting flares up again. L. Walczak.

Business Week. p 32–3. S. 24. '84. A one-sided debate on the deficit.

Business Week. p 34. S. 24, '84. Can the U. S. grow its way out of the deficit? S. H. Wildstrom.

Business Week. p 37. O. 22, '84. The deficit keeps spooking Wall Street—no matter what. A. Bianco.

Business Week. p 62+. O. 22, '84. Local surplusses won't slay the monster deficit.

Business Week. p 17–18. D. 3, '84. The house of cards supply siders built. L. Chimerine.

Business Week. p 26–7. D. 3, '84. Reagan's deficit dilemma. S. H. Wildstrom and L. Walczak.

Business Week. p 62–4. D. 31, '84–Ja. 7, '85. Washington will keep dancing around the deficit. S. H. Wildstrom.

Changing Times. 36:8. N. '82. That balanced budget amendment: down but not out.

Changing Times. 37:8. My. '83. How serious is the federal deficit?

Commentary. 77:60–2. Je. '84. Deficit thinking. M. J. Ulmer.

Commonweal. 111:549–50. O. 19, '84. Deficit debating.

Congressional Digest. 63:33–64. F. '84. Controversy over the federal budget deficit.

Esquire. 101:82–5. My. '84. The shadow over the trillion-dollar honeypot. A Smith.

Esquire. 102:87–8+. Jl. '84. Alice and Bill and the struggles at budget gap. A. Smith.

*Federal Reserve Bank of Atlanta Economic Review. 67:6–17. Ag. '82. A primer on budget deficits. J. R. Barth and S. O. Morrell.

Federal Reserve Bank of St. Louis Review. 63:3–10. Mr. '81. Deficits and inflation. S. E. Hein.

*Forbes. 132. Sp. issue: 23. Fall '83. The wealth of the nation can handle the deficit with ease. Malcom S. Forbes Jr.

Forbes. 132:287. D. 5, '83. Ready for a move? B. Weberman.

Forbes. 133:311. Ja. 2, '84. Bond market and Martin Feldstein. A. Bladen.

Forbes. 133:31. Mr. 12, '84. One promise Mondale would keep. M. S. Forbes Jr.

Foreign Affairs. 62:1037–57. Summer '84. Trade and debt: the vital link-
   age. William E. Brock.
Fortune. 101:9+. F. 25, '80. Ballooning federal deficit this year.
Fortune. 105:41–2. F. 22, '82. Making room for the deficit.
Fortune. 105:50–5. F. 22, '82. How to cut those deficits—and why.
   A. F. Ehrbar.
Fortune. 105:31. Mr. 8, '82. Skywriting. D. Seligman.
Fortune. 105:73. My. 31, '82. What's at stake in the deficit now?
Fortune. 105:71. Je. 14, '82. A straitjacket (with some zippers) for the
   budget.
Fortune. 105:77–8+. Je. 14, '82. Americans' hate affair with deficits.
   E. C. Ladd.
Fortune. 106:50–3. N. 15, '82. Stymied by the deficit. A. F. Ehrbar.
Fortune. 106:33. N. 29, '82. The coming battle over the deficit.
Fortune. 108:74–7+. O. 17, '83. The Reaganites' civil war over deficits.
   R. I. Kirkland Jr.
Fortune. 108:38. N. 28, '83. The deficit denouncers.
Fortune. 108:51–2+. N. 28, '83. The grass-roots revolt against federal
   deficits. T. Alexander.
Fortune. 108:25–6. D. 26, '83. Crisis ahead for the dollar. S. Marris.
Fortune. 109:113. Mr. 5, '84. Do deficits matter?
Fortune. 109:193. Mr. 19, '84. A modest proposal for the deficit. J. Ro-
   back.
Fortune. 110:39–40+. O. 15, '84. Why you can't love the deficit. B. Stein-
   berg.
Fortune. 110:205. O. 15, '84. Business doesn't buy Mondale's deficit
   plan. P. W. Bernstein.
Fortune. 110:52–3. D. 10, '84. Facing up to the budget mess.
Fortune. 110:155+. D. 10, '84. Down with the deficit. A. Cifelli.
Fortune. 110:205+. D. 10, '84. Beware of plans to cut the deficit. R. J.
   Genetski.
Maclean's. 95:23. Ag. 9, '82. A timely balancing act. M. Posner.
Maclean's. 96:20. Ja. 17, '83. Reagan's mounting deficit. M. Posner.
Maclean's. 96:33. D. 12, '83. Of deficits and disloyalty. M. Posner.
Money. 11:68–70. Ag. '82. Who cares about the budget deficit? R. Eisen-
   berg.
Nation. 234:391–3. Ap. 3, '82. The dangers of a "runaway convention."
   L. M. Baskir.
Nation. 235:129+. Ag. 21–28, '82. The secret history of the deficit. J. Mc-
   Dermott.

Nation. 238:209+. F. 25, '84. Why liberals should hate the deficit.

Nation. 239:233–5. S. 22, '84. If you think it can't happen here, think again. M. Waldman.

National Review. 34:15+. Ja. 22, '82. Dialing for deficits.

National Review. 34:70–1. Ja. 22, '82. Mr. Reagan's deficit? William F. Buckley.

National Review. 35:921. Ag. 5, '83. Reagan's spendthrift Congress. T. Bethell.

National Review. 36:18–19. My. 4, '84. The Republicans bite.

National Review. 36:44–5. Ag. 24, '84. A good word for deficits. E. van den Haag.

National Review. 36:13 S. 7, '84. The lowdown on the deficit.

National Review. 36:24. S. 7, '84. The unmentionable convention. T. Bethell.

Nation's Business. 70:36. Jl. '82. Deflating the deficit figures.

Nation's Business. 70:32–4. S. '82. Weighing a balanced budget amendment. B. Crickmer.

Nation's Business. 72:52. Ja. '84. The coming crunch in housing finance. M. Wantuck.

*New Leader. 65:12–13. Mr. 8, '82. Why deficits matter. G. P. Brockway.

New Leader. 65:8–14. My. 31, '82. The budget balancing act. G. Tyler.

New Leader. 67:12–13. F. 20, '84. Getting the red out. E. Zupnick.

New Leader. 67:9–12. Jl. 9–23, '84. Reagan's counterfeit Keynesianism. G. Tyler.

*New Leader. 67:3–5. Ag. 20, '84. Why deficits hardly matter. P. Davidson.

*New Leader. 67:9–10. O. 29, '84. All you need to know about the deficit. G. P. Brockway.

New Republic. 186:5–6. My. 19, '82. Moral deficit.

New Republic. 187:10+ Ag. 16–23, '82. Deficits anonymous. B. Gellman.

New Republic. 188:8–9. Ja. 24, '83. The deficit depresses.

New Republic. 188:10–12. F. 14, '83. By deficits possessed. J. Faux.

New Republic. 188:4. Mr. 21, '83. The deficits debate.

New Republic. 188:7–8. Je. 13, '83. Deficit of sense.

New Republic. 189:6+. O. 10, '83. Deficit? what deficit?

New Republic. 189:9–11. O. 17, '83. Deficit duel.

New Republic. 189:15–17. D. 31, '83. Liberals and deficits. M. Kinsley.

New Republic. 191:5–6. Jl. 9, '84. Low down payment.

*New York Review of Books. 31:16–21. N. 8, 184. The debtor economy: a proposal. F. G. Rohatyn.

New York Times. p 10. Ag. 3, '82. Budget deficits: a "solution" raises new questions. S. V. Roberts.

New York Times. p A1+. Mr. 2, 1983. Governors ask U. S. to reduce deficit in federal budget.

*New York Times. S. 10, '84. Statement on deficit reduction program. Walter Mondale.

*New York Times. p A 25. S. 11, '84. Mondale's plan: the middle class is not exempt. Jonathan Fuerbringer.

New York Times. p B 2. D. 2, '84. The priority is stemming the red ink. Walter W. Heller.

New York Times. p E 20. Je. 16, '85. The deficit. Remember the deficit?

New York Times Magazine. p 34–5+. Mr. 18, '84. Why Feldstein hangs tough. A. Smith.

*New Yorker. 60:47–55. Jl. 30, '84. Reflections: the deficit. R. L. Heilbroner.

Newsweek. 97:70. F. 23, '81. Deficits and inflation. M. Friedman.

Newsweek. 99:22–4. F. 22, '82. The deficit rebellion. P. McGrath.

Newsweek. 99:22. Ap. 12, '82. The budget balancer's meat-ax amendment. M. Beck.

Newsweek. 100:20. Jl. 26, '82. A balanced-budget law. T. Morganthau.

Newsweek. 100:72. Ag. 9, '82. The balanced-budget diet. M. Greenfield.

Newsweek. 100:49. Ag. 16, '82. An unbalanced proposal. Lester C. Thurow.

Newsweek. 100:75. S. 13, '82. The uses of hypocrisy. M. Friedman.

Newsweek. 100:70. D. 20, '82. How to handle the deficit. Lester C. Thurow.

Newsweek. 101:26+ My. 2, '83. Balancing the budget. M. Friedman.

Newsweek. 102:20–1. Ag. 15, '83. Doing nothing about deficits. M. Starr.

Newsweek. 102:77+ S. 26, '83. Congress: ducking the deficits. H. Anderson.

Newsweek. 102:81–2. N. 21. '83. Congress fiddles, the deficits burn. H. Anderson.

Newsweek. 102:65. D. 5, '83. Deficits: what, us worry?

Newsweek. 102:36–8. D. 12, '83. The deficit: out of control? W. Shapiro.

Newsweek. 103:50+ F. 20, '84. Manuevering over the deficit. T. Morganthau.

Newsweek. 103:26. Ap. 23, '84. Congress takes on the deficit. M. Starr.

Newsweek. 104:62. Ag. 27, '84. Teflon triumphs and failures. R. J. Samuelson.

*Newsweek. 104:78–9. O. 15, '84. The deficit's siren song. E. Gelman.

Newsweek. 104: 84. O. 22, '84. The politics of escapism. R. J. Samuelson.

People Weekly. 21:36+. F. 6, 84. Risking the ax, economist Martin Feldstein speaks out for chopping the deficit.

*Progressive. 47:10. Mr. '83. In praise of deficit spending.

Progressive. 48:10–11. Ap. '84. Paying the piper.

Reader's Digest. 121:123–6. Jl. '82. Red ink in Washington. I. Ross.

Time. 115:29. My. 19, '80. Balancing act.

Time. 115:69. Je. 16, '80. Balanced budget charade. Alan Greenspan.

Time. 119:34–5. F. 15, '82. The great deficit dilemma. C. Byron.

Time. 119:16–20+. My. 24, '2. A debt-threatened dream. G. J. Church.

Time. 120:11. Jl. 26, '82. Balancing the budget by decree. G. J. Church.

Time. 120:30. Ag. 16, '82. Twilight zone.

Time. 121:19–20. Ja. 24, '83. Down with the deficits. G. J. Church.

Time. 121:14–15. My. 23, '83. Untamed monster. Wilsaacson.

Time. 122:13. Ag. 15, '83. Grumbling about deficits.

Time. 122:17. S. 26, '83. Taking the easy way out.

Time. 122:23+ N. 21, '83. Cowering before the deficit. S. Tifft.

Time. 122:18–20. N. 28, '83. We're unable to act. E. Magnusan.

Time. 122:58–9. N. 28, '83. A lusty, lopsided recovery. C. P. Alexander.

Time. 123:62+. Je. 18 '84. Cut and tax. C. P. Alexander.

Time. 124:21+. S. 24, '84. Serving up a bitter pill. G. J. Church.

Time. 124:22–3. O. 3, '84. Plunging into the red ink. G. J. Church.

Time. 124:88–9. O. 15, '84. A beastly question. C. P. Alexander.

USA Today. 111:22–5. S. '82. Balancing the budget. Ernest Hollings.

USA Today. 111:29. Mr. '83. Understanding federal deficits. J. A. Schnepper.

USA Today. 112:35–7. Mr. '84. Deciding about deficits. W. Proxmire.

USA Today. 112:7. Ap. '84. Deficit not a major problem yet.

USA Today. 112:42–4. My. '84. Who's afraid of the big bad deficit? H. B. Ehrlich.

USA Today. 112:45. My. '84. Deficits and the election year blitz. T. D. Kane.

USA Today. 113:16. D. '84. Nation teeters on brink of disaster.

U. S. News & World Report. 88:25–6. Mr. 24, '80. Balancing the budget: Congress has its own ideas.

U. S. News & World Report. 88:23. Ap. 14, '80. Balanced budget is no cure-all. M. Doan.

U. S. News & World Report 90:58-9. Ja. 19, '81. Deficit spending—a hard habit to break.

U. S. News & World Report. 92:88. F. 8, '82. $100 billion deficit is too much. M. Stone.

U. S. News & World Report. 92:20. F. 22, '82. Do budget deficits really matter? M. W. Karmin.

U. S. News & World Report. 92:74 Je. 28, '82. What's a mere $100 billion? M. Stone.

U. S. News & World Report. 93:34+. Jl. 26, '82. How to fix a budget out of control.

U. S. News & World Report. 93:72. Jl. 26, '82. 27th amendment to the Constitution? M. Stone.

U. S. News & World Report. 93:8. Ag. 9, '82. Ahead: recovery or just more red ink?

U. S. News & World Report. 93:52-3. Ag. 9, '82. Budget Limit bandwagon picks up speed. C. R. Sheldon.

U. S. News & World Report. 93:63-4. Ag. 30, '82. Do we need a budget amendment?

U. S. News & World Report. 93:69-70. N. 1, '82. Drastic action needed to cut budget deficits.

U. S. News & World Report. 93:15. N. 8, '82. Record red ink—and worse to come.

U. S. News & World Report. 94:13. Ja. 17, '83. Reagan's wrong: a red-ink revolt.

U. S. News & World Report. 94: 24-5. F. 7, '83. Budget deficits: the endless river of red ink.

U. S. News & World Report. 94:85-6. Mr. 7, '83. Do federal deficits really matter?

U. S. News & World Report. 94:13. My. 9, '83. Red ink thickens.

*U. S. News & World Report. 95:33-34. O. 17, '83. Do $200 billion deficits really matter?

U. S. News & World Report. 95:14. N. 7, '83. Government's rising river of red ink.

U. S. News & World Report. 95:13. D. 12, '83. White House zips lip of its own economist.

U. S. News & World Report. 95:85-6. D. 12, '83. Europe's advice to U. S.: tax more, save more. A. Zanker.

U. S. News & World Report. 96:72. F. 6, '84. Budget deficit needs a quick fix—the quicker the better. E. Janeway.

U. S. News & World Report. 96:18–27. F. 13, '84. Budget '85.

U. S. News & World Report. 96:11 Ap. 2, '84. Deficits: now it's Democrats' turn.

U. S. News & World Report. 96:96. My. 14, '84. Amend the Constitution? M. Stone.

U. S. News & World Report. 96:64. Je. 11, '84. Pan amendment requiring balanced budget?

U. S. News & World Report. 97:22–3. J. 9, '84. Standing the red ink. M. W. Karmin.

U. S. News & World Report. 97:73–5. Ag. 13, '84. Ballooning deficits—what the real danger is.

U. S. News & World Report. 97:7. Ag. 27, '84. The great guessing game over deficits.

U. S. News & World Report. 97:59. S. 17, '84. Soak the rich? It wouldn't balance the budget.

U. S. News & World Report. 97:18. N. 5, '84. Washington red ink—official figures.

U. S. News & World Report. 97:73–4. D. 31, '84–Ja. 7, '85. We are going to need more revenue.

U. S. News & World Report. 97:74–5. D. 31, '84–Ja. 7, '85. Make people realize: deficits do matter.

*Vital Speeches of the Day. 47:290–3. Mr. 1, '81. The state of the nation's economy: we are out of time. Ronald Reagan.

Vital Speeches of the Day. 47:329–32. Mr. 15, '81. Fraud, waste, and abuse and the federal deficit. Elmer B. Staats.

Vital Speeches of the Day. 48:450–2. My. 15, '82. The budget problem. Ronald Reagan.

Vital Speeches of the Day. 48:458–63. My. 15, '82. Facing reality: today is the result of yesterday. G. C. Wiegand.

Vital Speeches of the Day. 48:687–90. S. 1, '82. A federal capital budget: an idea whose time has come. David Mahoney.

Vital Speeches of the Day. 48:714–17. S. 15, '82. Why can't government be run like a business: never mind the party. Edward V. Regan.

Vital Speeches of the Day. 48:731–4. S. 15, '82. Man the pumps: sound fiscal responsibility. Robert T. Powers.

Vital Speeches of the Day. 49:627–31. Ag. 1, '83. Our tax and spending policies: a call for change. Duane R. Kullberg.

Vital Speeches of the Day. 49:654–9. Ag. 15, '83. Looking beyond the current recovery: stop squandering our energies on destructive infighting. William F. Ford.

*Vital Speeches of the Day. 49:701–4. S. 1, '83. The problem of big gov-
    ernment: are we losing our marbles? J. Peter Grace.

Vital Speeches of the Day. 50:692–4. S. 1, '84. The United States: debtor
    nation. Lawton Chiles.

Vital Speeches of the Day. 51:106–9. D. 1, '84. The iron triangle's impact
    on the federal budget: Congress, bureaucrats and lobbyists. George
    Marotta.

*Vital Speeches of the Day. 51:470–3. My. 15, '85. Deficit reduction: a
    national imperative. Robert D. Kilpatrick.

Vogue. 174:308–9. Mr. '84. Cash crunch. S. Lee

*Wall Street Journal. Ja. 25, '83, p. 40–1. To the president and Con-
    gress: bi-partisan appeal to resolve the budget crisis. From an adver-
    tisement by The Bi-Partisan Budget Appeal, an organization whose
    founding members are former Treasury secretaries W. Michael
    Blumenthal, John B. Connally, C. Douglas Dillon, Henry H. Fow-
    ler, and William E. Simon and former Commerce secretary Peter
    G. Peterson.

World Affairs Journal. p. 5–10. Winter '84. The challenge of the deficit:
    America at a crossroads. Willard C. Butcher.

THE
REFERENCE
SHELF

4/96